Miss EX-Yugoslavia

Miss Ex-Yugoslavia

A MEMOIR

SOFIJA STEFANOVIC

ATRIA BOOKS

New York   London   Toronto   Sydney   New Delhi

ATRIA
BOOKS

An Imprint of Simon & Schuster, Inc.
1230 Avenue of the Americas
New York, NY 10020

First Atria Books hardcover edition April 2018

ATRIA BOOKS and colophon are trademarks of Simon & Schuster, Inc.

For information about special discounts for bulk purchases, please contact Simon & Schuster Special Sales at 1-866-506-1949 or business@simonandschuster.com.

The Simon & Schuster Speakers Bureau can bring authors to your live event. For more information, or to book an event, contact the Simon & Schuster Speakers Bureau at 1-866-248-3049 or visit our website at www.simonspeakers.com.

Interior design by Amy Trombat

Line art by Payton Cosell Turner

Manufactured in the United States of America

10 9 8 7 6 5 4 3 2 1

Library of Congress Cataloging in Publication Control Number: 2017045539

ISBN 978-1-5011-6574-0
ISBN 978-1-5011-6576-4 (ebook)

AUTHOR'S NOTE

This is a memoir, not a history. It's a collection of memories: a story from my point of view, and not necessarily one that others would relate. I have changed some names and distinguishing details. Though my intention has been to convey the essence of everything I recount, certain events and scenes have been compressed or expanded to fulfill the needs of the story. Finally, as is the nature of memoir, dialogue is an approximation.

Contents

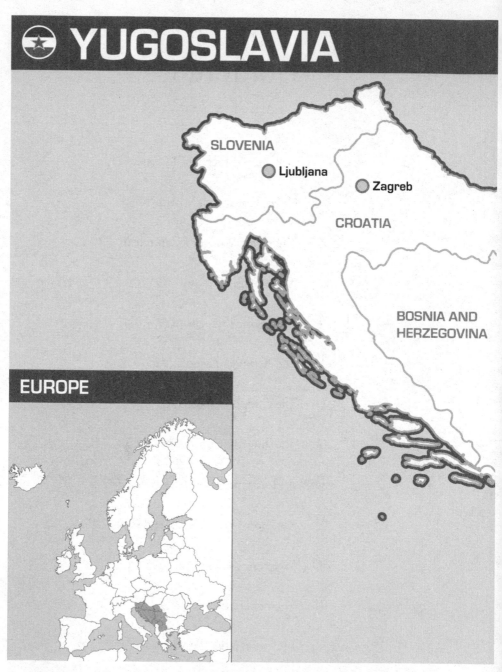

YUGOSLAVIA

SLOVENIA

Ljubljana

Zagreb

CROATIA

BOSNIA AND
HERZEGOVINA

EUROPE

Yugoslavia as it was in the 1980s. Following the wars, this region is now
divided into separate countries: Slovenia, Croatia, Serbia, Bosnia and
Herzegovina, Montenegro, and Macedonia (FYROM). Kosovo declared
independence in 2008, which is still disputed by Serbia.

Miss
EX-Yugoslavia

Prologue: Princess of Disaster

I wouldn't normally enter a beauty pageant, but this one is special. It's a battle for the title of Miss Ex-Yugoslavia, beauty queen of a country that no longer exists. It is due to the country being "no more" that our shoddy little contest is happening in Australia, over eight thousand miles from where Yugoslavia once stood. My fellow competitors and I are immigrants and refugees, coming from different sides of the conflict that split Yugoslavia up. It's a weird idea for a competition—bringing young women from a war-torn country together to be objectified, but in our little diaspora, we're used to contradictions.

It's 2005, I'm twenty-two, and I've been living in Australia for most of my life. I'm at Joy, an empty Melbourne nightclub that smells of stale smoke and is located above a fruit-and-vegetable market. I open the door to the dressing room, and when my eyes adjust to the fluorescent lights I see that young women are rubbing olive oil on each other's thighs. Apparently, this is a trick used in "real" competitions, one we've hijacked for our amateur version. For weeks, I've been preparing myself to stand almost naked in front of everyone I know, and it's come around quick. As I scan the shiny bodies for my friend Nina, I'm dismayed to see that all the other girls have dead-straight hair, while mine, thanks to an overzealous hairdresser with a curling wand, looks like a wig made of sausages.

"Dođi, lutko" ("Come here, doll"), Nina says as she emerges from the crowd of girls. "Maybe we can straighten it." She brings her hand up to my hair cautiously, as if petting a startled lamb. Nina is a Bosnian refugee in a miniskirt. As a contestant, she is technically my competitor, but we've become close in the rehearsals leading up to the pageant.

Under Nina's tentative pets, the hair doesn't give. It's been sprayed to stay like this, possibly forever. I shift uncomfortably and tug on the hem of my skirt, trying to pull it lower. Just like the hair, it doesn't budge. In my language, such micro-skirts have earned their own graphic term: *dopičnjak*, which literally means "to the pussy"—a precise term to distinguish the *dopičnjak* from its more conservative subgenital cousin, the miniskirt.

Though several of us barely speak our mother tongue, all of us competitors are ex-Yugos, for better or worse; we come from Bosnia, Croatia, Macedonia, Montenegro, Serbia, and Slovenia. I join a conversation in which Yugo girls are yelling over one another in slang-riddled English, recalling munching on the salty peanut snack Smoki when they were little, agreeing that it was "the bomb" and "totally sick," superior to anything one might find in our adoptive home of Australia.

The idea of a beauty pageant freaks me out, and ex-Yugoslavia as a country is itself an oxymoron—but the combination of the two makes the deliciously weird Miss Ex-Yugoslavia competition the ideal subject for my documentary film class. I feel like a double agent. Yes, I'm part of the ex-Yugo community, but also I'm a cynical, story-hungry, Western-schooled film student, and so I've gone undercover among my own people. I know my community is strange, and I want to get top marks for this exclusive glimpse within. Though I've been deriding the competition to my film-student friends, rolling my eyes at the ironies, I have to admit that this pageant, and its resurrection of my zombie country, is actually poking at something deep.

If I'm honest with myself, I'm not just a filmmaker seeking a story. This is my community. I *want* outsiders to see the human face of ex-Yugoslavia, because it's my face, and the face of these girls. We're more than news reports about war and ethnic cleansing.

"Who prefers to speak English to the camera?" I ask the room, in English, whipping my sausage-curled head around, as my college classmate Maggie points the camera at the other contestants backstage.

"Me!" most of the girls say in chorus.

"What's your opinion of ex-Yugoslavia?" I ask Zora, the seventeen-year-old from Montenegro.

"Um, I don't know," she says.

"It's complicated!" someone else calls out.

As a filmmaker, I want a neat sound bite, but ex-Yugoslavia is unwieldy. Most of my fellow contestants are confused about the turbulent history of the region, and it's not easy to explain in a nutshell. At the very least, I want viewers to understand what brought us here: the wars that consumed the 1990s, whose main players were Serbia, Croatia, and Bosnia and Herzegovina—the three largest republics within the Yugoslav Federation.

Like many families, mine left when the wars began, and like the rest of the Miss Ex-Yugoslavia competitors, I was only a kid. Despite the passage of time, being part of an immigrant minority in Australia, speaking Serbian at home, being all too familiar with *dopičnjaks*, I'm embedded in the ex-Yugoslavian community. Yugoslavia, and its tiny-skirt-wearing prone people, have weighed upon me my whole life.

Most of these young women moved to Australia either as immigrants seeking a better life (like my family, who came from Serbia), or as refugees fleeing the effects of war (like the Croatian and Bosnian girls).

"Why are you competing for Miss Ex-Yugoslavia?" I prod Zora.

"That's where I come from," she says, looking down, like I'm a demanding schoolteacher. "And my parents want me to."

In the student film I'm making, I plan to contextualize the footage of the Miss Ex-Yugoslavia competition with my own story. I've put together some home footage of me in Belgrade, before we moved to Australia. The footage shows me aged two, in a blue terry-cloth romper handed down from my cousins. I'm in front of our scruffy building on the Boulevard of Revolution, posing proudly on the hood of my parents' tiny red Fiat, with my little legs crossed like a glamorous grown-up's. To accompany these scenes, I've inserted voice-over narration, which says, "The Belgrade I left is still my home. I was born there and I plan to die there." But really, though I like the dramatic way it sounds, I'm not sure it's true. Would I really go back to that poor, corrupt, dirty place, now that English comes easier to me than Serbian?

I am quick to tell anyone who asks that I find beauty pageants stupid and that I'm competing for the sake of journalism. However, I am still a human living in the world, and I would like to look hot. I've had my body waxed, I've been taught how to walk down a runway, and I've eaten nothing except celery and tuna for weeks, in the desperate hope that it will reduce my cellulite. I've replaced my nerdy glasses with contacts, and I'm the fittest I've been in my life. A secret, embarrassed little part of me that always wanted to be a princess is fluttering with hope. I've reverted to childhood habits of craving attention, and, for a second, I forget all the things I dislike about my appearance. As I observe my fake-tanned, shiny body in the mirror and smile with my whitened teeth, I think, *What if somehow, some way, I actually win Miss Ex-Yugoslavia?* I allow myself to dream for a moment about being a crowned princess, like the ones in the Disney tapes my dad would get for me on the black market in socialist Yugoslavia.

This highly amateur competition is the brainchild of a man named Sasha, who organizes social events for the ex-Yugoslavian community.

He has managed to gather nine competitors aged sixteen to twenty-three who found out about the event through the ex-Yugo grapevine: a poster at the Montenegrin doctor's office, an advertisement in the *Serbian Voice* local newspaper, their parents, chatter in the Yugo clubs where young people go to connect with the community.

Sasha is Serbian, like me. Earlier today, he was bustling around the nightclub with his slicked-back hair and leather jacket, ordering people to set up the runway. I pointed a camera at him and, like a hard-hitting journalist glistening with recently applied spray tan that left orange marks on the wall, asked, in our language, why he decided to stage a Miss Ex-Yugoslavia competition.

Sasha turned to the camera with a practiced smile and said, "I'm simply trying to bring these girls together. What happened to Yugoslavia is, unfortunately, a wound that remains in our minds and in our hearts. But now we're here, on another planet, so let's treat it that way. Let's be friends."

"Do you think we will all get along?" I asked, hoping he'd address the wars he was tiptoeing around.

"I don't know, but I'm willing to try. I am only interested in business, not in politics." He looked at the camera to reiterate, to make sure he wasn't antagonizing any party: "I say that for the record, I am *only* interested in business and nothing else."

His interest in business is so keen in fact, that he's making me give him my footage after tonight. He is planning to make a DVD of the pageant, separate from my documentary. Unlike my film, with which I hope to encapsulate the troubled history of Yugoslavia in under ten minutes, he intends to skip the politics altogether. Instead, he will pair footage of us girls in skimpy outfits with dance music and then sell the DVD back to us and our families for fifty dollars.

Now it's eight o'clock, and the peace Sasha was hoping for reigns in the dressing room. Here, girls help each other with their hair, they attach safety pins to hemlines, and share Band-Aids to stop blisters. The event was supposed to begin an hour ago, but we are still waiting for audience members to be seated. There's a security guard who is searching each guest with a handheld metal detector downstairs, and I suspect it's taking so long because all the gold chains are setting it off.

My camera operator, Maggie, asks me quietly who she should be getting the most footage of, meaning, who's likely to win this thing? I think it will be Nina from Bosnia. She's not soft and fresh-faced like Zora from Montenegro, but she is certainly one of the most beautiful competitors. She is very thin, with big eyes, high cheekbones, and a pointed chin. Nina reminds me of the young woman in Disney's *The Little Mermaid* who turns out to be Ursula the witch in disguise, which is to say, she's both attractive and a little dangerous. At rehearsal, she casually mentioned getting into a fight with some girls at a club, to the awe of some of the more straight-laced competitors (myself included). Nina is wise, in many ways more mature than the rest of us, and I'm simultaneously drawn to her and repelled by her. With her gaze that is always calm, almost lethargic, she makes me feel especially neurotic and weird. And she isn't nervous about going onstage to be ogled—she's got a clear purpose in mind: "Definitely the ticket," she tells Maggie when asked about her motivation for competing. The winner of Miss Ex-Yugoslavia will receive a ticket back home, to whichever part of that former country she desires, and Nina is itching to visit Sarajevo, which she left ten years ago when it was a bloody mess.

Partly, it's my guilt—for not experiencing war firsthand, for having been born in Belgrade instead of Sarajevo—that makes me crave Nina's affection. My family left not because our lives were in danger, but because my parents wanted their daughters to have opportunities greater than those offered in wartime Yugoslavia. I know that Nina and I share ex-Yugoslavia, but the piece that belongs to her is more damaged than the piece that belongs to me. I wonder if she feels this injustice too, if she has a desire to punish me for the privileges I had, as I, deep down, feel a need to be punished.

"I can talk about being injured by a Serbian bomb if that would be good for the film," Nina offers, and as Maggie pivots her camera to face her, there's a knock at the dressing-room door, and Sasha pops his head in. Tina from Slovenia, the only blonde among a sea of brunettes, addresses the camera in English, like an on-the-ground reporter.

"That's Sasha, the organizer of the event."

"Just pretend the camera isn't here," I say, with a touch of irritation, as I've explained this about a thousand times already, and I have a specific vision for this film, namely, for it to look like a fly-on-the-wall masterpiece of observational cinema.

"Are you ladies ready?" Sasha says, in his accented English, staring straight at the camera, confirming that this will not be a fly-on-the-wall masterpiece after all. He clears his throat and continues his down-the-barrel address. "Now, you all know there is only one winner tonight," he says, and I imagine he's prepared this speech so that he can include it in his fifty-dollar DVD.

"You are all beautiful," he says with gravity, sweeping across the room with one arm. "But my job is only—for one winner. To . . . give her the crown." He pauses, as if confused by his own clumsy turn of phrase. "That is my job. You have five minutes," he says solemnly, hurriedly exiting the room and closing the door, as an excited cry rises from the girls, who rush to put the finishing touches on their outfits.

I ask Maggie to follow Sasha and capture some footage of the nightclub filling with hundreds of people. She comes back minutes later, with a worried look. She says she opened the door of the staff bathroom, and interrupted two businessmen snorting cocaine. Those who have seen the mafia portrayed in popular culture would be forgiven for thinking that half the people at Joy tonight are involved in organized crime. And considering how brutal the Yugoslavian wars were, an observer might also wonder—how many of these tall, strong men, in their leather jackets and open-collared shirts, were involved in the violence?

I peek out of the dressing room door to watch the patrons, who have all paid thirty-five dollars a ticket and are demanding the free glass of champagne they were promised on arrival.

I know that some of the people in this room, all dressed up, smoking cigarettes and knocking back Šljivovica plum brandy, were ethnically cleansed from their villages. When they were fleeing to refugee camps, starving under house arrest, or huddled in basements to avoid bombs, could they have guessed they'd end up here years later, in a club on the other side of the earth surrounded by ex-Yugoslavians from all sides of the war? Yet here they all are, waiting to pick a queen among the young women who will soon be parading their flesh onstage, in a country where bodies are not in danger of being blown up. If they are thinking these things, people aren't saying them. The horrors of war are generally something people keep to themselves; they are the secrets that wake them up at night, not topics to be discussed on a Friday night out, when turbo-folk music is pumping.

The person who knows these secrets best—what people did to one another in the war—is sitting out there tonight. From my vantage point, I can just make her out, her heavy frame coming into focus through a cloud of cigarette smoke. It's my mother. She's at a table surrounded by her friends, and every now and then, as if she's Marlon Brando in *The Godfather*, someone comes up to her. They're saying, "My respects, Dr. Koka," which is what they call her, even though she's not a doctor. Thanks to my mother's status as beloved counselor, I am, by default, respected in the community, too.

"Dr. Koka's older daughter is competing tonight," people are saying to their friends. I know it already, people are resolved to cheer loudly when I take the stage, out of love for my mother.

I spot another member of my crew, Luke, who I've enlisted to record sound. "This is like a Kusturica film," Luke says with glee, when I wave him over to the dressing room. He's a fan of the Serbian director who is known for the surreal depictions of ex-Yugoslavians. Luke looks around at my community, clearly hoping a pig will appear and start gnawing at the bar, or that someone will smash a bottle over his own head.

Sasha waves—it's time. The first stage of the competition, Casual Wear, is in fact just an opportunity to get up onstage wearing a mini-skirt and a T-shirt advertising Sasha's Yugo events business. At the last minute, Nina comes up with the genius idea of tying the front of our T-shirts in a knot, allowing us to show off our midriffs, and at the same time to quietly sabotage Sasha's attempt to turn us into commercials. We follow her lead. As we rehearsed, we walk single-file out of the dressing room. There is no actual "backstage" area, so the audience can see us as we walk out and stand in line at the side of the stage, waiting to be introduced. Already, it's embarrassing; as all eyes turn to us, we hear the whooping calls of boyfriends, family, and friends, and the whistles from strangers, while we stare straight ahead.

The emcees take the stage. Sasha planned on finding hosts from two ex-Yugoslavian countries, but it seems we have ended up with a random host-for-hire called Monica, a "true blue" Australian in a red cocktail dress, and a confused Serbian man in a suit named Bane, who I suspect is onstage not for his charisma but because he is a friend of Sasha's.

"Are you ready to go crazy and cheer for some babes!?" Monica screams, and the crowd answers with a roar. Does Monica know what ex-Yugoslavia is, who these tall, shouty foreigners are? Perhaps she doesn't care, and is just here to do her job: get the crowd worked up, make a couple hundred dollars, and then walk out of Joy and never think again about this little community. She could just as easily be hosting a dog show, a bake-off, or a bingo night. I think how liberating it would be to be a regular Aussie and stand in Monica's position—able to free myself of the ties that bind me to everyone in this room, even people I've never met, but whom I feel obliged to hug and kiss, because we come from the same troubled little piece of earth.

I notice a man waving enthusiastically, and it takes me a second to recognize him as a patient who had a cyst removed from his groin last week. I'd been working my weekend shift at Peter the doctor's clinic and was required to hold a little sterilized dish while the offending cyst was removed. I wave back. As if the sudden change from "groin-cyst patient and disgusted assistant" to "ogler and oiled-up young woman" were a perfectly normal progression of our relationship.

"Let's bring these girls up here, one by one. Can I hear a big round of applause for Contestant Number One!?" Monica shouts, and Nina steps lithely onto the stage, the pointy heels of her knee-high boots holding steady as she strides down the runway. She pauses at the end, puts a hand on her hip, raises a thin, arched eyebrow, and smiles at the judges. *That's how you do it*, I find myself thinking, as if I'm a beauty-show connoisseur.

"Let's hear it for Nina, from Sarajevo!" Bane says. The resounding cheer from the audience can be largely attributed to her fellow Sarajevans, refugees who make their presence known with whistles and shouts of solidarity. Many non-natives also cheer in support of Sarajevo, knowing what that city endured during the war.

Onstage, Nina smiles and blows a kiss to her fans, receiving applause so thunderous it makes the floor shake.

The crowd is riled up. They've been drinking, and shouting, and when Zora from Montenegro takes the stage, she too receives an uproarious welcome.

Montenegro is mountainous and beachy, war-free, and once a vacation destination for many Yugoslavians. Montenegrins are known for being tall and dark, and Zora's height, her tan, the nearly black hair that falls down her back like a horse's mane, are a definite hit with the crowd.

When it's my turn to go up, I take the stairs carefully, remembering that I slipped during rehearsal and praying I don't repeat the humiliation. I don't like taking chances, so I walk at half the pace of everyone else, out of time with the pop music that plays. The applause slows, but not in a mocking way—the crowd simply matches it to the speed at which I'm walking, clapping to a beat that propels me along. I get to the end of the runway, and mouth *hvala* at the crowd, which means "thank you," and I am answered with whistles and cheers. I'm supposed to greet the judges, so I nod to one of them, Peter the doctor, a dark Montenegrin in an Armani suit. He's told me sternly not to expect special treatment just because I work at his clinic—most of the other girls and their families are his patients. Beside him is the middle-aged Macedonian owner of Joy nightclub. At the end of the judging table is the woman who runs Fantastic Face Beauty School. Two of her students were conscripted to do our makeup, and I find her regarding my hair, trying to work out if I'm wearing a wig. I toss my head, attempting to flick my hair over my shoulder as I've seen other girls do, but it barely moves. One of the sausages just hits me gently on the side of the face, and I turn inexpertly on my spiky heel, making my retreat slowly back down the runway.

Backstage, everyone is euphoric, thrilled by the positive reaction of the crowd. We have half an hour before we're onstage again, for the Evening Wear portion of the show. I'll be wearing a long red silky dress, which I bought with the intention of returning to the store tomorrow and getting my money back. Someone points out that the patrons are eating *ćevapčići*—delicious skinless sausages—and we realize that, even though we've been here for hours, no one has offered us anything to eat. Sasha promises to bring us food, and as we wait, Zora and a couple of others start preparing for the next part of the evening, during which we will be asked questions.

"Describe yourself," one of the girls quizzes Zora, as the sausages arrive and we pick them up daintily with our fingers.

"I'm ambitious, confident . . ." Zora says, then rolls her eyes. "Yeah, right."

To avoid staining a dress I don't actually own with a greasy skinless sausage, I stay in my casual wear for a bit longer. I slide onto the floor next to Nina, and we chat in a mix of English and our native languages, both of them varieties of Serbo-Croatian—for me Serbian, with my clipped Belgrade accent, for her Bosnian, with her melodic Sarajevo accent. Before the wars started, when Nina and I were kids, Yugoslavia was held together under the optimistic slogan of "Brotherhood and Unity."

Yugoslavia, which had been formed after World War I as part of a long-cherished dream to unite the Southern Slavs, was re-formed into a Communist whole after World War II. That's despite the fact that its people had been at one another's throats during World War II, due to deep religious and cultural differences. In Tito's new, socialist Yugoslavia, the people were expected to live in "Brotherhood and Unity," and nationalists who held on to past hatreds were punished with death or jail for their insubordinate grudges. Marriages between ethnicities were encouraged and celebrated, symbolic of a unified Yugoslavia. Nina herself is the product of a mixed marriage. But the policy of "Brotherhood and Unity" alone could not eradicate the pull toward nationalism. Many wanted to be independent from a greater Yugoslavia. Hence, the wars. The messy wars that sprouted up in varying degrees of intensity, from Slovenia, to Croatia, to Bosnia, to Kosovo.

As Maggie crouches near us with her camera, Nina starts to tell me about the war. She was ten years old, playing in a parking lot with neighborhood kids, when a grenade exploded.

"The boy in front of me died straightaway," she tells me, and Nina felt something hot in her foot. "I looked down at my leg, and saw it was covered in blood."

As she says this, I can't help but look down Nina's leg, skinny and veiny up close, to her foot, on which she now wears strappy high-heeled sandals, showing carefully pedicured toes and a faint scar. After seeing the blood on her leg, Nina fainted, and lay unconscious surrounded by dead, wounded, and crying children.

"When there's an explosion, no one comes to help, because there's always a second one coming," she says.

Lucky for Nina, the second explosion missed them. The bomb, Nina tells me, was most probably set off by the Serbs.

"How do you feel about Serbs?" I ask, even though I know that Nina wouldn't be here, at an ex-Yugoslavian event, if she hated Serbs. I'm asking the question for the benefit of the camera, because I know my audience of non-Yugos has no idea how our community works. I asked Nina the question to highlight a contradiction: not only do we not hate one another, but we actually love one another. And while there are nationalists out there (known for clashing at sporting events, or in nightclubs), those people are not here tonight. Nina, and most of the people at Joy nightclub this evening, are Yugo-nostalgics: they remember, and pine for, Yugoslavia as it was before the wars, before politicians and crazy people took over, when kids of all nationalities played in the parking lots without fear of death.

"Just because I was wounded by the Serbian side," Nina says dutifully, glancing at the camera, "doesn't mean I hate Serbs."

She asks if I want to touch the shrapnel that is still lodged in her foot, and she guides my finger along the side until I feel a little lump, like a pebble under her skin. It moves around freely, and she says it hurts when the weather changes.

The other girls can hear our conversation, but continue doing their makeup. For most of us, war has always been present, if not in the foreground, then as a constant background noise, the details of mass graves, bombings, rigged elections buzzing like an old fridge, always there in the form of radio news, infiltrating our parents' arguments. It's not surprising to me that these women keep curling their eyelashes while Nina talks about being wounded. Or that the two of us can then get up from the floor, hug each other, and keep idly chatting without pause, turning a conversation from tragedy into something like breast tape, as we slip into our evening gowns, for part two of our evening of objectification.

Showtime. Nina is introduced to the audience again, now wearing a sparkly, cream-colored dress that plunges low between her breasts. This time, instead of walking offstage, she pauses by the microphone to answer questions. She waves at the crowd happily, like she was born to do this. "She's good," I whisper to the camera, falling into the on-the-ground-reporter style myself.

"What is your unfulfilled wish?" Monica asks, placing the microphone to Nina's lips.

As if Monica isn't there, Nina looks out at the crowd and says, in Bosnian, "For Yugoslavia to be like it once was."

The cheer from the Yugo-nostalgics is so loud and long that Nina laughs, beaming out at the audience.

Waiting by the stage, I feel my eyes prick with tears, the fantasy of a Yugoslavia "like it once was" taking me to my happiest memories, of all of my family and friends in one place, before phone calls were long distance and expensive, before my parents became angrier at each other, before my dad got sick. Is the cheering crowd crafting Nina's wish into their own fantasy, bringing back loved ones, making themselves un-foreign and loved, telling themselves: everything would be fine if only Yugoslavia was still around?

Monica the Aussie host cheers as well, as if the answer Nina gave makes complete sense to her, even if it was in a foreign language. Gushing at Nina in a way that suggests she's partaken in some recreational drug use with members of the community, Monica asks: "And why do you think you should win the competition, and this ticket back home?"

"Because I'd like to see my family, which I haven't seen for ten years," Nina says, this time in her Bosnian-accented English.

Next up: Zora, her thick hair now up in a dark, elegant bun, answers the same question with her prepared answer: "Because I think I deserve to win, and I *can* win, and I think going overseas would give me the opportunity to appreciate not just what I have here, but what I left back at home." Boom. Holding her head high, she spins around, strutting down the runway, and judging by the cheers, gathering a solid faction of supporters in her wake.

When it's my turn, I feel grossly underqualified. I stand with my hands on my hips to stop the sweat from staining my expensive red evening gown. "Why do you think you should win?" Monica asks.

"Well, I believe I should win because I've never actually won anything." I'd thought it was a good answer when I planned it (and it was true), but the crowd and Monica seem to be waiting for me to say something more to win hearts and minds, because there is silence. "Ever. Before." The crowd starts to laugh and I shrug, starting my walk down the runway, forgetting that I'm supposed to stay and answer another question. I am now pretty much resigned to the fact that I'm not going to win this thing, though I send out an appreciative kiss to my mother, her clients, and the man with the cyst, all of whom continue to clap out of sympathy and nepotism, even though it's painfully obvious I'm the losing horse in this race.

Back in the safety of our dressing room, we pose for a photo. In our beautiful gowns and our carefully made-up faces, we look like we're dressed for prom. Except we don't have dates. Like nuns are the brides of Christ, we are the brides of a dead Yugoslavia.

The evening gowns come off, and the bikinis come on, nervous energy spreading through the room. One of the Fantastic Face Beauty School students is using concealer and a tiny brush to cover the stretch marks on my thighs, while I, following the advice of my fellow contestants, slip rubbery inserts, called "chicken fillets" inside my bikini top, to make my breasts look bigger. During rehearsals, every now and then, a chicken fillet would become visible from the side, a rubbery mass trying to escape from under my armpit. I consider walking down the runway without moving my arms, to prevent the fillet from flying out into the audience and smacking a refugee in the face.

1

Hello, Collapsing World

I was born into a country destined for collapse. It was November 1982 and the timing was incredibly inconvenient, not only on a geopolitical level, but also because I picked a particularly bad night for it. Due to gasoline shortages, the people of Belgrade had been ordered to drive in shifts: only half the cars were allowed on the roads each weekend, and the license plate on my parents' Fiat 650 was not on the list that day.

To make matters worse, my mother, Koka, went into labor in the middle of the night, when the lights had all gone out thanks to electricity shortages. As the contractions started, my parents threw off their gray polyester blankets, revealing my mother, in her giant maternity nightgown, and my father, his skinniness accentuated by his saggy, brown cotton pajamas. My parents, like the rest of Yugoslavia's citizens, were used to inconveniences such as blackouts, but still, they started squabbling. They'd been married two years, and this was their go-to form of communication: my mother with her "constant nagging," my father with his "negative energy." And on this night, the familiar bickering offered some comfort in an unfamiliar situation.

Luckily, my mother was a dedicated smoker, so the apartment was full of lighters and matches, which they now started striking to illuminate their home.

"How dilated would you say your cervix is?" my father asked, grasping wildly at any useful phrases he could remember from that birthing book they had read.

In our language, we call the stare she gave him *gledati ga kao da ti je ubio oca* ("Looking at someone like they've just killed your father"). I believe the term in English is "murderous." How the hell was my mother supposed to know how dilated her cervix was? All she knew was that she was having a contraction and her insides hurt like she might die.

Moaning with pain, my mother put on the navy maxi-dress she'd been wearing every day since she became huge, and layered her purple fall coat over it. Her stomach parted the coat like curtains; I was ready to be born, shoving my way into life like a bald diva, with little regard for the logistical challenges I was creating for my parents.

Some months ago, my mother had made the inadvisable early eighties decision to regularly shave her eyebrows, and then draw them on in thin arches. But tonight, she remained eyebrow-less—the blank forehead giving her an expression of endless surprise, as if her eyebrows were raised so high they'd disappeared under her hairline and were hiding in her perm. In the soft light of a flame, she panted, her pointy eyeteeth bared, nostrils flared in panic. She fiddled with her thin gold necklace, where a small golden dachshund charm dangled. The trinket was a present from her mother that she never took off, and she grasped the loyal little dog now like some religious people might a gold cross. Even though she was technically Serbian Orthodox, like many people in postwar socialist Yugoslavia, she was not religious. But tonight she hedged her bets, looking upward and muttering, "If you're there, help me."

My father put on his glasses, which magnified his blue eyes in the fallen darkness, and scratched at his light-brown beard. Lola was my father's nickname, a girlish moniker to Western ears, but it was his preferred, unusual shortening from his old-fashioned name: Slobodan, meaning "he who is free." He could have called himself "Sloba" or "Boba," which were both common shortenings, but in a quiet way, my father liked to be different. In another life, he would have studied literature, and in his ideal life, he would have just lain around reading fiction all day, inhabiting imagined worlds.

When the lighter that my mother was holding got too hot, she snapped it out and dropped it, and was forced to feel her way along the walls toward the bag she'd packed. Her hands touched the frame of a painting: an abstract watercolor of Belgrade as seen from the Danube, in serene light greens and blues. She collected art, in the modest way that people with limited resources and high aspirations do: she kept her eye out for artists, she attended gallery openings, and every now and then she twisted her husband's arm to let them buy something that she knew he considered a waste of money. Yes, Dad's family was poorer than hers. They'd come to Belgrade when they'd had enough of the sulfur from the mine in the Serbian town of Bor, where my dad's father worked as an engineer. But my mother's parents didn't have much money either, and certainly no savings.

In 1980s Yugoslavia, no one was wealthy—regardless of profession. *Gastarbeiter* ("guest workers") left the country to earn money, but otherwise there was enough money only to put food on the table, and sometimes for a trip to the hairdresser, or a holiday nearby in Europe. Beyond this, there were no savings, and my family was no different. People were used to not having much—it had been like this for decades.

There were no baby things in the home yet. In our culture, you wait until you have a healthy living baby before you get stuff, so as not to tempt fate. And my parents hoped I'd be one of those healthy babies, so healthy that people would pretend to spit on me three times, making a noise like *"poo-poo-poo,"* to scare off witches or the devil, who might want to steal such a delectable newborn. It was grandmothers who followed such superstitions mostly: spilling a bit of alcohol on the floor before drinking to someone who'd died, turning on the faucet when someone was in labor to provoke a smooth "flow." And now, like an old lady, even though my dad rolled his eyes, my mother hobbled to the bathroom and turned the tap on, releasing a slow trickle, and leaving it to flow while she was gone. What's the harm?

As my mother kicked over a pile of books she had brought home from the university where she worked as a psychology tutor, my dad shook his head. If he had his way, the apartment would be spotless, minimal, stripped of the "junk" my mother accumulated: rocks from vacations lined up on the bookshelves, all those vases from her aunts. To her, that rock meant the beach in Croatia, the smell of whitebait and the taste of ice cream. But my dad kept his memories deep inside—he didn't need an object to stir his imagination, or a rock to remind him.

As my dad shoved his skinny bowlegs into old Levi's, he stubbed his toe in the dark.

"This fucking country!" he said, because of the darkness, because of his toe, because of his lack of a ready car to take his wife to the hospital, because of his dying Yugoslavia.

"Why don't you move to America if you hate it so much?" my mother said.

Even though she laughed at the unceasing "Brotherhood and Unity" propaganda of her own country, which had faded in luster over the decades, my mother was nevertheless a loyal child of the Socialist Federal Republic of Yugoslavia. She'd been brought up with free health and education under the authoritarian head of state, Marshal Tito, who was much better than what the Soviets had. In fact, my mother had always seen Tito as a sort of embarrassing uncle character. Yes, he said things like "You must guard Yugoslavia like the pupil of your own eye!" And he organized ludicrous parades of rural dancers in national costume. Yet still, when it came down to it, my mother's life had been pretty good under his rule. She'd grown up counting her lucky stars that she wasn't born in a country like Poland or Hungary, which had ended up behind the Iron Curtain. She'd take Tito over Stalin any day! Tito had resisted the Soviets and kept Yugoslavia relatively unscathed by all the other crazy dictators around the globe.

And as for the other side—capitalist America? My mother would admit that there was some appeal to it. Sure, she liked watching *Dynasty*, with its juicy plots, great shoulder pads, and Americans scheming and bickering. But she'd never want to live in a place like where the women on her television lived, in their mansions and Jacuzzis, where they could be lulled into self-obsession, tortured boredom, and anti-intellectualism. Belgrade, for all its faults, was my mother's home. And she couldn't imagine her child being brought up anywhere else. Her husband, she was beginning to suspect, however, had been thinking increasingly about going west. At first it seemed like a joke, but recently he wouldn't stop talking about how Yugoslavia was going to shit.

And he *was* a fan of the West. While my mother was wary of those fat cats, Dad, on the other hand, thought: What's the problem with becoming a self-made man? He was educated, he worked hard, he'd studied hard. Imagine if he was rewarded for that, rather than receiving his measly paycheck from the Mihailo Pupin Institute, where he developed software. It was work he could be paid ten times as much for in the West. He had tried his own little extra moneymaking ventures—as a student he'd worked as an usher in the cinema to fund vacations to Morocco and Italy, and there was something sweet about saving up money and watching it grow. He saw himself as an entrepreneurial thinker in a country that was built on an idealized concept of community. In a capitalist society, you could profit off your brain, your talents. Plenty of fellow engineers at his work talked of going west, and he'd join enthusiastically in the conversations, pretending for a second that his wife would ever agree to it.

"Maybe I will," he said, as my mother wobbled out the door. "Maybe I will move to America." And he took the stairs, two by two, to find a neighbor with a car that kept opposite days to the Fiat. It would have to be Branko from the first floor, with his beat-up old Renault. Branko's baby kept the household of 1C up regularly, so my dad hoped that tonight was no different, and that his knock on the door would be a welcome distraction from baby wails.

My mother waited in the dark. She had grown up in this building, her grandparents looking after her while her parents worked (in the fifties her mother was a successful professional thanks to the equal opportunities offered by the socialist system), three generations living happily under one roof.

She breathed the familiar smell of the building's foyer. And as another contraction seized her, she said to herself that she could do this, readying herself to walk slowly down the stairs as soon as it passed.

Minutes later, Branko from 1C was speeding my parents down their street: the Boulevard of Revolution. The boulevard, lined with tall buildings, plane trees, trash cans, and kiosks, was the longest street in the city. Trams dinged joyfully, despite the power outages all around. They passed the farmers' market, where old ladies with scarves tied around their heads and old men with missing teeth would peddle their wares tomorrow, like they did every day. They brought produce from the countryside, and cheese, which they would slice and offer on the end of a knife, Belgrade customers nibbling at the soft "young" feta or the harder, sharper aged one. Now, at night, the market was dark, black puddles reflecting the moon, cats mewling—the market napping while the rest of the city stayed up. The radio blared news: *"Unemployment is above 14 percent, while inflation is at 40 percent."*

"I can't listen to this shit!" my mother howled, and Branko switched to a station playing Bijelo Dugme, a band from Sarajevo. New wave and punk rock songs were becoming increasingly disgruntled, to match the attitude of the nation, and Branko and my parents, distracting themselves from the contractions that were becoming worse, sang along with the husky-voiced Bosnian singer Željko Bebek, who belted out, *"I don't have a dragon, a white horse, or a sword."* My dad and Branko nodded their heads to the beat, while my mother breathed to it, in and out. My dad sang along to the chorus, asking along with Bebek—how is a person supposed to be a hero, in these mangy times?

Branko delivered my parents to the hospital. My mother was taken away by nurses. Not even fathers were allowed in the crowded maternity wards of Yugoslavia, and my dad, like many men of the 1980s, was happy to be excused from the bloody scene, and went to wait at his parents' place.

In his shabby shoes and brown wool hat, my dad took the tram to his parents' neighborhood, biting his fingernails as he looked out the window.

Even in the small hours, Belgrade, as always, was buzzing. Drunk people spilled out of a *kafana*—a typical Yugoslavian tavern, where you could eat, drink plum brandy, smoke, and sing into the night. There were twenty-four-hour kiosks selling *burek*, and fresh bread with *ćevapčići*, delicious served with raw onion, cheese curd, and a spicy sauce called *urnebes*, which means "pandemonium."

Belgrade's party scene was strong; young women with fluffy Joan Jett haircuts, young men in turtlenecks, singing, "I Love Rock and Roll" and "Billy Jean." Cigarettes tucked behind ears, they stumbled along the streets with cracked pavements, buildings covered in graffiti, doorways smelling like piss.

During the decades following the Second World War, Yugoslavia was a hub of arts and culture, a great transnational experiment. Though known to some as a dictator, Marshal Tito was also the country's bodyguard, shielding his people from the escalating face-off that came to be called the Cold War. Tito ushered Yugoslavia away from the Soviet Union, but also away from the United States, and we became part of the Non-Aligned Movement, an informal organization that refused to become a puppet of either superpower. Joining Tito in its establishment were the leaders of India, Indonesia, Egypt, and Ghana. The idea was for these developing countries to stick together, in a spirit of non-aggression and mutual respect, and to take a middle ground between the Cold War giants. Because of our nonaligned status, and his generally light-touch dictatorship, Tito allowed influences from both the East and West to enter, and so we became the only socialist country not behind the Iron Curtain. This was our special place in the world; there was much to love about our distinct mixture of openness and peculiarity. We were the only socialist country to sell David Bowie records: young Russians traveled to Belgrade to stock up on their illicit copies of *Ziggy Stardust* and *Diamond Dogs*. The English came to enjoy our beaches, where liberated Yugoslavian women sunbathed topless. We were inexpensive, laid-back, built on hope.

The tram reached the suburb of Dedinje, and my dad hopped out. From the tram stop, he took a shortcut, walking around the perimeter of Red Star soccer stadium. The cold felt stronger around the stadium. There were no tall buildings to protect him from the wind whipping around. The trees dropped their leaves, and it smelled like rain was coming.

Dad walked uphill toward his childhood home. The electricity never got cut in his parents' neighborhood, thanks to a handful of embassies nearby. Foreigners didn't have to endure the things Yugoslavia's citizens were expected to. He took a deep breath of the wet November air, and just as the rain started to fall, he rang the doorbell to apartment 2B to wake his parents up.

His mother, Beba, opened the door in her pajamas, her face greasy with creams. Behind her was Milan, my grandfather, whom dad called "Gonzo" after the famous Muppet he resembled. (Though Gonzo wasn't the only one with a big nose; my dad had one too, and the person being born at that moment—that's me—would inherit it also). Gonzo shuffled into the living room in his neatly pressed pajamas and his old brown slippers, turning on the big radiator and the lamps, which cast light over the glittery, blinking rocks placed around the room: souvenirs from his mining engineer days.

He settled into his chair, lit a cigarette, and flicked the television on. Tito had died in 1980, two years earlier, and they were replaying his funeral.

"Do they play this every single night?!" Dad said. "I swear this was on yesterday!"

"What else is there to do while we wait?" Gonzo said, and even though he hadn't loved Tito with the fervor of some of Yugoslavia's citizens, it was obvious he was proud of the grand funeral that put our country on the international stage. Tito's death was still heralded as the most emotional moment in our recent history. He died during a football match between a Croatian team and a Serbian team, which was being broadcast across the whole of Yugoslavia. Officials walked onto the field to make the announcement, the cameras that were broadcasting the match nationwide continued to roll. Marshal Tito was dead. As the packed stadium gasped, and then began to weep, players on both sides fell to their knees. Football matches regularly provoked tears among Yugoslavians, so the groundwork had been laid for an outpouring of emotion, in the stadium and by the people watching at home.

Now, the TV's voice-over recited: "*The funeral was attended by four kings, thirty-one presidents . . . Thatcher, Arafat, Brezhnev . . .*"

My dad shook his head, annoyed at the worshipful telecast. For my dad's circle of educated friends, as he aged Tito had become a joke. His bombastic speeches were laughable. Dad rolled his eyes at all those parades, with villagers from different republics dancing ecstatically, holding hands, in a show of childlike unity. Tito's supporters went on voluntary "working vacations" to build roads because the country was broke, yet they forgave Tito for everything. The country's infrastructure was crumbling, and yet Tito enjoyed the opera, invited Sophia Loren and Elizabeth Taylor to his residence, and wore fancy designer suits.

Under Tito the country went further and further into debt and unemployment. And the balancing act that he'd managed to pull off for nearly forty years, the keeping of nationalism at bay through repression by his secret police, and the arrest of his political opponents, would, in the years following his death, prove to be a failure.

Now the TV was showing crowds of mourners, in Slovenia, Serbia, Bosnia, Croatia, Macedonia, Montenegro, all the republics of Yugoslavia. My dad watched Tito's image, in military uniform, for the thousandth time, portraits held up by mourners, some of the bereaved kissing the image as they cried. There were identical squares, statues, streets dedicated to Tito all around Yugoslavia, as if, as this country became more and more divided, Tito was still trying to keep it together, if only with his name and image, repeated across the land—a ghost that wouldn't quit. Yet the nationalism grew, and my dad claimed it would boil over into violence.

"Why aren't they talking about *that* on TV?" he asked of Gonzo, suddenly frustrated, thinking about the future of his growing family. "There'll be a war here!"

"Don't say such things!" Gonzo said. "Haven't we had enough wars in this country?"

Some of the fluorescent lights at the hospital were dead, but others flickered, still holding on as my mother prepared for birth. In a room crowded with other women at various stages of delivery, she got undressed and put on a gown, and then her vagina was shaved. My mother was born in 1953, in this same hospital. She wondered with horror if the ancient razor that the nurse was using was the same one that was used on her mother. She glanced with concern at an old heart-rate monitor, and listened to the squeak of cots threatening to collapse.

My mother tried to distract herself from the pain of her contractions and the hospital smell of detergent masking bodily fluids. She thought about how as a teenager, she and her friends would take the train to Italy to buy jeans and eat gelato. Even if money was tight, my grandmother would slip my mother some change and tell her to buy a miniskirt. "When else are you going to wear one? When you're fifty?"

At that moment, my mother decided she would take the same attitude with her child. *What would the fashions be when this baby was a teen?* she thought. See-through clothing popped into her head as a viable option, and she decided: *My child will have the latest transparent wear.* Even if she had to fight her stingy, nerd husband all the way, she'd make sure her child felt special.

The contractions were coming faster now, and my mother was moved to the delivery room.

She pushed, and hours passed, as I had become stuck, having painstakingly tied my umbilical cord in a knot way back when I was a tiny fetus, adding an extra level of difficulty for the overworked hospital staff.

Thanks to a group effort, I was finally drawn out, a slick, silent bundle. A midwife held me tightly, so I wouldn't bounce back in on that short umbilical cord. I was alarmingly motionless until a midwife smacked my behind, and I let out a wail.

However, thanks to the effort of a rough birth, I was hideous, with a chafed face and a blue head. Also, my head was mushroom-shaped, the top of it resembling a sassy beret. My mother looked at me dumbfounded, uncertain whether this bizarre blue creature might forgo the breast and request a baguette instead.

"We'll fix that!" the midwife said as she observed my unconventional head shape. As she massaged my soft, newborn skull into a more mainstream silhouette, she said, "much better," admiring her work.

There were no wheelchairs to take her to the recovery room, so my mother shuffled there. To make matters worse, every bed was taken, so she was made to share one with a woman named Yoka, who had traveled all the way to the hospital from the countryside just in time to give birth. They lay back-to-back, their recently vacated swollen stomachs teetering off either side of the bed. My mother cringed whenever Yoka's calloused feet scratched her under the covers, and she eventually became so grossed out, despite the pain, that she snuck out of the room to observe me through the window to the nursery, where the newborns lay in rows. My mother found her daughter, the serious-faced bald one with the squishy skull, and she smoked as she looked lovingly through the glass, until the nurses, playing cards and smoking in their station, chased her away, and she had to crawl back into bed with Yoka's sharp heels.

When dawn had broken, my dad stood behind the hospital. Following my mother's telephoned instructions to a T, he'd brought along a basket of food and a ball of twine. Guests weren't allowed in the crowded maternity ward, for health and hygiene reasons, but my mother couldn't stand the hospital food and she was starving. She was waiting at the open window for the *gibanica*; a feta cheese and phyllo pastry pie, and "reform torte," a nutty, creamy dessert—both made by her mother, at her request. Dad spotted her and threw the ball of twine all the way up the gray building to the third floor. She didn't catch it.

"You didn't throw it right!" she yelled down, falling easily back into the irritated tone she used with her husband.

"You can't catch!" he yelled up, glad to see she was recovering well enough to gripe.

He threw it again and she caught it.

"If you'd thrown it like that the first time, I would have caught it," she said, hauling the basket up, eager to have the last word.

Many of the women in the maternity ward communicated with their families from the window like this, and the nurses turned a blind eye, easily bribed with snacks and treats. My mother took out the stash and lowered the basket back down again, having placed in it a little sketch of me. She had always been talented at drawing, and my dad keenly looked at the image of his daughter: her bald head, eyes shut tight, puckered lips, and little fists balled up.

The following day, our sanctioned day on the roads, my father picked us up in the Fiat, and got to see me in all my real-life glory.

My mother had wished for a boy, but Dad hoped for a girl; in this day and age women could do anything, and he would teach his daughter about computers, science, anything she wanted. In socialist Yugoslavia, women were called "comrade" just like men were, and they participated in the workforce, earning as much as their male counterparts. But the next generation, my dad thought, who knew what they had in store? Who knew what his child might invent, what exciting new world she would be a part of? The other good thing about girls was that they didn't go to the army.

That evening, family and friends came over in droves with hand-me-down gear and clothing from their older babies. Soon there was a crowd of people smoking and chatting over cake and alcohol to celebrate my arrival. I was passed from one grandparent to another. I was kissed by my mother's friends from the university: philosophers, psychologists, eccentrics. And then by my father's straightlaced friends: engineers, architects, mathematicians.

The discussion turned toward my name. Right away my father had come up with nicknames for me: Piglet, Gooseberry, Boy, Churchill—because of my alert, bald-headed resemblance to the statesman. My real name, though, was still undecided.

Stojan, a journalist, looked over at me. "These days, you might be wise to name her Serbislava," he said. My mother groaned. "It's true!" he said. "Call her *Glory to Serbs*. Let's not pretend it's not happening. We are living in a country where the words 'Brotherhood and Unity' will very soon be dead in the water."

"Why do you have to ruin everything with politics?" my mother said.

"What about Sofija?" my mother's best friend, Dada, said, as she peered into my serious face.

"Like Sophia Loren," my dad said.

"It's international, so she can travel the world," someone said, and my dad added, "Or emigrate."

"God forbid," both of my grandmothers said in unison.

"We're not going anywhere," my mother said, looking at my crinkled face. "Sofia: goddess of wisdom."

Nods around the room. Everyone agreed that more wisdom was exactly what we needed right now. But it's not what we would get. Whatever wisdom existed in our little country—as imperfect and weird as it was—would soon be replaced by chaos, and this pleasant world I was born into wouldn't last for long. Over the coming years, the people milling about in our living room would scatter all over the world.

2

The Fuzzy Worm of Capitalism

When I was a baby, my parents were featured on a Serbian television program about modern parenting. My mother knew someone at the TV station, and she jumped at the chance to show off her baby on TV. She was well connected to the "intellectual elite" of Belgrade, a gregarious group that would come to our apartment to talk and drink. For the TV shoot, my parents stood side-by-side, trying to look relaxed in Tašmajdan Park in Belgrade's center. My dad held me to face the camera in my white sun hat, my mouth open in wonder at the boom mic that loomed above our heads. My mother sported her new haircut—she'd lost the perm in favor of a trendy Rod Stewart style with fluffy bangs. An interviewer asked them questions about modern parenting, as elderly passersby peered toward the camera. My parents explained that, unlike the generation before them, they shared parenting duties. "Except breastfeeding," my dad added, and the interviewer laughed.

My mother enjoyed maternity leave and continued leading an active social life. Every few days, she and I would go to meet with her friend Dada and her new baby Marko, or to the café near the university, where she'd catch up with her colleagues and I'd smear ice cream on my face as the adults cooed. She continued hosting parties at our place like she'd done before I was born, and she tried to keep the political discussions to a minimum, calling them "boring" and choosing to ignore the news reports of rising nationalist tensions and increased unemployment.

In 1985, after one year of paid leave, and two years unpaid (another perk of Yugo socialism), my mother went back to work tutoring psychology students at the University of Belgrade a few days a week. While my parents worked, I was left in the care of grandparents.

My earliest memory is from when I was four years old, in Tašmajdan Park, where I'd been filmed as a baby. Still agape at the world around me, I sat beside my grandfather Gonzo on a bench, dangling my legs off the edge while he talked. Gonzo, the former mining engineer, explained that the word *Tašmajdan* derived from Turkish, and underneath where we sat there used to be a stone quarry during the Ottoman times. Many of Belgrade's century-old buildings were made from the stone that came from under where we sat, Gonzo said, and then suddenly he put his hand across my knees to stop my legs moving and put his finger up to his lips. I froze, terrified I'd done something wrong. Even though I was basically never scolded, the praise of adults was what I lived for. So now I watched my grandfather with bated breath.

Gonzo said: "Shall we catch a pigeon?" And to my astonishment, he got off the bench, tucked his tie out of the way, and, squat-walking in his brown suit, cupped his hands and slowly advanced toward some pigeons. Very gently, he encircled a pigeon with his hands and grabbed it, the other birds flying off in a burst, and Grandpa Gonzo sat back beside me, holding the captured pigeon. With pounding heart, I stared at the bird, as he brought it closer to my face. I'd never considered a pigeon this closely, with its smell of feathers and straw, its head cocking from side to side in a panic. Gonzo told me I could touch the bird—despite being ravenous for experiences, I was not one to take initiative. With Gonzo's encouragement, I brought my finger up to the pigeon's chest and stroked it, feeling the bird's soft feathers and quickened heartbeat, which was similar to my own. He let the pigeon go and it cracked its wings open and flew away. I would never look at a pigeon the same way, now that I knew about their heartbeats, those beady, strange eyes, and the musty smell.

My grandfather died not long after that, and whenever I thought of him after he was gone, I would remember either that thrilling day in the park, or when, for my fifth birthday, the doorbell rang and I found a bike on the doorstep—my grandfather running up the steps flailing his arms, saying "She got away from me!"—implying that the bike had climbed up on its own. That day, there was a party at our place and I was the center of attention, our home filled with family and friends gushing over me, like they did every birthday. That was only a few weeks before Gonzo was diagnosed with lung cancer, and only six months before we left our comfortable world, but I had no inkling of these things, and I ran down the stairs followed by my grandfather carrying my bike, bursting to take it for a ride around the block.

In my preschool years, my parents split their spare time between obsessing over me—praising me for my vocabulary, taking my childish monologues seriously, talking to me like I was an adult; more modern parenting methods that they believed in—and falling into fits of argument about money, politics, or our family's future. During those latter times my advanced conjugations of the plural forms of tricky words like "buffalo," which had impressed endlessly, would fade into the background as my parents' gazes would turn from me to each other.

In 1986, the news reports warned that the radiation from the Chernobyl nuclear disaster might reach us over in Yugoslavia, even though we were over six hundred miles away. My mother, who was in the early weeks of her second pregnancy, booked an abortion because she was terrified of the possibility of her child having birth defects from the radiation. In a panic, my parents rolled up the carpets as the news instructed, and my mother ran to the grocery store and bought every canned good they had, determined to save her living child from the poison that might be floating our way. The contaminated cloud however went north, toward Sweden and Finland—a rare case of wealthier countries suffering while we went unscathed. Nevertheless, for the next year, my mother remained shaken, and she insisted that all my milk, fruits, and vegetables come from cans. Every now and then, she would pull me close and look at my eyes and throat as if she was a doctor, and if ever I coughed, her eyes would widen with terror.

That summer, like many Yugoslavians, we went on our annual vacation to Croatia. With my mother's mother, Grandma Xenia, we headed to Cavtat, where her sister Olga lived. Olga's husband, Great-Uncle Marko, had been born into a rich Croatian family, and they were among the people who'd had their wealth stripped from them by Tito's army, the Partizans, after the Second World War. Old money had been seized, in line with the Communist ideals that the Partizans held sacred. Though Great Uncle Marko's family had once owned half of Cavtat, he had been left only with this little house surrounded by oleander bushes and hydrangeas. A tortoise lived in the garden bed, and I fed it slices of tomato.

Grandma Xenia and Great Aunt Olga sat together in the courtyard in their matching cotton summer dresses, their skinny legs crossed at the ankles and reminisced as I listened. "When we were children," they would say, "our mother made us brush our hair with fifty strokes each night. Our hair would be beautiful and shiny, as if we were going to a party. But we never went anywhere . . ." I would imagine these wrinkly, veiny old women when they were little girls just like me, with tightly braided hair and strict parents. I savored their stories, which they told through clouds of smoke as they inhaled cigarette after cigarette; there was the one about a tiny old relative who, when she came to visit, would walk off the train wearing five dresses one on top of the other. She said it was more practical than packing a suitcase and having to crease all the dresses. "She was so small, she slept in a washing basket," Grandma Xenia said, and I pictured this Thumbelina snoring in a soft bed of clothes.

Each day we left the old ladies talking in the little house and went to the waterfront. My parents sat in cafés by the sea, wearing not much and laughing with their friends, while we kids splashed in the water, or sat bored beside them as they stayed for one last drink or cigarette.

On the beach, my parents always read *Time* magazine, which was sold in the local store, where you could buy Croatian, Serbian, and foreign papers. Dad loved learning about Bill Gates, and the other entrepreneurs making it in the West, reading snippets out loud to my mother, who feigned great boredom. She, on the other hand, furrowed her brow looking for bad news, now that Chernobyl was behind us. *Time* is where she first read about the deadly new disease AIDS, which caused her to stop getting pedicures: who was to say it couldn't be transmitted via nail hygiene tools? She read darkly about the hole in the ozone layer as I waded carefully into the shallows, naked except for my arm floaties.

The world was becoming a terrifying place, she decided, squinting at an ad for a "microwave" and announcing it was probably yet another source of radiation. "I would never buy one of these, even if they *were* available in Yugoslavia."

"*Nothing* is available in Yugoslavia," Dad laughed, looking over his glasses at her.

At Belgrade University, as well as teaching, my mother was getting her master's in clinical psychology, focusing on analyzing children's drawings for their psychological content. She would come home with the drawings of damaged or abused children whom she'd interviewed, and when I asked about the children, she would give me the details, treating me like an interested colleague rather than a preschooler. One of the drawings that my mother particularly admired was framed in our hallway, the work of a girl who was five, just like me, but who'd had half her brain removed due to a tumor and was now disabled. Her drawing was a surreal representation of people at a beach, their colorful bodies bent into unnatural shapes, throwing a ball to each other. Another of my mother's case studies was a troubled eleven-year-old boy who drew hyperrealistic images of people who looked like superheroes performing acts of violence. Among his drawings strewn out on our dining room table I once saw an eerily accurate sketch of my mother with a knife plunged into her head. When I gasped, my mother snapped it up, laughing. "It's *symbolic*," she said, as if that would reassure me.

Often, she'd bring home diagnostic tests and subject me to them, eager to make sure I was developing well, and not going the way of her deranged clients.

"Sofija," she said, and I looked up from the princess I'd been drawing. "If you were a flower, what flower would you be?"

"A rose?"

"Would you have thorns?" she asked, and I thought, *What does Mama want me to say?*

"Yes."

"Oh my god," she said, scribbling something in her notebook, shaking her head sadly. Having given what was obviously the wrong answer, I tearfully went back to drawing, distressed that I'd failed her. Her detailed notes on my progress stated that for my first four years I was above average as far as my language, comprehension, and problem-solving was concerned. A rooster I drew at the age of two was proudly displayed on the psychology faculty notice board, beneath it my mother's handwritten caption: "Sofija, two years old, drawing at four-year-old standard."

By the age of five, however, my glory days were behind me. My mother's notebooks presented me as having regular intelligence, but being a bit of an emotional mess:

"She watches the scene in Disney's 'Dumbo' where the mother elephant is shackled, and cries. Once it is over, she insists we play the scene again, and cries again."

"When other children in kindergarten are reprimanded by the teacher, Sofija will often cry."

"When her grandmother gave her a book she already had, she cried because she thought she'd disappointed her grandmother," and so went my mother's notes; her pride at my empathy intertwined with concern at my lack of emotional robustness.

At the age of five, I had a long face and dark blond bangs that stretched from ear to ear. As for my ears, they were always perked up, trying to make sense of the conversations around me. I listened keenly to my parents' conversations, trying to piece together what "inflation" meant, and how it related to shitholes, the cost of cigarettes, and a mysterious place called *zapad* ("the West"). This was the place my dad and his friends talked about, where people who knew about computers were seen as heroes and received fat paychecks.

Although the Serbian language has a smaller vocabulary, it contains much more profanity than English does, and in general treats cursing as a more accepted practice. Walking the streets of the neighborhood where I grew up, it's not unusual to hear someone's grandma shout "To cock with it all!" when she drops her groceries. And in my case, it wasn't unheard of for my mother to tell my father (with the same potency as "Take your visa and piss off!"), "Take your visa and go back to your mother's cunt!" This was how my mother responded to my dad's suggestions that our family should procure visas and emigrate somewhere far away.

"But in the West," my dad shouted, "you can live like a normal person—you don't have to line up for detergent, like we do in this shithole!"

She knew this. She knew that Dad was eager to join the technological revolution, that he wanted his children (there was a baby on the way) to speak English, to have access to the liberal Western style of education. She also knew that the West was an unknown place, far from family and friends, where there was violence and disease and where she would have to speak in a foreign language to be understood—yes, a language she'd learned at school, but it was also a language in which she felt clumsy and inarticulate. She could put up with lining up for detergent if it meant being at home. So Belgrade was gritty and politicians were always snapping at one another—big deal, she'd rather her children grow up in an environment full of familiar faces than be torn from their roots, living the lives of *Dynasty* characters and stuffing themselves full of McDonald's.

My go-to mode was introspective distress mixed with bursts of extroversion. I loved to express myself, and, as always, relied on the encouragement of adults around me to boost my confidence. When I got the doting attention of a kind adult, I would go forth like an excited puppy, telling stories and espousing theories that would make grandparents cluck, "You're so clever, Sofija!" But when an adult was busy and brushed me away, I would recoil, withdrawing like a pup smacked on the butt with a rolled up newspaper, crawling into myself anxiously, before replenishing my excitement for the next time it was desirable. At age five, I had taken a serious interest in Lepa Brena, an icon of the contemporary folk genre known as "newly composed music"—an urbanized version of folk that would later transform into the even more frenetic turbo-folk. In the late eighties, singers like Lepa Brena were enjoying huge success with hits including "Long Legs" and "Mile Loves the Disco." The news increasingly showed politicians arguing about things that made no sense to me. Nationalism was rising in parliament as well as among militant peasants, who I watched on TV, shouting their grievances in villages, and there were grim reports on the economic crisis—the country's debt, the rising unemployment, the scarcity of goods. Many people in Yugoslavia liked to turn away from these unpleasant reports of ethnic unrest and increased poverty and would flip the channel to the gyrating performers and folksy beat, letting their minds drift to a simpler world. It was the contemporary version of Tito's parades, washing over troubling issues with explosions of dance and goodwill, a pacifier for the whole nation. My Grandma Beba and I liked to watch the performers on TV, or hum the earworm melodies while sitting in the dark, a frequent occurrence due to the ever-increasing electricity shortages.

On the tram on the way home from Grandma Beba's one day, I couldn't help myself. I'd had a day of grandparental attention and several slices of my favorite, walnutty "Rozen torte," and I was feeling relaxed and energized. When I wasn't cautious or distressed, concerned about my parents' arguments, disturbed by what was unsaid but hung in the air: that all roads were leading out of Belgrade and into the unknown—I felt a great energy inside, a desire to tell stories that were as thrilling as the picture books I memorized, or the Disney films I knew scene-for-scene. When I shook off the tension that encroached from the television and the adults, I felt bursts of uninhibited lust for life.

Now, on the tram, full of cake and generally pleased with myself, I caught a woman's eye and winked at her. I put my hands on my hips, stuck out a foot, and jigged my leg up and down in the style of Lepa Brena, singing the words to one of her hits: "*Miki, Miki, you have such a good body . . .*" I crooned, to the surprise of the woman, and the mortification of my mother. I had expected the entire tram to break into applause as I sang and danced—"Look! A tiny replica of the great Lepa Brena!"—but in reality, most people ignored me, my voice came out as a squeak, and my mother pulled me onto her lap and asked what had got into me. Often, the way I imagined things was not the way things turned out, and despite my occasional unbridled attempts, my actual life was so much less dazzling than that of my favorite characters from books or films.

While my mother tried to keep one unblinking eye on my inner life and the other on her child psychology and global disasters research, my dad had his own unrelated obsession. He'd gone halves with a friend to buy a computer and he'd glassed in our balcony to make what he called "the computer room"—a tiny space dominated by the large, whirring PC, on which he programmed when he came home from his job as a software engineer. It was the eighties, we were among the first in our circle to have a computer, and Dad's nerd friends would come over to marvel at it. Through the computer room's glass you could see our building's backyard, where I would go out and play with kids, looking up every now and then to see my dad's face glowing green before his screen.

"Just you wait, one day everyone will have a personal computer!" my dad would say to my mother.

"What idiocy! Why would *anyone* want a computer?" my mother would respond, looking at the horrible bulky machine, with its green text rolling down the screen, and, like most people in the era before email, finding it hard to conceive that she would one day have her own laptop, from which she could access information about the world, communicate with her friends, and whittle away hours looking at animal videos.

I would sit on Dad's lap while he programmed with zeal, both of us admiring the script running down the page by itself. His engineering skills and passion for trying to conquer developing technologies made him a sought-after employee in the booming field of information technology. While Yugoslavia itself wasn't experiencing corporate growth, Western countries on the brink of the information age were keen to get their hands on plucky programmers from overseas—to drain the brains of smaller, poorer countries just like Yugoslavia, luring the talent to enjoy their towering skyscrapers and large paychecks.

One night, I was eavesdropping on my parents while pretending to play with the Lego set that my mother had got for my birthday from the international store, which also sold the latest editions of English-language psychology books that were not translated into Serbo-Croatian, that she would save for. I felt special for having the Lego, as none of my friends did. Even though my clothes were hand-me-downs, and my toy supply was limited, my mother spoiled me as much as our means allowed. Despite her love of our homeland, she admired things that came from other countries, saying "Look at that quality." Even though, unlike the West, we didn't have ads that overwhelmed us with choice and fueled materialism, my mother still recognized that luxury items from abroad were superior to some of our shoddy local products, and she wanted me to have the best.

Not only did I have Lego, I also enjoyed Lindt chocolate elephants mailed to us by my businessman uncle Misha, who lived in Paris. The chocolates were luxurious compared to the locally produced chocolate banana candies which we bought less frequently ever since my mother had found a steel nail in one that we were sharing.

I was playing with my special toys when, out the corner of my eye, I saw my parents standing around the dining room table with brochures from the Australian embassy spread out across the surface, where the drawings of mentally compromised children normally were.

"Australia!" my dad said in the adventuresome tone he used when trying to get me to eat food I didn't like, this time trying to engage my mother. He had applied for an Australian visa, just to see if he could get one and to both my parents' surprise, it was approved. My mother, with her pregnant belly sticking out, was now waving around an image of Uluru, the great desert monolith of Central Australia, asking with venom in her voice whether *this* was where he expected us to live.

In those preinternet days, my parents knew nothing about Australia, except that it was quicker to get a work visa for there than it was for America and Canada. But at least my parents knew about those countries from reading and watching films. For Australia, their main references were *Crocodile Dundee* and *All the Rivers Run*, a television show about a female paddleboat captain.

Ignoring my mother's negativity, my dad called out to me. "Sofi, look what I got as a souvenir from the Australian embassy," he said, tossing a tiny heart-shaped soap wrapped in fragrant tissue paper in my direction. "When we move to Australia, you can have soap like that all the time." As my mother's nostrils flared with fury, I sat on the floor of our living room, on the rug that had been there since my mother was a girl. I looked down at my little Lego village, just as the heart-shaped soap landed in the middle of the scene like a meteorite from space.

In the evenings, my parents' friends would come over, and there'd be the usual laughter, punctuated more frequently now by arguments about politics. They talked about Kosovo, a region that had long been a point of contention and debate. Unrest due to ethnic tensions had persisted between the Orthodox Serbs and Muslim Albanians in Kosovo throughout the twentieth century, but after World War II, Tito "solved the problem" by doing what he did best—quashing nationalism (or at least sweeping it under the rug). To curb Serbia's dominance, he made Kosovo an autonomous province within Serbia, with its own government. Tensions between the growing Albanian population and the minority Serbs simmered until 1987, when an ambitious Serbian politician named Slobodan Milošević went against Communist Party lines and took the side of the Serbs. Favoring one group over another was a violation of Yugoslavia's guiding principle of "Brotherhood and Unity." "No one will beat you," he said to the Serbs who claimed they'd been mistreated by Albanians.

This single act—of taking the Serbs' side—was a dangerous thing to do, and he knew it. Much of the tension in Yugoslavia was based around the fact that the Serbs were numerically dominant, but the country couldn't function if they were also politically dominant: the principle of "Brotherhood and Unity" that had held the country together more than forty years was based on a pact that the groups would be given equal weight, without one looming over the others. And now, here was someone taking the side of the Serbs, and many were eager to hear it. The other groups within the country, afraid of impending dominance, were not.

Milošević's statement, which was broadcast nationwide, was enough to unravel everything Tito had done to quiet nationalism, and all over the country, nationalist rumbles began, from Kosovo to the republics of Croatia, Bosnia, and Slovenia.

This is what my parents and their friends talked about in our smoky living room. My dad brought up our last vacation in Croatia, when his friend Miki, a Serb like us, had showed up to the café in a fury. He'd been to a nearby bakery and had asked for *hleb*—the Serbian word for bread. The Croatian baker pretended not to understand. In Croatian dialect, the word was *kruh*. Everyone in Yugoslavia knew both of the words—the language was called Serbo-Croatian and both words were acceptable. Miki was offended by the Croatian baker, who was expressing his separatist feelings by pretending not to understand him. *Brotherhood and unity, my ass*, the baker probably thought, deciding to show the Serb where he could shove his *hleb*.

"A war is brewing," my dad said now, as they all sat in the living room.

My mother tried to downplay it: "If anything, there'll be a separation, like what happened in Czechoslovakia, and we'll still go to Croatia every summer and laugh about it." But she hadn't been through military service like Dad and some of their friends had. She didn't know how broken the country was, they told her now. Especially in the rural areas. Pockets of Serbs living in Croatia were still sore from the Second World War, our friend Boris said. "A Serbian living in Croatia said to me, 'I love Belgrade. Over there, everything seems so nice and harmonious, you're always going to galleries and embracing each other like everything is just fine. Over here, the graves are still fresh from the war. I know the people who killed my grandparents.' And he pointed to where they lived." Boris's story was met with concern.

Serbs and Croats had been on opposite sides during the Second World War—the puppet Croatian fascist state fought with the Axis powers, while the Allies supported Communist and Serbian resistance movements. The new, socialist Yugoslavia was formed afterward by Tito's Partizans, under the understanding that former feuds would be forgotten. And as far as urbanites like my mother were concerned, it had worked—she had Croatian friends and Bosnian friends, and they all loved one another. She'd gone to Croatia her whole life and never had a problem! But not everyone felt the same, especially those living in areas where Serbs and Croats had fought during the war, and where memories of the war were still strong.

As the months passed and the discussions at our apartment got bleaker, my mother, heavily pregnant with my sister, seemed willing to admit that our country was fucked, and she would throw her hands up in the air, for once without words, and glance at my dad, who would inevitably mention emigration.

People always stayed late at our place, and when he got tired of the drunken conversations, my dad would go to bed early with a book. I would peek from my room into my parents' and see his familiar form propped up in bed, his glasses on the bedside table. He seemed to be mirroring the framed illustration above him: a boy in bed reading. Except the boy in the fanciful illustration didn't have a lamp, as my father did, but a bright-eyed cat, who lit up his manuscript. The illustration was from a children's book about the famous Yugoslavian inventor Nikola Tesla; my parents had been given it as a wedding present, and both loved it.

When he went to bed to read, my dad became oblivious to the noise, lost in the world of fiction. My mother had become used to this, one of her husband's quirks that everyone knew: at any point in the evening, Lola might disappear, unapologetically choosing the company of a book over that of people.

On the days my parents worked, often my mother's mother, Grandma Xenia, picked me up in the morning. Sometimes she glowered at my dad, because she disapproved of his shouting at my mother, and their arguments did not stop for company. Although I was used to my parents' disagreements, and I'd certainly heard neighbors and friends' parents fighting too, it would take some time for me to realize that my parents argued more than other people. Once, my mother's friend Divna said point-blank to my dad, "You're rude to her," and after Divna went home, my mother said to me, "Sometimes people who love each other shout at each other, and then there are people who don't say a mean word to each other, yet they hate each other."

The other thing Grandma Xenia did not love about her son-in-law was his eagerness to leave Belgrade, and the possibility that her daughter and granddaughter might suddenly be transplanted to the other side of the earth did not sit well with her. Three mornings a week, Grandma Xenia took me to French kindergarten. Multilingualism was considered important, and throughout their schooling, Yugoslavian children learned two languages. My parents were planning to send me to a primary school that taught French and English, so I was, like many of Belgrade's kids, getting a head start on the French part. Following socialist ideals, kindergarten was free, equal, and inevitably, overcrowded. Grandma Xenia spoke French, and on the way to kindergarten, she would quiz me on the simple phrases we repeated daily as a chorus. We walked hand in hand—my mother secretly following us, I later discovered, peeking from behind the plane trees that lined the street, late for work but determined to observe the state of what she referred to as my separation anxiety.

I would request that Grandma Xenia recount my favorite stories, and as she told them, letting her voice rise or fall with emotion, taking dramatic pauses, I was a rapt audience, repeating the stories to myself and imagining telling them to my parents, or even to a crowd of children who could in turn watch *me* create a magical world.

There was the story about how when she was living in a small town, despite being forbidden to by her parents, young Xenia would sneak into the high school gym at night and tumble across the mats, vault over the horse, all by herself in the darkness, determined to become an Olympic gymnast. I marveled at her bravery, her disregard for rules. There was the story of how when Grandma Xenia was pregnant during World War II, she left her husband Novak in Belgrade (she was angry at him because he'd been gambling) and convinced a German officer to pretend she was his wife so she could sneak across a Nazi checkpoint to be with her parents. Then there was the story of when she was traveling for work and met a hemophilic peasant boy on a train, and helped hold a towel to his throat, which had been sliced by a blade of wheat and would not stop bleeding due to his disease. Every now and then, Grandma Xenia and I would break into full-throated renditions of Serbian love songs from her youth.

It wasn't just Grandma Xenia who told dramatic tales. Ex-Yugoslavians are prone to telling melancholy stories and singing songs about heartbreak. Most ex-Yugos have in their arsenal tales that feature something alarming conveyed in a jovial tone, be it murder, infidelity, or, in the case of my own great-grandfather's life story, kidnapping. Great-Grandfather Aleksandar was a swaggering young pilot who would go to villages and "abduct" a pretty woman, then fly with her *under* the bridge of the town, skimming the water of the river below. Observers would scream, concerned he was going to bring down the bridge or crash, and then they'd applaud wildly when he passed the plane under the bridge, like threading a needle. He'd get put in jail for his delinquency, and come out days later a hero. The kidnap victims, apparently, would swoon. Even my other grandma, Beba (the kidnapper's daughter), who was known for her sunny disposition, liked telling Grimm-like stories, such as the one in which a family came to her cosmetics salon bringing their daughter whose face was covered in hair. "She was a freak who had been living locked in a room because of her unsightliness, and they had come all the way from their village to see if I could help," Grandma Beba whispered. "I got out my wax, and started. Little by little, we revealed a nose, mouth, a beautiful face that had been covered in bearlike fur."

These were the stories I grew up on. Stories that entwined tragedy and comedy with chaos, set in a land many times battered by war, where people were poor, often drunk, and frequently heartbroken. I played these stories in my head, imagining my family as protagonists in thrilling scenarios, in my very own Belgrade; or in villages, forests, or caves by the Danube River; or even farther, in glamorous parts of Europe, where Grandma Xenia's work as an agricultural expert took her to exciting conferences. On her travels she saw beautiful French women at a Parisian hotel, wearing matching chic bathing suits. She attended a circus performance in Hungary featuring little people, some of them clearly miserable. And she went all the way to America, where she was the only woman in a conference room of men talking about agriculture, who were forced to respect her when she appeared as the representative of the entire country of Yugoslavia to express her opinions on the cross-pollination of fragrant flowers.

And even if some of the adult-themed stories that I savored chipped away a little at my innocence, they generally enriched my inner life, and played in my head when I daydreamed.

The story that knocked the breath out of me, however, wasn't one of Grandma Xenia's, though I heard it on a day like any other, not long after Grandma Xenia and I walked up the steps of the gray building where other grandparents dragged little children to their classes.

When we got to the echoey hallway, my grandma joined the other grandparents. She was following my mother's instructions not to leave, in case I got upset, which happened often, so, amazingly, for my three-hour kindergarten stint she stayed. The old people sat on vinyl chairs, where they would smoke and complain about their pensions and the cost of eggs. I went into the classroom, where there was a long table and chairs. I found my friends Milica, Ana, and Eva, and we all sat with our notebooks open, ready to copy down words Madame Marie wrote on the board. I considered Madame Marie very beautiful and glamorous. She wore a navy suit jacket with shoulder pads, matching blue eye shadow, hair in a voluminous bob, coral lipstick, and strong perfume mixed in with the smell of cigarettes (the base smell for everything in my childhood). For good work, we would receive heart stickers in our notebooks. I liked to flick through the pages of my book and admire those hearts.

As usual, that day I stared down the long table at Nemanja. I had first been drawn to him at our kindergarten concert a month earlier. I had been dressed in my finest outfit for the concert: a dark blue woollen dress with a pinafore, hair held back with colorful clips, and, like all little girls at that time, white socks with lace at the top and black patent shoes. During our performance, I stood in the "tall row," staring at him in the shorter-people row before me. In a white shirt and bow tie, Nemanja sang along to *Alouette,"* the sadistic song about plucking a lark, one body part at the time: *"First I pluck your back, then I pluck your head . . ."* Everyone sang but me. I didn't care about the performance because all I could concentrate on was Nemanja's delicate ear. I didn't know what I wanted to do; reach out and touch it, and then take it from there? But of course, I didn't. I just watched breathlessly, admiring his half profile, his soft hair. *This must be love,* I said to myself then, comparing the emotions I felt with those Snow White had for the Prince, or the singer Lepa Brena had for Miki with the good body.

Now that it was months later and we were back in class, a curveball was thrown at my unrequited romance. Short-haired Dina put her hand up to go to the bathroom. Nemanja's hand shot up straight after, and he followed her out of the room. Smelling a rat, I threw my hand in the air. *"Le toilet s'il vous plaît!"*

I ran down the hallway, past my grandma, who held a cardboard cone containing fried whitebait, something I normally loved, but now I ignored the delicious fish, hurtling toward the bathroom, looking to all the world like I was having a toilet emergency.

I threw the door of the bathroom open and was greeted by a tender scene that rendered me speechless.

Past the tiny stalls with the child-height toilets, Dina was washing her hands at the sink. Leaning against a wall, Nemanja stood there watching, entranced.

"Wash, wash," he said.

I watched, agape. Okay, yes, as five-year-olds, we were used to being told to wash our hands. But I had never heard an instruction said with so much adoration. As far as kindergarten exchanges go, Nemanja's utterance was positively romantic. It was like the Tramp had come out of my television screen and was talking to Lady, right in front of me. His love was palpable.

I wanted Nemanja to say "wash, wash" like that to *me*. I wanted him to look at *me* the way he looked at Dina. I imagined him turning from her, and seeing me, realizing his mistake—realizing that *I* was the one he loved. And then he would come over and—something. A hug?

But they didn't even notice me, their attention focused on Dina's meticulous washing. She did everything right.

I thought of all the wonderful things about Dina. How she could scrunch up her mouth and move it side to side like a sassy cartoon character. How she had nice short, dark hair. My hair was long, with massive bangs—because my hairdresser was my mother, and she wasn't very good.

Suddenly, I was filled with the fury of the unloved. I slammed the door of the bathroom as hard as I could, hoping that the force would snap them out of it, or at least that it would banish the image of the two of them from my mind.

I marched down the hallway and back to class, too heartbroken to even glance at my smoking grandmother, who tilted her cone of whitebait in my direction. I just grabbed a handful and shoved it in my mouth, the delicious saltiness turning to ash on my tongue.

Once everyone was back in class, it was nap time. We put our arms on the table and crossed them over, using them as a pillow to rest our heads, legs dangling under the table. I kept my miserable eyes open, staring at Nemanja, then at Dina. Nap time usually gave Madame Marie a chance to talk to Madame Violet from the class next door. They hovered at the doorway, chatting in low voices about money or men, while we pretended to sleep. But today, Madame Marie was sitting at her desk, alone, even more testy than usual. For whatever reasons of her own, suddenly, she interrupted our nap and said: "Let me tell you the true story of the Hunchback of Notre Dame." We raised our heads like little meerkats. We'd never heard of the Hunchback of Notre Dame. The Disney film wouldn't be released for another eight years, and as five-year-olds we were not familiar with the literary works of Victor Hugo.

Madame Marie sucked on her cigarette in the way she did when she was angry. Her legs were crossed—one of her high-heeled shoes jiggling from the end of her raised foot, as she launched into her own version of the story.

"The Hunchback was a young man who had a big humpback," she said. "He was nice, and smart, but horrible to look at. He was in love with a beautiful girl. But she didn't love him back."

Yes, I thought, eager to hear the tale of a kindred soul.

"The girl didn't love him because of his disability. Who wants to be seen with someone like that? With a big humped back?" she asked our class, several small heads nodding along in agreement (except mine, as I was 100 percent Team Hunchback).

"The Hunchback thought if he could just lose the hump, she'd like him." Madame Marie inhaled on the cigarette.

"So he decided to have it surgically removed."

I held my breath for what came next.

"He gathered money. He begged for it and borrowed from his relatives." A murmur of understanding went around the classroom—lack of funds was a familiar issue in many of our households. We listened to our parents argue about it, we heard rumors of pensioners eating pigeons.

Madame Marie continued. "So he went to the hospital to have the hump removed, but the surgeon warned the Hunchback: 'This operation is very dangerous. If it is not successful, you will die. You will lose a lot of blood.' But the Hunchback just said: 'Do it.'"

I felt tears building in my eyes. I repeated it to myself, moved: "Do it!"

"Anyway, then the surgeon performed the operation and it was a failure."

We stared at her.

"He died," she said, to drive the point home.

I looked down at my notebook, so Madame Marie wouldn't notice I was crying and send me out to my grandma, as per usual.

"That should teach you to use your money wisely," Madame Marie said obscurely, looking pleased with herself.

I don't know why Madame Marie chose to tell this story to a group of five-year-olds that day. It could be that she was having financial problems, or cosmetic problems, or relationship problems. Or she was just fed up with her job, like a lot of people.

What had shocked me most, apart from the gruesome image of someone dying from bleeding to death on an operating table, was the injustice of it all: injustice that I had been rejected by Nemanja, and that the Hunchback had been rejected by his love and then died, for no good reason. Why were we not good enough? I pondered, allying myself with the tragic hero. It was the first time I felt the sting of being rejected, of being denied acceptance into something I wanted to be part of. Still, there was a strange comfort in being able to dramatize my personal pain through the lens of the Hunchback's story. I believed my heartbreak and the Hunchback's were equivalent, and I felt some luxury in that pain, in having my own tragic story to tell.

I don't know if it was the birth of my little sister Natalija in 1988, or the mounting pressure from my dad, but somehow, when I was five and a half, my mother finally buckled under the pressure, and we were leaving Yugoslavia. The thought of bringing up two children in a country that was becoming poorer and more politically unstable spooked her. The deal my parents struck was that we would go to Australia, where it took two years to get citizenship, and then we could return to Yugoslavia, knowing the door to Australia was always open. My mother was going to take maternity leave anyway, and her job would be waiting for her, as long as she returned within the generous three-year period allotted by the university. As for me, since I had never left Yugoslavia before, the concept was abstract to me, and the only thing I could compare it to was when we left Belgrade to vacation in Croatia, so I imagined a similar sort of trip.

Dad's professional visa arrived the day my mother went into labor. "So many exciting new things, kid," Dad said, as we waited for the phone call that would tell us Natalija had been born, red-faced and chubby.

Dad and I went to the hospital parking lot, threw a ball of twine, and sent my mother food in a basket. But instead of having a party at our place afterward, we came back to our bare apartment, where my parents had taken down some of our paintings to sell. Dad quit his job the next week and got a ticket.

Friends came over and told us we were crazy to leave. My mother's best friend, Dada, showed up one day and tearfully took photos of me and her son Marko, with our arms around each other. "Who knows when we'll be together again?" she asked.

Three weeks later, my dad was gone. He would search for a job and a home, and the three of us would follow. In my mother's mind, we were going overseas for two years, *no more*. Only if there was a war, as my dad darkly predicted, would we stay there. If he could show his wife what living in a liberal democracy was like, surely she'd get used to it, surely she'd appreciate the stability, and the calm. "But there won't be a war," my mother said defiantly. All those speeches about "Brotherhood and Unity" and how our people stuck together. Those weren't just words, those were principles embedded in our people, people who enjoyed free health care and education, who cherished Yugoslavia just like she did. There would be no war, she repeated to herself.

Now Natalija was two months old, with a tuft of dark hair on her head, like a cake decoration, and we were about to join my father. The night before we were to leave for Australia, my mother put me to bed, and before embarking on her repertoire of lullabies, she said: "The smell of your birthplace is something you'll always remember, and it will make you feel at home."

"What about if you were born in a dumpster?" I asked.

"Then the smell of garbage will feel like home," she said, and tears filled her eyes, as if she'd been born in a dumpster herself and was getting sentimental about it.

For me, the smells of the old, dark city of Belgrade were, indeed, home. The smell of the Boulevard of Revolution: chestnuts roasting by the side of the road, piss in the doorways, wafts of women's perfume and Lucky Strikes, mixed in with new snow. But I didn't realize that, because I'd never *not* smelled those things. Yet.

On the evening of our departure, Grandma Xenia held my face in her hands and said, "You will never see Grandma again." When my face crumpled up at this horrible thought, she continued by way of explanation: "It's because I'm old, and I will probably die soon." I sobbed. Grandpa Gonzo had died several months earlier from lung cancer, and my parents presented the concept of death to me by saying he had gone far away. Now we were going far away, and those we left behind might disappear the way of Gonzo.

At the airport, the three of us, my mother with Natalija in her arms, and me with a little backpack—all of us red-eyed and puffy—joined another tearful family we'd been introduced to via friends. This family's dad had also gone to Australia, and they were now following, just like us. The mom, Branka, was thinner than my chubby mother, with a short haircut, a cigarette clamped in her lips. She held a big-eyed baby, Aleksandra, who was Natalija's age, but also notably thinner. And the son, Miloš, was my age, both of us had big noses and long bangs, though for once I felt like less of a baby, as Miloš had never been on a plane and was even scared of vacuum cleaners. I told him that we had made previous airplane trips to Cavtat and that the noise of the plane was indeed similar to a vacuum cleaner.

On our last trip to Cavtat, my mother had gathered rocks from the beach, in case it was our final visit, and then insisted on packing them in boxes of our things that were sailing to Australia. Something to remember all the happy family vacations. That summer, I helped her collect rocks and wished my name was Sanya, because of the popular song that was playing everywhere at the time, and which we sang along to as we collected: "*Boats sail down the Danube, is one of them called Sanya?*" That trip felt so fresh in my mind, but now we were at Belgrade Airport. Instead of our summer clothes and a light duffel bag, we were holding everything we owned. Instead of traveling for one hour to a place we knew, we'd be traveling almost thirty hours, to the other side of the world.

During the flight, sensing my mother's anxiety and eager to make the trip smoother, I kept my crying to a minimum despite my devastation at leaving home and possibly never seeing Grandma Xenia again. Instead, I thought about seeing my dad soon, and tried to lose myself in the new books my mother had bought me for the trip. Our fuel stop was in Singapore, and as we got close, the plane's air-conditioning stopped working. The rest of the descent is a terrifying blur: as the temperature rose, my mother screamed for the flight attendants to bring ice, stripped my sister down to her diaper, and rubbed ice on her while Natalija howled like a demonic version of those fat greeting-card cherubs. Finally, we landed. Sweaty and exhausted, we walked off the plane and through a tunnel— two worn-out mothers toting newborns, and two sullen, exhausted five-year-olds, one of whom had just vomited (me). The powerful air-conditioning in the tunnel turned our sweat into a chill on our bodies, but then we were inside Singapore Airport, and my whole world changed.

Everything I knew up until then had been confined to crumbling, socialist Yugoslavia. It was my home and I loved it, but that's because I'd never been to the Singapore Airport. It was like a humongous version of the international store in Belgrade, full of colorful, delicious products. I felt like we had been plopped into one of the Disney films I was obsessed with.

"It's so clean!" my mother said, forced to admit that there were, in fact, some perks to shiny capitalism. She'd traveled around Europe before, but this was something new, and like the rest of our group, she was impressed.

"You could eat off the floor," Branka agreed, and I was inspired to grab a snack and do so.

It was in this glorious place that I had an earth-shattering realization: everything I'd thought was good up until then was actually terrible. I was suddenly gripped with a crazy delight. The world was a massive, fun, bright, beautiful place and I'd been stuck in a small gray corner of it. Until now.

"Orchids!" my mother exclaimed, referring to the perfect white flowers growing out of planters every few steps.

I wanted to get down on my butt and scoot across the shiny white tiles. I wanted to jump on the escalator and travel up and down, up and down, singing and dancing to the pleasant music that seemed to be playing wherever we walked. Why were the other travelers not marveling like we were? Everything smelled like perfume, and as we walked through the airport, a beautiful Singaporean woman dressed in a suit spritzed my wrist with some when I held it out tentatively, copying my mother.

Everywhere we looked, there were marvels of capitalist beauty: gigantic glass-walled stores, full of colorful apparel; screens advertising entertainment systems, shoes, Walkmans, and most enticingly to me: a fuzzy worm. The ad featured a bunch of happy children laughing while the most gorgeous fuzzy worm wriggled around, climbing up their arms and over their faces. Up close, the worm looked adorable: little googly-eyes on a pointy face, sweet fluffy fur. My mother must have seen my face as I watched the ad in stunned silence, while in my imagination I was having one of those Looney Tunes moments, in which my jaw dropped and my eyes turned to love hearts and popped out of my head, accompanied by a loud "A-roo-ga!" My mother understood.

Then and there, she apparently became an immediate convert to consumer culture. We marched to the currency exchange counter, where my mother slammed her dinars down, procured some dollars, and bought me the worm. Had my dad been present, there might have been a discussion about money, about a need to exercise caution as we didn't have much of it; about how we were picking up and moving to a whole new, expensive country. An argument would certainly have ensued. But it was just my mother there. Her eyes glistened, remembering my tears as I said goodbye to Grandma Xenia, remembering her own childhood, which was uninterrupted by politically spurred migration, feeling sorry for me and thinking—*Why should my child be any worse off than the other children at this airport!?*—And even though the worm wasn't expensive, she didn't even look at the price tag; however much the worm had cost, my mother would have bought it for me in that moment.

It was curled up in a little round plastic box. My heart pounded as I held it, desperate to get on the plane again because that's when I would be allowed to open it and start playing.

As the gentle music of the airport played, the babies finally dozed off, and our mothers collapsed on a bench and sipped coffee in take-away cups. Then, we heard our names over the loudspeaker, and the announcement that our connecting flight was about to leave us at the airport. Amid the excitement of discovering this heavenly place, our mothers had lost track of time.

"Run!" my mother shouted, and we all made a mad dash toward the gate.

On the plane, as my mother caught her breath and Natalija slept, I took out the little box that contained the worm. I opened it ever so carefully. I touched the worm gently, and its fuzzy fur felt as soft and delicate as the feathers of the pigeon my Grandpa Gonzo had once caught. And then, quietly, I whispered one of the three words I knew in English: "girl . . ."

My mother looked at me.

"Girl . . ." I said again, waiting for the worm to wake up, to start wriggling around, climbing up my arms, tickling me under the nose like it had done to the kids in the ad.

"Sofija, for a smart child, you are sometimes very stupid," my mother said, and showed me that the worm was not in fact alive, or robotic as I had thought, but that it moved with the aid of a nylon string. Pulling the string along made the worm crawl, and when you did this, it did indeed tickle you, wriggling up and around. I got Miloš's attention from across the aisle and then stuck my arm out, making the worm crawl up it. He watched solemnly, impressed.

And so, with my enchanted worm on the tray table in front of me, I dreamed about my future in Australia. I imagined a scene as best I could: a shiny white classroom, full of little children like me. "Wow, did you see that magic girl?" the kids would say to each other. And I would stand there with my worm, the new kid on the block. In my head I repeated the words "hello," "tomorrow," and "girl," my entire English vocabulary. I smiled, content, looking out the window into darkness, as we flew farther away from our small bubble of a world, heading for our exciting future at a great speed.

3

Asshole of the World

"Well, I guess this is it. The asshole of the world." That was what my mother had been calling Australia, because it was so far from Belgrade, which, to her—bickering populace and economic crisis aside—was the earth's beating heart. As we got off the plane, she and Branka glanced around for a place to smoke, with the desperate eyes of addicts who'd been forced to go cold turkey, and the added torture of babies and preschoolers whining at them. The Melbourne Airport was clean, and busy, full of locals wearing flip-flops and big T-shirts, some of them overweight and sunburned, their hair in little braids after vacations in Bali or Thailand. A woman with bare feet walked by—the sign of a true-blue Aussie—and my mother concluded that she must be schizophrenic.

At the luggage carousel, friendly airport officials stood and uttered greetings like "G'day," which baffled foreigners, who tried to link the bizarre language they were hearing to the phrase books they'd studied, or words they'd heard on an English-language tape. The Australian accent was formidable to my mother, who had just flown across the earth with a vomiting five-year-old and a cranky newborn attached to her, and was just about ready to eat a cigarette. My mother—who had learned English at school and used her knowledge of the language mainly for watching the import shows that hadn't been dubbed and reading academic books she got from the international bookstore— was now squinting suspiciously at an elderly airport employee wearing shorts and socks to his knees, who called her "love" even though they'd only just met. *Was he a sex addict?* my mother wondered, sizing up the eager old man. Meanwhile, I had never seen an adult dressed like that. I was fascinated by his exposed elderly legs, and his red, scabby nose. I would soon learn that Anglo skin does not take well to the hole in the ozone layer, and elderly Australians often have to have their skin cancers removed, losing small chunks of nose skin in the process. The old man pointed toward the exit to indicate there would be no smoking until we were all the way out of the airport.

Finally, we had the bags on a trolley, with Natalija strapped to our mother like an angry troll, her hair wild from the static of our mother's nylon sweater. We crept through customs, toward a set of metal double doors that opened automatically, taking us suddenly into the free world, or more specifically, into the giant, bright arrivals hall. We paused, getting our bearings. Self-consciously, new arrivals ran their hands over their unbrushed hair, straightened their wrinkled clothes, wished their breath was fresh and that they could get the smell of airplane toilet out of their nostrils. The spectators, on the other hand, were waiting for loved ones, full of anticipation as each person walked out, their faces falling whenever the metal doors spat out a stranger. Feeling those disappointed eyes, the three of us couldn't do much but keep going along the walkway, hoping to spot Dad and scamper to him.

I looked at the waiting faces along the way, so many more ethnicities than I had seen in homogeneous Belgrade. Families were waiting with balloons and flowers, toddlers in their best clothes ready to meet grandparents for the first time, people holding signs, crying or laughing, grown men yelling "Mama!" and waving maniacally to little old ladies with heavy European coats. A plane ticket to Australia in the eighties cost a huge amount of money. If a person had come all the way to Melbourne, they meant business.

And then, there was my dad at the end of the walkway, wearing his old jeans and smiling through his beard. He stepped out from the crowd, squatted down to my height, and opened his arms. The people around me blurred as I ran to him, throwing myself into his loving embrace. When we walked out of the terminal, we said good-bye to Branka and her family, and my mother finally got to light her cigarette, all the troubles of the world temporarily leaving her as she exhaled them in a blessed stream of smoke, going out into Australia's unpolluted air. We looked up at the sky, which extended above us like a vast blue dome. Gone was the small gray sky of Belgrade that hung low like a blanket. Gone were the tall buildings that had surrounded us, the crowded streets and concrete. The sun shone bright above us. This was our introduction to Melbourne winter: fifty-five degrees Fahrenheit and snowless with a cold, unfamiliar wind.

My dad led us proudly to a silver secondhand Holden Commodore that would be our family car. "Look at that tacky stripe!" my mother said, pointing at the orange trim running along the side.

"I thought it looked good," Dad said, looking again at the orange stripe, which had held so much charm until that second. My mother rolled her eyes, keeping to herself the nice things she had said about him when he wasn't there. ("Lola is a genius," I'd overheard her saying to friends. "Can you believe he rented a car the day he arrived in Australia and drove himself to a job interview? And he *got* the job straightaway, even though he was jet-lagged and speaking *English!*")

Leading up to the move, my dad, who always made an effort to read English-language novels and magazines in the original, had cranked up his studies, constantly looking up strange spelling rules ("*i* before *e* except after *c*") and conversational sayings. He wanted to be the kind of guy who could say, "a bird in the hand is worth two in the bush" and know exactly what it meant, rather than just staring dumbly, like a sad immigrant, as those around him bantered. He felt empowered that first day as he drove the rented car toward a job interview in Melbourne's downtown with the window down, making his way from the sparse suburbs where we would eventually live, through leafier inner suburbs, to the guts of this large city. The building where my dad was headed stuck out from the rest, a high-rise towering above high-rises— the headquarters of BHP (Broken Hill Proprietary)—a giant multinational mining company, which was arming itself with nerds who could automate systems. While someone with an accent like my dad's was regarded as a "wog" by certain Australians (who used this derogatory term for those from the Mediterranean and Eastern Europe), a *tech* guy with an accent like Dad's was regarded as "a good bet"—programmers from Slavic countries had a positive reputation in the world of software engineering. He left that day with a job offer and a salary of thirty-six thousand dollars—about ten times more than he had been earning in Belgrade. That afternoon, he bought the secondhand Holden Commodore with orange stripe and went back to the suburbs to find a home to rent for his family.

Our new home was a three-bedroom, low-roofed brick house in a cul-de-sac opposite a small park. Melbourne is a large city—back then the population was about 3 million, but it was spread thinly and our home was ten miles from the city center. Back in Belgrade, our apartment had been considered large, but it was tiny compared to this place. Our yard in Belgrade was shared by two buildings that backed onto each other, where the resident kids went wild when they came home from school. But now we had a yard that was just for us, a lonely, large expanse of green grass with a bizarre structure in the middle. It was an Australian institution—the Hills Hoist washing line. Essentially, it was a pole with rotating blades resembling those of a helicopter, and clotheslines strung in between. Dad showed us how it turned, and I imagined swinging from it. "That," my mother said, "is the ugliest thing I've seen."

"I thought the curtains were the ugliest thing you've seen," Dad quipped, recalling a comment she'd made minutes ago, and offering her a spoonful of the Nutella he had bought from the supermarket earlier that day. "Oh, I love Nutella!" she said, remembering the treat Uncle Misha had once sent from abroad, and suddenly she had a mouthful of Vegemite, a brown, yeast-based spread that tastes as opposite to a chocolate hazelnut treat as possible. While she shouted curses at my father from the bathroom, where she was now brushing her teeth, I sampled a tiny bit; the bitter saltiness of the Vegemite both thrilling and shocking.

Now wise to my dad's prankster mood, my mother walked over to the wall, and reached her hand up toward a gigantic, furry spider. She'd assumed it was a prop set up by my dad, but as her fingers brushed it, it scuttled off and we all screamed. This was our introduction to the huntsman spider, an impressive beast often spotted on Australian ceilings. I wasn't scared of spiders, having trapped many of them in glasses to observe them carefully with my grandma Xenia, but the size of this one, and the horrified reaction from my parents, made me think that, like the backyard, and the house, perhaps everything in Australia was bigger and scarier than back home.

When darkness fell that first night, we went outside to look for the Southern Cross constellation in a sky that was, according to my mother, all wrong: "It's like someone threw a stone up there and upset everything." I realized I hadn't paid enough attention to the sky before, because to me it looked as I imagined a sky should look. As I stood there gawking up at the heavens, trying to connect the stars that were meant to be a cross, Dad broke a leaf off the eucalyptus tree and snapped it in two. I inhaled the beautiful fragrance and touched the moisture from the leaf with my fingers, rendering them sticky and lovely smelling. And then we heard a deep breathing sound from very close by. This was a time when "sex predators" were a staple of news programs, and my mother, who believed Melbourne was an isolated backwater, did not doubt that the suburb of McKinnon would be the perfect lurking ground for a sex maniac, a creep breathing his frantic breaths from behind the bushes as he watched the young immigrant family. She clutched sleeping Natalija to her chest and drew me to her and my heart sped up, as Dad walked over to a plum tree. Was someone going to jump out from behind it? Instead, Dad discovered a cat-sized, bug-eyed creature with a curled tail sitting on a branch, breathing as loudly as a human pervert might. This was an Australian ring-tailed possum—a marsupial often found feasting on the fruit in people's gardens. On a nearby branch was another possum, and what we had overheard was a plum-related face-off, a territorial dispute among curly-tailed creatures. We stood for a while staring at the possums, animals that reminded me of nothing I had seen until then, as they stood still, watching each other intensely, apparently unaware we were even there.

We learned more about the possums soon enough, from fellow Yugo-slavians eager to share local knowledge about these fruit-gobbling pests. A party was thrown in our honor, at the house of an older, established Serbian couple. The guests were members of the old guard who had been here since the sixties and seventies. They had left Yugoslavia for vari-ous reasons: so they could start businesses in a capitalist society, because they were nationalists who opposed Tito's policy of "Brotherhood and Unity," or because they were royalists opposed to Tito's presidency. This old guard was comprised of a hodge-podge of Yugoslavians who lived in large houses in the outer suburbs of Melbourne and spoke Serbo-Croatian with English words thrown in. "Havaya," a man with slicked-back hair explained to my dad, "is an Australian greeting." It was months before my parents worked out that "havaya" was actually a mutation of "how are ya," a phrase uttered in the Australian accent and misheard by Yugo ears, which had become a greeting in the Aussie-Yugo community.

These were the seasoned immigrants, whereas we were the first trickle of a new wave, the brain drain that would soon fill out the diaspora. One of my parents' new acquaintances gestured proudly in the direction of the piglet roasting on a spit and said, "Just like home!" Later, when we were in the car, my mother said, "Not like *my* home. Do they think we come from a village?" Even though the ex-Yugos were, technically, "our people," they were not the small circle of Belgrade's intellectual elite that my parents had hung around with. Melbourne was not the place for parties with loveable drunks talking about philosophy, politics, and art—at least not our part of Melbourne, anyway. According to my mother, the only thing she shared with the diaspora was a common language. "There's only so many conversations I can have about recipes," she would say after parties like this, and before she could finish her sentence, Dad would call her a snob.

The diaspora was out of touch with the things that were going on back home, so my parents couldn't talk to them about their dislike of Slobodan Milošević, who had recently become the president of Serbia, after managing to unseat his predecessor and set the path for his ascent to power in Yugoslavia. They couldn't speculate on when he'd fall and withdraw to whatever nationalistic hole he'd crawled out of. Until other new immigrants started to arrive in the months that followed, with fresh news and opinions from back home, my parents could only have their speculative political arguments with each other, which made them frustrated, snappy, and stir crazy. The only world news program on Australian TV was focused on the Iraq-Iran war, so my parents' information about Yugoslavia was based on the scraps they heard over the phone or in letters: Milošević was gaining more support from nationalists, but he was on his own against the majority. Any second, my mother reasoned, he would fall and the nationalists would be silenced. "Don't be naive!" my father responded. "This is just the start of something bigger!"

But when they tried to initiate political conversations at our welcome party, my parents found that Australian Yugoslavians preferred to speak about buying houses, the price of cotton clothing, and gossip within the diaspora. A man proudly informed my mother that he'd been jailed for smuggling racing pigeons from Yugoslavia into Australia. "Plucked, anesthetized, and tucked into a sock!" he said, beaming, and my mother remembered the horrendously long flight we'd taken to get here, trying to picture what it would have been like if we were seated next to someone with sedated bald pigeons sticking out of his socks.

As he regaled my mother, every now and then, the pigeon-smuggler would kiss his watch. Eventually, he stuck his arm out to show her that it had a hologram of Marshal Tito on it. When his adored leader died, this man decided to make Australia his home, having no desire to live in a Tito-less Yugoslavia. In Melbourne, he turned to pigeon racing as a lucrative hobby, finding that birds from his beloved Yugoslavia were champions at high flying, and starting to smuggle them over.

"What happened to the pigeons you smuggled when you were caught?" my mother asked, now genuinely taken by this eccentric and keen to write about him to her friend Dada.

"The customs officials broke their necks," the man said with tears in his eyes.

Since getting out on bail, he had stopped smuggling live pigeons. "But," the pigeon fancier said, glancing at my mother's thick, Rod Stewart–like locks, "it's quite easy to pin an egg in someone's hair. Or hide it in a brassiere."

The party marked the beginning of a weird new phase of my parents' lives, and it felt a bit like they were in the film *Casablanca*, surrounded by expats gone wild, far from home. They were now part of an ethnic minority, alienated from mainstream society and bound to the diaspora by their accents and their status as new immigrants. For the first time they lived on the periphery of the city, ill-equipped, shackled by their linguistic and cultural shortcomings, and unable to muscle their way into its center.

After he helped himself to the roasted piglet, Dad discovered some engineers and got into an excited discussion about tech, and my mother eventually extricated herself from the pigeon man and started quizzing some women about sunscreen, as she was now living beneath the hole in the ozone layer.

Meanwhile, I was in a room with two girls my age, sitting around a pile of Barbies. The girls, who were born in Australia, to Yugo parents, had been instructed to speak Serbo-Croatian with me because I didn't understand English. As soon as we were left alone, however, they started speaking in English. They waved their hands in front of my face like I was an idiot, shouting words I didn't understand. "Shall we speak in our language?" I suggested, in Serbo-Croatian, thinking that they might have forgotten the instruction left by the adults. They continued their English chatter, while my ears filled with the impossible words and I sat there staring at a Barbie in my hand, as if she might have some idea of what I should do next. But Barbie delivered nothing but a perky smile, and I was left sitting there like a fool. Mute and humiliated, I imagined shrinking to the size of nothing, and I was seized with an impulse to flick Barbie in her joyful face a couple of times, hard.

I remembered that my baby sister was in another room, hidden in her stroller, away from the thick smoke of the roast outside. In her two months on earth, Natalija had not held much interest for me, but blood was fast becoming thicker than water, and I found myself suddenly warming to the boring newborn who was my biological teammate. I went and stood by her stroller and talked quietly to her in our language, as if she was not a baby, but my friend. The two little girls soon appeared, and tried to come into the room, impressed by the baby. "No," I said, in English, waving my arms around like an air traffic controller. Yes, I was an outsider, and couldn't play their foreign-language games. But as far as *this* room was concerned, where *my* personal sister was lying, farting and gurgling in response to my conversation, in that space, *they* were the outsiders, and they stepped back as I chased them out, swinging my arms maniacally.

The next week, my parents took me to Bentleigh West Primary School, where I would join the "prep" class, the Australian equivalent of kindergarten in the U.S. I now spelled my name "Sofia" because the principal, an older gentleman in a bright red sweater, suggested we remove the *j*, explaining that even though it was pronounced "y" where we came from, it would be confusing to Australians. He showed us around the big schoolyard, full of multicolored play equipment, and a large, friendly brick building with a mural on it, painted by students. As we walked, he picked up a discarded bag of chips, placing it in a trash can and deeply impressing my family. ("The *principal* picking up trash!?") Even though we had come from a place where everyone was a "comrade," a school principal would never pick up trash, and children were expected to talk to adults using formal address, so we were particularly taken aback when a child ran past and called "Hey, Mr. B!"

Unlike everything else about the school, which seemed futuristic and liberal, the students wore uniforms, something that didn't exist in Yugoslavian schools, and it was strangely old-fashioned: white-and-blue checked dresses for girls; gray shorts for boys, or blue sweatpants, a yellow T-shirt with the school logo, and a yellow cap with a long train for extra sun protection. Instead of sitting at desks, they sat on the floor with their legs crossed.

Unlike the glamorous and icy Madame Marie with her meticulous makeup, my new teacher, Mrs. Melville, wore no makeup, had a red nose, and wore large, bright shirts and sandals that she would remove, wiggling her toes near where we students sat on the ground. However, in my eyes, even though she was aesthetically opposite, she was equally as cruel as Madame Marie.

During my third week at school, frustrated at my slowness with a word-recognition activity, I started to cry. I understood when Mrs. Melville, who had witnessed my breakdowns daily, said to the other children: "Ignore her," as the word "ignore" is similar in Serbo-Croatian. Rather than celebrate my private victory of having actually comprehended a word, I cried even harder. Not only was I dumb but others were instructed to treat me like I didn't exist. I stared at the page in front of me and sobbed. In Serbian I conjugated words and tenses perfectly, according to my mother's notebooks. I was asked trick grammar questions by my parents' friends, which I answered without a glitch, and I bathed in the applause. Now suddenly I was the dumbest kid in class, and the other students snickered, turning their heads away as I sat there like a fool.

During playtime, they called me names I committed to memory, so I could repeat them to my mother and ask her to translate. Up until then, I'd been just another kindergarten wailer, crying because I was tired, or I missed my mother, or for reasons that now seemed microscopic. Now, for the first time, I stood out as the weirdo, and I was ridiculed, called "dummy" or "stupid," and I didn't know how to retaliate except to yell "*you* dummy," to the laughter of my taunters. I wasn't crying along to a Disney film in the comfort of my own home, distressed when Dumbo was teased for his big ears; I now *was* Dumbo, facing the taunts of schoolyard bullies. And there was no Grandma Xenia waiting in the hallway to take me away, to tell me stories and buy me a treat. In the past I had flinched when I was not given 100 percent of an adult's attention, or when I made a tiny mistake; these days I was like a dog that had been hit with a scrunched-up newspaper so many times I no longer wanted to come out and play. I wanted to make myself small and invisible. I didn't feel brave like my Grandma Xenia in her stories, and I was certainly not like any of my fictional heroes, a plucky Disney princess who would call upon her inner strength and teach bullies a lesson.

In the mornings, as my mother pushed Natalija's stroller, we walked to school together, past suburban houses with flowering gardens. Tearfully, in Serbian, I speculated to my mother what might happen that day.

Would they call me "stupid Sofia" or "idiot"? Would I understand a single word? My mother would cry with me. My sensitive personality was taking a beating, and she feared I would carry these memories with me for a long time.

My mother had tried her best to control my environment so far. Whether it was installing my grandmother at French kindergarten, or how she told me the truth about Santa Claus when I was three so I could learn this upsetting news in a safe, controlled environment. But she was now experiencing helplessness. She couldn't protect me the same way when she herself was struggling. "I can't speak English!" she would shout at my father—always blaming him for this whole mess—recounting some exchange she'd had at the pharmacy that resulted in the purchase of sanitary pads instead of diapers. When he told her she *could* speak English, reminding her that she read books in English and that she had learned the language since she was a child, she would snap back: "I only know the hardest words from academic books! I know what gerontophilia is, but I don't know the word for face cream! Or apple core!" And if he corrected her for saying something wrong— "It's not 'How you are?' it's 'How are you?'"—she would yell back: "I am sick of this English colonization! They are trying to get the whole world to speak their language, but I refuse to! I refuse to fix my mistakes for them!" And he'd laugh, amused and exasperated at the same time.

The dynamic of my parents' relationship was changing. While in Belgrade, they had stood on similar footing—both of them having solid friendship groups and work friends—now Dad had the upper hand. He was respected at his workplace, he earned a good salary, and my mother was suddenly reduced to lonely housewife status. She knew no one except for the women of the diaspora, whom she found boring, and limited, and whom she complained about bitterly.

Her colleagues were not rapidly leaving Belgrade like the people in Dad's field, and her friends back home were still struggling at their university jobs, still smoking and laughing in the face of Yugoslavia's growing crisis. My mother felt that she stood out like a sore, artsy thumb, among people she insisted she had nothing in common with. Now that my parents were on unequal footing—Dad having a relatively good time, my mother having a bad time—their arguments became more intense, and more often than not, my mother cried.

From the moment we landed in Melbourne, my mother found herself homesick, frustrated, and frequently on the brink of tears. She blinked them back at the supermarket because there were too many choices. (We were used to one type of yogurt; now we were forced to search through a hundred of them!) She cried when she tasted some parsley she was planning to put into chicken soup. "What have they done to this parsley!?" she shouted (with a level of outrage similar to that of Mia Farrow in *Rosemary's Baby* when she beholds the demon child and yells: "What have you done to his eyes!?"). She'd actually bought cilantro, and if someone had told her then that she would grow to love it, she would have laughed in their face, as she threw the whole bunch into the trash.

When she wasn't crying, my mother wrote letters to Grandma Xenia, plotting when Grandma would come visit us, salvation dangling on the horizon. That is what she clung to in the early months when she was struggling with losing parts of her identity. She spent the rest of her time at the local park with Natalija, who soon learned to crawl all over the fresh grass while my mother would sadly smoke. She couldn't blame Dad entirely for her misery, as they'd agreed to try Australia together. But she was depressed, obsessed with the idea that she'd become something she never thought she'd be: an isolated, powerless housewife.

One day, a letter came with an opportunity: it was from a woman who ran a matchmaking agency in Belgrade, who had a mutual acquaintance with my mother. She was asking if my mother would partner with her to find eligible Yugoslavian singles in Melbourne who were interested in hooking up with someone from back home. My mother, eager for something to distract her from her tedious existence, grabbed this lifeline and snapped into action. She drafted an advertisement in a notebook as she sat on a park bench, paying little attention to good-natured Natalija, who was toppled every now and again by a friendly dog. Her business partner was happy for my mother to take the lead, and my mother took it upon herself to design pamphlets for the matchmaking enterprise, which she named YugoLove—the logo printed in rainbow-colored font against the image of the famous hands reaching toward each other from *The Creation of Adam* fresco in the Sistine Chapel.

Even though she shied away from the diaspora, which she insisted she had nothing in common with, she now put an advertisement in the local Yugoslavian newspaper. In the advertisement, she invited Yugoslavian singles to put their faith in her, a professional with a background in clinical psychology. She requested that singles send a detailed description of themselves so that my mother could scrutinize the profiles and match each lonely-heart with the perfect partner. But even though she thought this might be her way of connecting with the community: putting her psychological skills to work, giving her something more interesting to do than gossiping with the Yugo mothers, her ad was a flop. She received a single reply, from an elderly Macedonian man, who had misunderstood the concept behind YugoLove. Using the familiar form of address, he wrote a semi-legible love note: "Hi girl. So, I see you put an ad in the paper. You're trying to find yourself a husband. Well, I'm available." For the first time in a long time, my parents laughed so hard they cried. My mother framed the note, and with no other takers and dwindling enthusiasm from her partner overseas, the YugoLove business fizzled months after it began.

And my mother, who been temporarily drawn out of her depression, now slumped back into it. Dad's efforts to get her to persist were met with a sharp, "No. Maybe I'm just lazy." He did manage to convince her to submit her University of Belgrade clinical psychology degree to the Australian Psychological Society (APS). Her qualification was recognized, and she was accepted as a member. "It's not like I'm going to be working anytime soon," she said, because she didn't have anyone to look after us two. But privately, she was pleased with her APS membership certificate. She was, after all, a professional.

Meanwhile, in the hellhole known as school, I spent lunchtimes hanging out by a little barbed wire fence where the school pets lived: a goat (Josephine), a sheep (Mimi), and a pony accidentally named Matilda by school vote even though it was very clearly, and fascinatingly, male. I spent most of my time poking grass through the wire, hoping people would think I had a deep connection with animals, but really I did it so the teachers wouldn't notice I had no friends. Just as I'd pretended to be interested in my baby sister at the Yugo party, I pretended I had something to say to Mimi and the others, gravitating to the stupid farm animals so I wouldn't have to face the children. The school pets and I were dummies, but their apparently relaxed attitude to this fact somewhat calmed me. Eventually, I became a nonentity, a quiet background figure by the fence, and my classmates grew bored of bullying me. Pretending to focus on the animals, I became invisible to them, and keeping my eyes on the poop dangling off Josephine's butt, or on Matilda's pendulous penis so no one was the wiser, I perked my ears up and started spying on the other kids, picking up bits of language, storing them away, and practicing to myself when I was alone. I knew I couldn't hang out with the farm animals forever.

My mother had called the school to discuss my secret life as a friendless mute, and the second she said "Hello," the receptionist had sighed and said, "Ah, it's you, Mrs. Stefanovic," recognizing her accent before my mother had a chance to introduce herself and ask to speak to the principal. In our neighborhood, there were not many families who spoke a language other than English at home, and the school wasn't used to dealing with tearful non-English-speaking students. But, after consulting with my mother, Mr B. tried a special tactic. He would come into class, sit next to me, and, every now and then, point to something (scissors, whiteboard) and say the word, as if he was just making a casual observation to himself, totally unrelated to me. "See Rebecca?" he'd say, pointing. "She has a ponytail. And Jessica has pigtails." Sometimes, I'd preempt him and get a word right, in which case he'd act extremely impressed, and I felt like a watered flower, sucking up the nourishment and praise I longed for, growing. I'd store away the information Mr. B imparted, and on the walk home with my mother and Natalija—the time when I transformed back into an anxious blabbermouth—I would talk about the day, dotting Serbo-Croatian with the English phrases I'd learned "So, even though *'pony'* makes sense, because a 'ponytail' *looks like a pony's tail, why* would you call *two* ponytails *'pig'* tails, when a pig has only one tail!?"

To encourage my ESL education, my mother chose a two-pronged approach. One was cultural immersion: I was allowed to watch as much English-language television as I wanted. As soon as I got home, on came *Play School, Sesame Street, Monkey Magic,* and *Masters of the Universe.* Not only did these shows provide me with entertainment, joy, and linguistic skills that I desperately needed, they also offered the beautiful and comforting formula of beginnings, middles, and ends. I recognized the formula from books, films, and the stories I heard from Grandma Xenia. And even though I didn't know all the words, I could make predictions based on my knowledge of storytelling, and learning English became less of a chore, more of an adventure. Watching TV brought some order into the chaos. I turned into a devoted couch-potato; the screen became my most loved teacher.

My mother's second tactic for my English development was social immersion. One day in the park, she started talking to the only neighbor we had who also smoked. I assumed they bonded over their mutual love of the life-threatening Marlboros they favored, and our neighbor agreed to send her daughter Anthea to our place after school so I could learn English from her. I liked playing with Anthea. Every afternoon we would watch TV, touch tongues in secret pretending we were grown-ups kissing, and play with the secondhand My Little Ponies my mother procured through her new favorite activity: rummaging around at garage sales. Soon I knew English well enough to argue with Anthea, and my mother caught me, waving a toy dog who held her puppies in a Velcro-sealed stomach, emphatically shouting: "It is *PREGNANTED* not PREGNANT!" My misguided confidence was confidence nonetheless, and it showed that I was leaps and bounds away from the sobbing weirdo of a few months before. Having the language to express myself made it suddenly easier to define myself in the world. I rediscovered that part of myself that loved the spotlight, that wanted to be heard, and that felt her opinions and stories were valuable.

By the time my first school term was ending, I spoke English fluently, and my parents' pride at my genius swelled once again. I warmed to Mrs. Melville when I found that teachers in Australia lavished far more praise on students than Madame Marie, with her halfhearted handing out of heart-shaped stickers. Children were commended not just for correct answers but for just *trying*, and in fact, while Madame Marie would deal in absolutes ("correct" and "incorrect"), Mrs. Melville would dole out the term "nice try" in a way that didn't make you feel foolish. I stopped being afraid to use trial and error, and I began to talk, sitting happily right up front near Mrs. Melville's bare feet, no longer terrified of making mistakes.

One particular day, I had managed to engage in a full conversation with other kids about *Masters of the Universe*, opining on the hero He-Man and his nemesis, Skeletor. No one laughed, and the other children offered the respect my observations deserved.

I was excited to tell my mother about it, as we walked home under blooming bottlebrush bushes while Natalija gurgled in the stroller. In rapid-fire Serbian I launched into my story.

"Today, the kids were talking about He-Man, and I joined in!"

I expected my mother to break out into applause, or high-five me.

"What?" she said instead, sharply.

"The kids were talking about He-Man, and *I* joined in!"

"Oh my god," she said, in the way she did when someone mentioned something about the hole in the ozone layer.

She stopped pushing the stroller. "This, I did not expect," she said, sighing, and I tried to work out what I had done wrong.

"What those children were talking about," she said, looking me in the eye and putting her hand on my shoulder, like she had when she'd told me Grandpa Gonzo had died, "is a thin membrane covering a woman's vagina, which is penetrated by a man's penis when she has sex for the first time."

What.

Oh God, I thought. *What?*

My rudimentary picture of the human anatomy was enriched in my mind's eye as these new and cruel elements she had described were added to it. A giant rocket-style penis, for one.

My mother sighed. "I am surprised those children are talking about advanced sexual concepts, but you know I have always been straightforward with you. Now you know," she said, in the same no-nonsense tone she'd used when telling me that Santa Claus didn't exist. The word He-Man, to my mother who was more familiar with academic language than with popular culture, sounded an awful lot like "hymen," and her anxious mind had gone right there.

"He-Man," I said, weakly, thinking about furious penises, ". . . his sister is She-Ra."

"Oh," she said, the penny dropping, as she remembered the show I watched. "Right."

Then, cheerfully: "Forget what I just said. So, you joined in talking about a television show, and the other children were receptive. Great work!"

But it was, of course, too late for praise.

So it was that my mother, whose goal was to protect me from trauma, presented me with some terrifying truths: there was such a thing as a hymen, it could be penetrated by a penis, and there was nothing He-Man could do to stop it.

Instead of walking home crying, or talking over each other, like we'd done so many times before, we walked in stunned silence.

By the time I was in grade one, when we called my relatives on the phone, they said that I sounded like a foreigner when I spoke Serbian. It made me feel ashamed, but it was also validation that I was an English-speaker. I was speaking English all day at school, and even though we spoke Serbian at home, my tongue had softened up and my Rs came out unrolled, my consonants soft. But at thirty-six years old, my mother's brain wasn't as absorbent as mine, her tongue was less flexible, and she felt her foreignness more than ever.

A ten-minute walk from our place, the shopping strip on Centre Road was where we'd go most days after school. One day, I darted into Benn's Books to see if there was a new *Baby-Sitters Club* book. I had gotten into these books thanks to Anthea, who was two years older, and I started to read them voraciously, dreaming I would one day be a thirteen-year-old babysitter, too. My mother, pleased I was reading at an above-average level, happily bought the books for me whenever a new one came out. We walked past Buci boutique, a shop whose window mannequin often wore a beret and fancy tights, a place where I imagined only very fashionable people went. Then we went to the supermarket. Natalija was placed in the cart where she would eventually become surrounded by grocery bags, reaching into them and sinking her new little teeth into fruit, and I hung off the side of the cart, letting my mother push us along, until I spotted a musical lollipop. I asked my mother if I could have it, and in my excitement, I assumed she'd said yes, when in fact she hadn't heard the question. I grabbed it as we rolled past, like some sassy skateboarder, I thought. At the register, after my mother paid, the shop assistant asked whether we would be paying for the lollipop as well, which was still in my hand. My mother grabbed her wallet, paid, and when we got out on the street, she snatched the lollipop out of my hand, hurled it in the trash, and for the first time in my life, slapped me across the face. Her nostrils flared and she hissed near my ear, though no one would have understood her anyway, as she was speaking Serbian: "What do you think those people in there think of me!? They think, *Look at that ethnic woman, stealing from us!*"

Back then, I couldn't shrug off my mother's outburst as paranoia. I didn't have the insight to tell her that they didn't think she was a thieving ethnic, that they could see she just forgot to pay. Instead, I thought that because of me, people thought my mother was an ethnic thief—a label which, thanks to my mother's tone, sounded even more pejorative than a native-born thief.

The truth is that she felt worthless, and she imagined others saw her that way, too. In her own esteem, she was no longer a respected, witty, professional; she was an inarticulate, lonely, funny-sounding stay-at-home mom who, as far as anyone knew, was as dumb as those Bentleigh West farm animals her daughter had communed with. Everything was strange, and being foreign, she was powerless.

To everyone's delight, Grandma Xenia came to visit, paying for her ticket with the cash she kept in an envelope under her couch. Grandma Xenia, who had told me I would never see her again because she would probably die, was very much alive and en route to Australia! We stood at Melbourne Airport arrivals and waited. She came out onto the walkway, the most glamorous of all the travelers, in the Chanel suit she'd purchased thirty years ago when she was a working woman, when she flitted around the world, coming back from New York with the latest haircut, knowing her children were being looked after by their grandparents. "I have now been to every continent except Africa," she told us, lighting a cigarette and looking up at that big Australian sky once we were outside.

She was here to look after us, to take her rightful role as grandparent and give my mother a break. In Yugo culture, grandparents don't go on cruises, or have independent, active social lives like grandparents in the West do. And when they get *really* old, instead of going to a nursing home, Yugo grandparents stay in the family home, and are taken care of by those same people whom they took care of before. Still in the active-grandma phase, Grandma Xenia was here to help, immediately assuming the role of caretaker rather than guest.

She cleaned the house, cooked whatever we requested—from chicken schnitzels, to potato soup, to cakes—and cheered my mother up. My mother now had the enthusiasm to attend a Yugo party and quickly make a friend she actually liked: Davorka, a Croatian doctor, who had a toddler my sister's age called Ivan, and Dina, a girl a year older than me. When their family came over, the adults laughed in the living room and Dina and I hung out in my room, speaking English. Dina was the first person my age who genuinely found me funny. Even though I was still hesitant around my school friends, I would in time become more confident and preposterous in front of Dina, making jokes that would cause her to roll around on the floor laughing and farting simultaneously—a true measure of success. We would lie on my bed looking at the glow-in-the-dark stars that were stuck to the ceiling, listening to the New Kids on the Block tape Dina had brought over, and stuffing ourselves with the plum dumplings Grandma Xenia made.

Not long after she arrived, we took Grandma Xenia on "the tour." Now that we'd been here for a while, my parents had the authority to tell fresh immigrants and visitors like my grandma all about Australia, from an insider's point of view. In the evenings, we took Grandma to Brighton Beach, when the sun had already gone down and the hole in the ozone layer, a lingering obsession of my mother's, couldn't kill us. We took her to the Dandenong Ranges on the outskirts of the city, where rhododendrons grow, and Grandma Xenia examined various plants up close—amazed at how large certain species grew in Australia. I showed Grandma a "paper bark" tree. "People call it the bush toilet paper!" I explained, as I'd somehow got the idea that this bark was used in the Australian outback by people who had no access to toilet paper.

At this time of my life, an avid television watcher as always, I became obsessed with an ad for chewing gum. In it, happy, beachy people jumped around, smiling with their bright white teeth. "It's a piece of Australia, the clean, fresh taste of Australia," the jingle went. I was unaware that this was an international ad campaign, and that Wrigley's used the same visuals in various countries. The "clean, fresh" people I liked so much were not specific to Australia, as I'd thought, but generic. In the U.S., the same ad was running with the lyrics "the clean, fresh taste of America." But back then, I was convinced Australia was the promised land, and this chewing gum song was its unofficial anthem. When I saw anyone on the street who was brown or Asian, or big-nosed and pale like us Yugos, I would smile broadly, like the people in the ad. "Welcome to Australia," I hoped to convey with my smile. "You might be struggling right now, but just wait and see, we Aussies are a kind and welcoming people, clean and fresh."

Soon after our second anniversary in Australia, we went to an Australian citizenship ceremony at the town hall. I took my certificate to school for show-and-tell, unafraid to get up in front of the class and educate them on the intricacies of Australian citizenship.

With Alicia and Cara, the friends I'd legitimately made now that I was no longer just a crying foreign kid, I sat on a massive fallen tree that had been sanded down and repurposed as a bench. Simply because of its cylindrical shape, some boys had named this tree "the big dick," but it was our special place, where we made flower bracelets and talked about exciting developments in our lives, such as the upcoming premiere of a TV series that had been heavily promoted: *The Simpsons*. Meanwhile, Mimi, Josephine, and Matilda chewed on grass behind us, and if they'd been any smarter, they would have felt the sting of my lapsed attention. I had abandoned my very first Australian friends. Ruthlessly, I refused to look back.

Alicia and Cara had been suspicious of me back when I arrived, but eventually allowed me to join a game they had devised called "Goblins and Girls." I started off as a goblin, but was eventually promoted to girl, and now, two years after my arrival at the school, we were inseparable.

My mother gladly allowed me to go after school to Alicia's place, where we would read books from the school library, jump like loons on her in-ground trampoline, making up aerial dance moves to the tune of her dad's Roxette tapes, and, eventually, lie on the trampoline exhausted, shoving barbecue-flavored chips into our mouths.

And then one day when I was seven years old, everything changed. I was in the sunroom, leafing obsessively through the encyclopedia of dogs that my parents had got for me in place of the real dog I begged for, my legs up on the recliner we'd got at a garage sale, snacking on the cheesy Aussie snack Twisties, when my dad dropped a bomb. Now that we were citizens, we could go back home to Belgrade. My parents had been planning this for a while, but I'd been too occupied with my new life to eavesdrop. This was the deal they'd struck, and my mother was making Dad honor it. The war he'd long feared had been kept at bay and, as my mother insisted, it was time to go home.

The door to Australia was open, Dad said, and we could always come back here if we needed to. Even though I'd come so far—I'd gained the power of language, friends, an Aussie accent—I was powerless in the face of my parents' whims. I just lay there on the recliner—too stunned to cry, too confused to know what to think. "Home!" my mother said, reminding me of our Belgrade apartment, of our family and the kindergarten friends I'd left behind: Ana, Milica, and Eva. But I was scared to admit that I only vaguely remembered any of it, that as far as I was concerned, my friends were Alicia and Cara, not some girls I hadn't seen since kindergarten. But I didn't want to hurt my parents by acting like an Aussie. We were going home.

And so we packed up our clothes and our books and our rocks, we sold our furniture, and we made our way back to the Melbourne Airport. With our precious citizenship certificates, on the day before *The*

Simpsons premiered, we boarded a plane and began the long journey back to Belgrade, back toward a land where there were no Simpsons, no Twisties, no clean, fresh taste of Australia. Where we were headed, though my parents didn't know it, there was just the grisly taste of impending war.

4

Politics for Preteens

When we got back to Yugoslavia, 1991 had just begun, and there was still no war. To those in Belgrade, my dad's insistence on going to Australia to get our citizenship just became another one of his odd decisions, like how he put cotton buds in his ears when he was cold. From what we were told, nothing had changed in Belgrade—"It's still the same shithole!" my mother's friend Dada said, hugging my mother to her at the airport. "We'll see," Dad said, and Dada and my mother rolled their eyes in unison, their mannerisms so similar, Dad had to laugh. To me, however, the people waiting for us, who my parents embraced fiercely, were unfamiliar after several years spent in a different world.

We too had become different versions of ourselves, bearing the marks of our time away. My mother's homesickness had manifested in emotional eating. She'd always struggled with her weight, but her time in Australia had made it worse and lately she fought it with yo-yo diets, slurping revolting cabbage soups one day and standing in the kitchen looking defeated and eating slices of bread the next. She now wore baggy clothes that tried to hide her weight, looking longingly into shop windows that contained small, chic clothing, playing with the little dog charm that hung from her neck.

My dad now wore an Akubra, a sort of cowboy hat made from fur felt, with a wide brim to block the Australian sun and rain. He paired this with another Australian item: a long Driza-Bone oilskin trench coat. Though he worked in an office and this gear was technically only useful in Melbourne for walking home from the train station in extreme weather, he didn't mind that the getup had the people of Belgrade imagining him galloping through the stormy desert on a camel. We had, after all, been to the end of the world and back. Our friends were intrigued, and my dad liked the waft of the exotic we had about us after our travels to distant lands.

Natalija was now a toddler, gravitating toward pieces of poop, glass, or cigarette butts on the street, eager to put them all in her mouth. I assumed she'd get a disease here in Belgrade, far from the innocuous grass and paperbark she had been consuming in Australia, and I found myself constantly hissing at her, less sibling, more Dickensian matron.

As for me, I was eight: taller, chubbier, and lispy. My speech was affected by an Australian lilt, my sentences coming out not like the rough barks of the Serbo-Croatian language, but rising at the end, as if everything was a question. Since learning we were leaving Australia, I'd become increasingly anxious; I avoided cracks, counted my breaths, and divided stairs into sets of threes and fives in my head. When we returned to Belgrade, I became fixated on the spit and trash that lined the busy streets of my hometown, the Roma women sitting on the ground, breastfeeding babies and begging for money.

Now that we were back in this grim atmosphere, all of Australia's faults were forgotten and it became a faraway paradise in my eyes. I complained in my diary that my parents had grown lax in the safety of suburban Melbourne, and said that I now felt they weren't keeping a close enough watch over my sister: "I fear," I wrote, allowing myself to be inspired by the books and films I consumed, "that Natalija may be kidnapped." I didn't trust my parents, who, in my opinion, didn't keep a careful eye on my clueless two-year-old sister, with her tendency to hug strangers. I still got chills remembering when she'd wiggled out of my mother's grasp at Melbourne Airport, grabbed onto a moving escalator handrail, and was lifted into the air, whooping with joy, until my mother jumped and plucked her back down.

Though you wouldn't know it in Belgrade—where our family and friends gathered in our apartment the day we arrived, drinking and laughing like before—tensions were rising in the countryside. Thanks to my revived predilection for eavesdropping, I gathered that something was up between Serbia, where we lived, and another of Yugoslavia's republics: Croatia.

But really, it wasn't until years later that I was able to piece together how our country ended up at war. For one thing, two nationalist leaders came to power after Tito's death. Tito's Yugoslavia depended on an ethos of "Brotherhood and Unity" in which nationalism was illegal. With Tito gone, Serbia's president Slobodan Milošević was spouting nationalist rhetoric and trying to strengthen Serbia's position above the other republics. Meanwhile, the people of Croatia had voted for their own nationalist, a leader of the conservative Right named Franjo Tuđman. Now we had two nationalists leading the two republics that had always been at odds.

Add to that the long-standing grievances between ethnic groups, which had been swept under the rug for forty years by Tito and were now ready to burst out. Tuđman embraced the Croatian checkerboard flag from pre–"Brotherhood and Unity" times, which incensed the Serbs living in Croatia. (That was another ingredient for war: ethnic groups were not confined to their own republics, so there were, for example, many Serbs living in Croatia—about an eighth of the population.) The Serbs in Croatia were furious, because the checkerboard flag had last flown during World War II, when Germany's puppet Croatian state had killed hundreds of thousands of Serbian people, who were their enemies at the time.

Although recent tensions in Croatia had started as yet another uprising by poor, rural people—the Serbs protesting the flag—the kind of thing that Tito had quashed thousands of times, the uprising was still not resolved, months later. And now those who had asked fearfully "What will happen when Tito dies?" were learning the answer.

We were about to see that Tito's banning of nationalism did not destroy it; that, in fact, it may have inflamed it, and that there were plenty of people who were ready to jump at one another's throats like their forebears had done in the Second World War.

Yet my dad, who had predicted war three years ago, was still being told by family and friends that he was paranoid. "The international community is not concerned," my mother's friend Dada said, pointing out that the international press had paid Yugoslavia no heed. This will blow over, the intellectuals of Belgrade said, flipping through opposition newspapers where caricatures of Serbia's and Croatia's presidents abounded. My parents' friends assumed that most people felt the same way they did. Meanwhile, in the countryside, those people who had been ignored under Tito—who were crushed by unemployment, poverty, and ignorance, and spurred to nationalism—were learning how to use guns.

My former kindergarten gang, Ana, Milica, and Eva, came to our place on one of those first, disorienting days in Belgrade. They looked different to the photo I had been referring to for the past two years, where we all looked like a version of the same little girl. Ana, like me, had had a growth spurt. She was gangly, while Milica and Eva were still slight, asserting themselves with coordination, while we early developers suffered with our awkward bodies.

As my friends were observing the new me—with my accent, my rounder face, my manner affected and self-conscious—I presented them with a plan. From Australia, I had brought a brand-new *Baby-Sitters Club* do-it-yourself kit, which included membership cards and other tools needed to set up an enterprise like the one in my favorite books. I tried to explain the concept to my friends, who, while I was in Australia immersing myself in Western entertainment, had not been exposed to these American classics. In my Australian-accented voice, the plan came out flat: "We will look after neighborhood children, earn money, and have interesting adventures." I'd imagined resounding excitement, my friends high-fiving each other, putting together a list of clients, suggesting the names of boys who could join our ranks.

To their credit, even though my plan sounded dead-boring, and they were living in a culture where children babysitting other children for money wasn't a thing, my friends agreed. I opened the packaging I'd left untouched until now and declared that the four of us would be the Baby-Sitters Club of Belgrade. I grandly removed a sticker that read "Baby-Sitters Club Headquarters" and was meant to frame a light switch, only to find it didn't fit on the Yugoslavian switch, which was a different shape to the wide, flat switches common in Australian homes. I tried to smooth it over, but it bulged with air bubbles, the corners of the sticker coming off the sides of the light switch.

Undeterred, I handed out pieces of paper, so we could vote for our president, which I assumed would be me, as I was the brains behind this operation, not to mention the owner of the kit. I was taken aback to find that three of the slips said "Milica," except for the one written in my own careful hand, which naturally said my name. "Fine," I said, wobbly voiced, scrunching up the pieces of paper. My friends suddenly seeming infinitely stupid, childish, unaware that to be a teenager, they must follow my guidance as I was the one who had *read* about teenagers. "Why don't *you* run this meeting?" I said sourly, handing Milica the "President" pin that should have been mine. And that is how Baby-Sitters Club of Belgrade died that very day.

While Belgrade was turning out to be underwhelming from my perspective, my mother, who had felt suffocated for two years by her Australian cultural alienation, was back in her element. The parties resumed as if we'd never gone, and I listened from my bed and tried to make sense of the heated political discussions.

The adults spoke about the opposition to Milošević in Serbia, fronted by a man named Vuk Drašković, a conservative patriot, whom I'd seen in the opposition papers my parents read, a tall and charismatic figure with a wild beard. The name "Vuk" means wolf in Serbo-Croatian, a strong name that was given to infants in the olden days in the hope of warding off spirits, illness, and predators. Now when I considered the name, I thought it fit Drašković perfectly, with his fiery eyes and scraggly beard.

My parents supported Drašković, and also the recently formed Democrats, a center-left party of liberal academics, led by my mother's friend from student days, Zoran Đinđić, a handsome, silver-haired philosopher. My mother referred to him by the nickname "Zoki," and I soon adopted the language I'd overheard, lecturing to friends about the prominent democrat "Zoki Đinđić" as if I shared a close personal relationship with him.

I didn't understand the politics, except in black-and-white terms: Milošević was a bad guy who wanted war. The opposition were the good guys. I listened along to the opposition broadcasts, laughing when my parents did at the sketches making fun of Milošević, less because I understood them, and more because I felt this was a way to connect with my parents, and be part of something. When I drew a caricature of Milošević, or made a disparaging comment about one of his cronies, my dad would say, "Bravo, kid," and my mother would laugh, and my heart would swell. It swelled even more to see my parents getting along better now that their lives were "back to normal" as my mother called it. But for me, Belgrade was not normal.

I was home but it was strange. While I hadn't fit in in Australia, now I was confused to discover I didn't fit in here, either. I was anxious for my parents, myself, and especially Natalija, the smallest and most vulnerable member of our group. This was a child who had spent most of her life in the shiny playgrounds and soft lawns of suburban Australia, and now she was here, in a filthy city, where bits of metal stuck out from seemingly everywhere, ready to impale children.

When there weren't adult conversations to eavesdrop on while I was struggling to get to sleep, I would fixate my attention on Natalija's breathing across the room. I would grow panicky as I listened, imagining that she was suffocating or, if I was in a particularly strange mood, that her breath was actually the hissing of a predator awaiting us both in the shadows. So I'd tiptoe over to her bed, look under the bed, then open her eyelids. The presence of her eyeballs, which rolled back as she slept, was a satisfying sign, enough for me to go back to bed, my anxiety somewhat abated, my loneliness once again appeased by my unwitting little sister.

These were the days when my parents programmed their alarm clock to wake them up with the morning news. Which meant, usually, the whole family would wake up to a booming voice reporting on skirmishes among Croatian and Serbian populations or threatening speeches by nationalist politicians. If Natalija or I made noise while the news was on, we would get screamed at, or smacked on the butt or head, a response that my sister thought was driven by my parents' passion for news media rather than their obsession with monitoring the daily escalations of our political conflicts. Just as my mother used to wake little Natalija from her afternoon nap by saying "Get up, Nani, I'll put *Snow White* on for you!" my sister would climb into my mother's bed, bring her little face right up to my mother's, and say, in the same promissory tone: "Wake up, Mami, I'll put the news on for you!"

My parents went back to their old jobs. My dad returned to the engineering institute and my mother not only worked at the university but also landed a gig hosting a television show exploring the emotional development of children, called *Mom, Dad, Me, and Everyone Else*. She adored going each week into the TV studio, where she sat across from experts and explored the kind of issues that had always thrilled her, like whether you should play music for your baby, and why children wet the bed. Natalija and her friends were sometimes plonked in a playpen as cute extras, the camera cutting to them as my mother and her colleagues talked.

My parents resumed active social lives, as there were plenty of adults around to look after us. Though Belgrade had felt foreign and disappointing when I first returned, I soon realized it was *my* city, full to the brim with people who seemed programmed to automatically love me. Not only did our own neighbors (whom I had all but forgotten) kiss me and Natalija three times when they saw us, offering us jam and candies, the neighbors of my relatives smothered us too, welcoming us back from Australia like we were their own family. There were framed photos of us at both of my grandmothers' places—of me in my school uniform, Natalija looking jolly with a potty on her head. We were beloved here: the children who had gone away, who had broken hearts by doing so, and who were now back, like heroes returned from war! It was the opposite of how I felt in Australia, where we were nobody.

Grandma Beba's cosmetics salon became a key point of interest. Now, as an eight-year-old who dreamed of being a teen, it proved very relevant to my preoccupations. When I was in the salon, I stretched out on a spare reclining chair with my feet daintily crossed, enjoying my celebrity status of "granddaughter from Australia" while Grandma Beba tended to her clients, ladies who came to get their legs waxed with the dark brown, delicious-smelling thick, gooey substance that Grandma Beba mixed in a large heated vat.

Some of Grandma Beba's clients were into the increasingly popular musical genre of turbo-folk—so she put the television on in the background, and we watched men and women gyrating on screen while the clients patiently waited for the vibrating disks attached to their thighs and butts to cause their cellulite to disappear, as the brochure Beba handed out promised they would.

In between clients, Grandma Beba would squeeze my pores, or massage my face and then apply the special skin balms that she made herself, and I would inhale the scent of the balm, damp cotton balls resting on my eyes to soothe them. One day, Grandma Beba suggested we pierce my ears, and before I could think about the germs that might crawl into the holes, and the fact that my mother disapproved of children having pierced ears, she had clicked the gun twice, and it was done, my earlobes burning and my pride swelling at being suddenly grown up.

On the weekends, I often slept at Aunt Mila and Uncle Tim's place. Aunt Mila was my mother's sister, her husband Tim was an Englishman, and together, they were a television-making duo. She wrote and he directed some of the most famous Yugoslavian kids TV shows from the last few decades, and they were beloved figures in the city. Aunt Mila went every day to Radio Television Serbia, where she was head of children's programming, passing the office of the Milošević-installed news team who were in charge spreading pro-Milošević propaganda and keeping opposition opinion off the air. Because the children's department was apolitical, Aunt Mila managed to keep her job despite her contrary political opinions, while her Milošević-opposing colleagues in the news division were not so lucky, and got fired.

Thanks to a bit of nepotism, I was given a small role in one of my aunt's television shows, *Broom Without a Handle*, about child detectives solving a mystery involving a pet store robbery. I was featured in a scene at a birthday party, in which I was meant to catch a runaway rabbit that had snuck under the couch and offer it to the main character to pet. I also appeared in a scene where a group of children went to an eccentric old lady's home and she asked, "Do you like *šnenokle?*" (a type of dessert), to which I answered as somberly as if I was reciting a wedding vow: "I do." During the day's filming, I was breathless with excitement, but also suffering from conjunctivitis, for which one of the adult actors kindly squeezed cream into my eye. I went home as proud as I'd ever been, imagining that a Hollywood executive who happened to be in Belgrade would spot me in my fleeting television appearance and make me a star.

In my aunt and uncle's apartment, there were framed illustrations of the two of them which had appeared in newspapers over the years showing them in all their eccentric glory—Aunt Mila in one of her signature brimmed hats and bright red lipstick, Uncle Tim with his domed bald head and long pointy beard. The only person I knew who spoke Serbian with an English-language inflection the way I did was Uncle Tim Byford, who had quit his work with the BBC and moved to Belgrade to marry my aunt, after they met in Sarajevo in the seventies. Uncle Tim was known for his accent—which, in a country with not many foreigners, had been named the "Byfordian" accent. I adored my aunt and uncle and their sons, Andy and Jovan, who had just started university. At their place, I spent hours reading the English-language Asterix comics and Famous Five books that my cousins had long outgrown, but my favorite activity was watching films with Aunt Mila.

Like me, my aunt enjoyed watching films many times over, and she was happy to spend weekends showing me the classics, including all of Hitchcock's oeuvre, *Gone with the Wind*, and psychological thrillers like *What Ever Happened to Baby Jane?* If films and books had been important to me before, now they became sacred. A good film was able to ease out all concerns from my mind: my anxiety about living in Belgrade, the heated political debates, the prospect of Natalija meeting her end, and my own confusion about where I belonged.

Some of my favorite memories are of settling in on a comfortable armchair for a late night of film watching, swaddled in a blanket, my belly full of Aunt Mila's delicious food. We watched in complete silence, respectful of each other and of the scenes unfolding before us. Between films, Uncle Tim offered us "After Eights," thin squares of dark chocolate, with a smear of mint inside them, packaged in small envelopes: delectable and sophisticated. I would slip one onto my tongue while I watched the black-and-white scenes playing on the screen, and just for a while, I felt like a proper grown-up.

When the school year began, I was enrolled in third grade at Vladislav Ribnikar Elementary School. The differences between my new school and the one I'd come from in Melbourne were so stark they made my head spin. In Yugoslavia, children did not wear uniforms or sit on the floor. Instead, they sat at little desks, with a hard floor underfoot, and wrote with fountain pens. In some ways, I appreciated the more adult seating arrangement; we were elevated to the level of the teacher, rather than sitting by her wiggling toes, as we had done with Mrs. Melville. However, children at school in Yugoslavia were not expected to have a casual, friendly relationship with their teacher, but to be deferential and formal. They learned three languages during their schooling, including Latin. It dawned on me that after spending two years away from this multilingual education system, I was screwed.

A map and a blackboard were the sole decorations in our class-room. The décor was made slightly less depressing by one element: the familiar and enduringly handsome face of Nemanja, my unrequited kindergarten love who, having followed his French studies to this elementary school (other nearby schools taught Russian, German, English, and Italian), happened to be in the same class.

Well, well, well, I thought to myself, tucking my hair to show off a pierced ear, *we meet again—all grown up.*

However, Nemanja did not show any signs that he knew who I was. No matter. I took a seat at a desk behind him, where I could resume the role of silent stalker that I was born to play. When the teacher, Ms. Danica, walked in, we all stood up. Ms. Danica gave us permission to sit, and we began the first day of third grade with dictation. After that, we were instructed to open our textbooks, containing Serbian poetry we were supposed to memorize throughout the term. I didn't have a book yet, as the store had run out. "You're the one from Australia?" Ms. Danica asked.

"Yes," I said, expecting she might ask me to introduce myself to the class.

"Have the book by the end of the week, or you get a big fat fail."

Every day after school, sitting at our old dining room table, sobbing, I practiced the Cyrillic alphabet, learned to write with a fountain pen, and, with the help of a private tutor (one of the students from my mother's university who gave affordable lessons in French), caught up on two years of French that I' had missed while in Australia. In my diary, I wrote exclusively in Serbian and in fountain pen to practice. After several hours catching up on my Serbian education, I would spend some time on my English, thanks to a friend of my parents from the Yugo-diaspora in Australia, who sent me Baby-Sitters Club books by the boxful.

I raided my parents' library, each inside cover stamped by my dad with a neat, blue-inked "Library Stefanovic" in Cyrillic. I read Serbian and Croatian translations of English books, as well as the immensely popular Winnetou series, about an Apache Indian chief. These books were huge in Yugoslavia, and I only found out later that they were written by the German author Karl May, who had never actually been to the Wild West, which he wrote about so extensively. Not knowing this, I soaked up the details of the life of Native Americans and cowboys. Believing them to be true, I pictured myself riding on horseback, enjoying the delicious meat of grizzly bear paws, and inhabiting the vast planes of America, where the good guys ultimately won, a fantasy world that took me far away from the realities of school, family, and politics.

Every day I caught the tram in front of our apartment building, rode two stops, picked up two delicious pastries—a triangular *pašteta* filled with cheese, and a round *pogačica*, also filled with cheese—from a bakery, and walked the rest of the way to school gobbling them down. Unlike my mother, who was acutely aware of her weight, I didn't notice the weight I put on as a result of my decadent sampling of all the delicacies I was surrounded by.

One morning, still sated from my cheese pastries, I was sitting behind olive-skinned Nemanja as Ms. Danica explained the rules of Serbian spelling. "We are lucky our language is phonetic," she explained. "Certain other languages have very strange, unintuitive spellings. Take for example, in English, the word 'chair,' which we would simply spell ć-e-r. In English, it is actually spelled like this."

She wrote "SCHAIR" on the blackboard. My hand shot up, Aussie-style, one finger in the air instead of two.

"That's not how it's spelled," I said, excited to show my intelligence and elicit praise. "There is no *s*!"

"You are wrong," Ms. Danica said. "And you should only put your hand up if I have asked the class a question. I have had enough of your interruptions!"

The constant hand in the air, high and excited, was my thing. Asking questions and making observations had been encouraged in Australia, and it was something I'd embraced wholeheartedly at Bentleigh West Primary School once I felt confident speaking English. In Australia, I had my hand up constantly, my legs crossed, my back rod-straight, bursting to be allowed to speak. Knowing the answers and being able to express them in an articulate way was a source of pride for me, and a way to obliterate the humiliating traces of being the dumb foreign kid. Tolerant teachers indulged me, letting me show off my knowledge, ask questions, and enhance their lessons with sage but unnecessary observations like, "You say the sunset is orange, but I have also seen purple."

But now, when I finally felt I could make a contribution, when I'd hoped I could achieve some much-needed status in class even though I *knew* I was right about "schair" I was shot down. My arm wilted to the side of my little wooden desk in humiliation. I was done trying to be noticed, at least for a little while. Nemanja turned around and gave me a "ha, ha, you got in trouble" look, and despite my low mood, I thought perhaps this would turn into one of those teasing flirtations, and considered approaching him after class to remind him of our kindergarten past. But, as he turned away from me again, I figured he'd probably say "I don't care," or, more specifically, "my butt hurts," which is, inexplicably, the slang expression we use for "I don't care" in our language.

The only time we could rise from our seats during class was when we were called upon to recite a poem we'd memorized, or when Ms. Danica entered or exited the room. But one day, she announced that we'd be doing a drama exercise. Had my ears deceived me? We were actually doing something fun? I felt like bursting from my desk in rapture, mentioning my CV—that role on *Broom Without a Handle*, several monologues from old Hollywood films that I knew by heart. Could it be? Was this my Grace Kelly moment?

Ms. Danica spoke up: "The most talented children, please step up to the front: Jasna, Nemanja, and Nikola."

Apparently not.

Jasna, the girl every boy seemed to love, stood at the front of class, where she would be playing—what a surprise—a princess.

I observed her small, pretty nose and wondered why some people had all the luck. My mother had recently commented that I had a "prominent nose," which had stopped me dead in my tracks, because I'd never even considered my nose before. But from that moment on, I saw myself as nothing *but* a giant, walking nose—and now I seethed as I watched Jasna, convinced she had been chosen not for her skills but her appearance.

The drama these so-called "talented" students were called up to perform was a famous poem by the Yugoslavian author Dušan Radović called "The Ballad of Nađa and Kađa." It begins at sea, with a princess called Nađa.

The king, Nađa's father, was to be played by Nikola, whose nickname was "Dicksie" because we children knew the English word "dick" and we also knew that he was ruled by his. Nikola was the tallest boy in class, and even though he was only nine, he had taken the computer game *Leisure Suit Larry* to heart. Somehow all of us had managed to access this adult-only game (stolen from older siblings, played at friends' places, or painstakingly copied), in which Larry's goal was to have sex with women. When he succeeded, a "CENSORED" sign appeared across the screen, bobbing up and down to block the "sex" that was apparently occurring. It was illicit and thrilling, and we loved to huddle around computers while our parents weren't watching and giggle as the pixelated animated Larry did his thing. Whenever we waited for our teacher to arrive, Nikola, parroting Larry, would approach girls when they weren't looking and thrust his pelvis into their butts. The girls jumped away and screamed, "That's gross!" and he'd laugh.

Maybe it was because I was unpopular, or because I was increasingly fascinated by sexual things as I lurched toward teenage-hood, or I was just influenced by watching a lot of romance films, but I thought, *This is the closest thing to passion I have seen up close*—and every now and then, I leaned slightly over a desk, pretending to look at my notebook, and, inevitably, Nikola came up behind me and "humped" me. I always jumped away, saying "That's disgusting!" like the other girls did, but secretly, I felt a thrill, a flush in my cheeks, the addictive sensation of being singled out and wanted. Though I understood that there was positive attention—such as the satisfaction I got from being told I was good, or smart—and negative attention—like the bullying I'd faced in Australia—I miscategorized Nikola's advances as being in the good category: the sort of attention that made me feel both special and worthwhile.

Ms. Danica's final casting decision resonated with me: Nemanja was to play Kađa, a rugged, handsome bandit who wins the princess's heart. Ms. Danica began by reading the poem aloud while the "talented" children "performed" it, swooning around the front of the room.

I exchanged an eye roll with my sort-of friend Artur, who sat at the desk next to mine. Artur and I were both outsiders in the class, his outsider status due to his disability: a syndrome that left him with skeletal problems including underdeveloped arms, and mine because I had come from Australia. I felt that Artur, like me, saw through the classroom politics—the alliances people had, the hierarchy of popularity, how Ms. Danica was unwilling to dig a little bit deeper, to find some talent hidden among the *less* obvious students, who might just surprise her with the depths of their performances.

As Artur and I continued to exchange our knowing glances, it occurred to me that Artur was probably in love with me. It made sense: we walked to the tram stop together after school and I didn't tease him like some of the other kids did. I thought, *If Artur is in love with me, I could sigh and tell the other girls, "I think he* really *likes me,"* looking afflicted by the positive attention.

Meanwhile, at the front of the class, the princess Nađa was being swept overboard. To demonstrate this, Nemanja and Nikola reached their hands helplessly toward Jasna, as she spun round and round, enacting the experience of being in a whirlpool, I guess). I imagined myself in Jasna's place—not only receiving all the attention but being somehow so relaxed about it, as if she didn't notice the loving glances of both Nikola and Nemanja.

After the bandit saved the princess (a predictable ending, I thought), Nemanja and Jasna held hands, giggling as the class clapped. *Barf*, I thought, in English, using the lingo of a Baby-Sitters Club character, feeling some comfort that I still had this little thing, this knowledge of another language and another world that I could escape to, at least in my mind.

After school that day, Artur and I walked to the tram stop together. Our school wasn't large enough for all the students to attend at once, so we went in shifts: mornings one week, afternoons the next. Today had been a morning school day, so we had a whole afternoon off. I'd bought a creamy Čoko-Moko ice cream, which I slurped loudly, and I was planning to spend the afternoon reading and forgetting about the class play.

Enjoying my ice cream and the idea of a relaxing afternoon, keen to lift my mood further, I asked Artur straight up: "Do you like someone in our class?"

"I do, as a matter of fact," he said, and laughed.

"Would you like to tell me who it is?" I asked, with what I thought was gentle encouragement, as we reached the tram stop, where we would part ways. *He must be so nervous now,* I thought, turning to Artur and tucking my hair behind my ear, just in case he hadn't noticed my ears were pierced.

"Jasna, of course!" he said, blushing and trotting off toward home as I stood there, dumbfounded. He turned back, and yelled, "I'm *embarrassed* now!"

I wanted to yell back that I didn't care—that my butt hurt for his embarrassment. But instead, I tossed the ice-cream stick in the trash and boarded the tram.

I found an empty spot and stood there with my feet weirdly splayed. I wanted people to whisper to each other, "Look at that girl, she must be a ballerina." Or "What an unusual way to stand. It must be uncomfortable for normal people, but it's obvious, she is a dancer." Faux-absentmindedly, I started to mutter to myself in English. "I must remember to pick up some cigarettes for Mom on the way home," I mused out loud, hoping people would say, "Oh, she speaks English perfectly! This ballerina must be a foreigner, visiting our crappy city." Instead of looking at me though, people continued to look ahead. Old ladies talked to each other with bags full of market vegetables by their feet, and teenagers in Guns N' Roses T-shirts put cigarettes in their mouths, ready to light up when they got off. From the smell, it was evident that someone had brought pickled cabbage onto the tram and everyone looked around, searching for some old lady with a container of sauerkraut, so they could shake their heads disapprovingly. Less popular than some stinky cabbage, I stood there, waiting, unnoticed as always.

On March 9, 1991, Grandma Xenia was in charge of looking after a bunch of us neighborhood children while our parents went to a protest. Even though Milošević had won several months earlier in an election that purported to be fair, opposition leader Vuk Drašković barely received any airtime in the lead-up, thanks to Milošević's control of the media.

In response, Drašković's party invited the people of Belgrade to take to the streets to protest the lies of TV Belgrade, to demand press freedom and oppose Slobodan Milošević. The March 9 protests drew a crowd of about one hundred thousand. Every now and then the crowd broke into a chant of "*Slobo Sadame,*" likening our leader to Saddam Hussein. They also chanted "CNN" because they wanted the foreign press to document their protest, so that they wouldn't be forgotten within a dictatorship, like the countries behind the Iron Curtain had been. The protesters wanted the West to see them, to recognize their plight for press freedom and democracy, and support the opposition movement. They could not have known that it would take more than a decade until Milošević was gone, and that the push would come from within, rather than the Western powers they'd tried to engage.

In the middle of one of the speeches, the police threw a canister of tear gas into the crowd (which the protestors later claimed was a move designed to provoke violence). People began to run from the gas, clashing with the police, who had surrounded the perimeter. The television, which my grandmother watched as she looked after us, showed demonstrators turning cars upside down, young men throwing rocks at the police. In minutes, the peaceful protest had become a riot. Grandma Xenia watched openmouthed as water cannons blasted the protestors and we children gathered around her, trying to spot our parents in the crowd.

Soon, a policeman and a protestor were reported killed. "Good God!" Grandma said, turning on the radio to an opposition station so she could get more coverage of the event, hoping to hear the dead protestor's name, and praying it would be an unfamiliar one. The army was sent into the streets. The official line was they were sent to "discourage vandalism," but my grandma said, "Milošević is showing the opposition that he's willing to use violence."

Aunt Mila, who was at the protest with my parents, called our apartment for news from my cousins, who had been at the violent forefront with the other students. While my aunt was using the pay phone in the Hotel Majestic, my mother went to the hotel bathroom and vomited from the tear gas. It was there that she met Neboysha and Tamara, fellow vomiting demonstrators whose Melbourne-dwelling relatives my parents knew. How far Melbourne seemed now, with its large suburban houses and grassy backyards. Through the glass of the hotel lobby, my parents and their new friends watched the smoke and water and chaos in Belgrade's streets.

Back in our apartment, Grandma Xenia ordered all the children to shut up so she could concentrate on the phone and news. When our neighbor, a little girl named Mira, started crying, saying she feared for her parents, Grandma Xenia snapped: "You! You are the only child here with nothing to worry about. You're just here because you live in the building and I told your mother she could bring you! We know your parents are Milošević sympathizers, who are sitting comfortably at home while the rest of the parents put their lives at risk for our freedom!" We went to my room and shut up, staring at Mira with new eyes, while she cried.

That evening, as tanks rolled through the streets of Belgrade for the first time since World War II, my parents came home, full of adrenaline, repeating the chants they'd been shouting all day and cursing Milošević. I told my dad what Grandma Xenia had said about Mira's parents being Milošević sympathizers, not sure whether to sound shocked or as if this was common knowledge. In my mind, though the intricacies of the political situation were murky, I knew that the heroes were the opposition, and we supported the opposition. The villain was Slobodan Milošević, up there with Cruella De Vil and *Psycho*'s Norman Bates, and by extension, his supporters were villainous. But Mira's parents had always seemed so nice, I couldn't believe they'd tricked me into believing they were "one of us" when they were murderous jerks all along.

"Yes, they vote for Milošević," my dad said. "That just means they have different political views to us. Milošević supporters believe in his ideas, and we believe in the ideas of the opposition. They are still our friends." At first, this threw me, as it upset the neat narrative I had built of good versus evil. But somehow, that explanation also took a massive weight off my shoulders. It was just another one of those things that seemed contradictory but wasn't, I decided. Just like how people can still love each other even if they shout and use curse words, as my mother had once explained. People can have different political opinions, and still be our friends.

Later that evening, Slobodan Milošević went on television to explain that the army had been used on the people of Belgrade to combat the "forces of chaos and madness" that had taken over the streets. The opposition in Belgrade now knew that Milošević was prepared to take military action against them, and the people of Yugoslavia were reminded of who was in charge. Those in other republics were warned as well.

After the violence of March 9, the various opposition movements continued to build, though often they disagreed with one another, dissolv-

ing and re-forming. My parents and their friends had pins made with "Forces of Chaos and Madness" written on them, and wore them to their jobs at universities and other schools.

Meanwhile, in troubled Croatia, which wanted independence from Yugoslavia, the city of Vukovar was boiling over, and people were dying. There were six hundred thousand Serbs living in Croatia, and Vukovar itself had a large Serbian population. The local Serbs, with the aid of paramilitary forces from Serbia, were laying siege to the city. Their reasoning was that if Croatia wanted independence, then Serbs would take villages with a Serbian majority, link them up and attach them to a new Yugoslavia. So, as far as Milošević was concerned, Croatia could have its independence, it just had to leave a chunk of land behind. After he had sent tanks into the streets of Belgrade, it was becoming obvious that Milošević was willing to use force.

In the fall, I went to nightly protests with my dad while my mother stayed home to care for Natalija. They were small vigils, and it was explained to me that the aim of the protest was a call for peace and solidarity: the candles we lit were for the people dying in Vukovar. As my father stood in his Driza-Bone coat, I walked Leo, an Irish setter belonging to another protestor, pretending I was there on my own, that I'd come to this protest not as a child following her father, but as someone who knew about politics, and who, importantly, had her own dog. I'd recently read Serbo-Croatian translations of *White Fang* and *Call of the Wild* from my dad's library and I quietly talked to Leo as we walked, imagining that he could understand me in a way humans could not.

On the way to a protest one evening, Dad and I encountered a woman walking a tiger cub on a leash. The woman explained that the cub had been born in Belgrade Zoo, but had recently been purchased by none other than the dreaded Arkan—a paramilitary leader my parents talked about in whispers. Arkan was one of the leaders of the nationalist

Serbs in Vukovar; his volunteer soldiers, the "Tigers," were apparently criminals and psychopaths. The zoo had entrusted this woman with looking after the tiger cub while he was too young to fulfill his paramilitary mascot duties. She told us the cub woke in the night crying like a baby, and enjoyed baths, trying to grab the stream of water coming out of the faucet with his large paws. I was allowed to pet him, as he moved his giant, babyish head from side to side. This cub would grow up to live in the unsettlingly Disney-looking castle Arkan had erected right near my grandma Beba's house. Years later, I'd hear rumors of a full-sized tiger living in the compound that was guarded by Arkan's armed guards, and imagine an adult beast stalking back and forth.

The nightly vigils I attended with Dad were allowed to last for up to an hour, and the moment the hour was up, the police stamped out the candles we had planted in the ground. My dad and the other protestors laughed in their faces, calling them morons, but still we walked away, threatened with arrest if we stayed longer. We rode the tram home in our coats, Dad wearing his old beanie instead of the Akubra and with cotton balls stuffed into his ears now the weather was getting colder. We sang the unofficial anthem of the protest movement *"Don't cry, celebrate, with the people!"* to the disapproving looks of older Milošević supporters, and, more often in urban Belgrade, to the nods of approval of those on "our" side.

Even though I was only in third grade, I felt deeply involved in the political sphere, which made me feel closer to my parents and part of the adult world I longed to join. At my dad's request, I had written a call for peace in English. It said: "I AM A CHILD OF 8 AND A HALF YEARS OLD. I WOLD NOT LIKE MY COUNTRY TO HAVE A WAR. WHY SHOULD WE FIGHT BETWEN OURSELVS? BETWEN OUR FREINDS? I WAS BORN HEAR IN SERBIA AND I DON'T WANT ENY WAR TO START! AND I WILL DO MY BEST TO MAKE PEOPLE 'GIVE PEACE A CHANS!'" To my great pride, my dad photocopied it, along with a somber photo of me, and added an English caption: "Seeing her parents active in anti-war and

opposition movements in Belgrade 1991, a young girl decided to make her own contribution. She wrote this note in August 1991 and asked her father to send it to the world via computer (email)." He was proud of the email bit, as we were still another three years from the World Wide Web, and it made us seem technologically advanced. He sent it to media outlets in Yugoslavia and beyond.

At one of the protests I accompanied my parents to, I stood at the front, looking up at the podium where Vuk Drašković was making a passionate speech, spittle flying from his mouth. My parents were impressed by him, and their enthusiasm was enough to make me excited, too. I watched the fervor in the speech of this man whose name meant "wolf," and though the content of what he was saying was too complex for me, still I grinned, taken with the atmosphere of dissent, the passion of the crowd. I must have been one of his youngest, most visibly excited fans, because when he finished speaking, Vuk stepped off the podium, grabbed me, and kissed my forehead firmly, wetly, and everyone cheered.

In June 1991, Croatia declared its independence and asked the rest of the world for recognition. On the same day, Slovenia declared independence as well. The Yugoslav army was sent to Slovenia, and a ten-day war resulted, with Slovenia ultimately gaining independence from Yugoslavia. The small-scale conflict in Slovenia marked the beginning of the Yugoslav wars, and it was only a taste of the longer, bloodier wars that came. The real fighting would happen in areas that were more ethnically mixed, like Croatia, which would not gain its independence as readily.

As fighting in Croatia raged, my parents and their friends started to speculate that Bosnia would be next. Because Bosnia was the most ethnically diverse of the republics, there was always a fear that, if nationalism were to arise, Bosnia would erupt into war. We have a saying similar to the English "Don't stir the pot," except it's basically "Don't stir Bosnia." Bosnia was always seen as the bear of our country, asleep in a cave, and if you poked it, stirring up the nationalism that lay sleeping, there would be hell to pay. The people of Bosnia were now watching the rest of Yugoslavia start to implode, and the bear was stirring.

My favorite outfit when I was eight was a headband with tiny diamantés Grandma Beba had gotten from the market, a large color-blocked sweater, jeans, and loafers that made me look like a busy mom from the eighties. I'd been making regular trips to the video store, where I had been told that they didn't have *Grease*—a film that came recommended by Aunt Mila—but they might get it eventually, which made me feel justified in going and asking for it every few days. But one day I was banned from going there because the mafia had attacked the café next door and put hand grenades in people's mouths to terrify them while they robbed the place. To my parents it was a further sign of the country falling apart—organized crime taking over—but the incident had seemed strange to me, like something out of fiction, and I found myself struggling to believe that violence was something real.

That all changed when I went to school one day and Nikola, aka "Dicksie," wasn't in the classroom, harassing girls as usual. He wasn't at school, we soon learned, because his father was dead. As Ms. Danica made the announcement, several of us gasped. Nikola's dad had died on the front line in Vukovar. Ms. Danica said she would take our class to the funeral the next day.

And with that, the war in Croatia became real to me. Thinking about Nikola's dad, it suddenly occurred to me that my dad could die as well. My dad, who was so involved in the protests, who stood in front of the police holding up three fingers, the anti-Milošević salute of the opposition movement. My cousins Andy and Jovan had left college and moved by themselves to London, so they wouldn't have to do army service and, God forbid, be sent to the front lines. It was only now dawning on me that if they'd stayed, my eighteen- and nineteen-year-old cousins could have been shot, as Nikola's dad had been. I thought of Nikola, foolish Nikola, so eager to fake-hump girls and make stupid jokes, who was now at home crying because his dad was never coming back.

Back at home, in a shaky voice, I told my parents the news, and then just sat in my room, not sure what to do.

I heard them in the living room making calls to other parents of kids in my class.

I wrote in my diary in large full-caps Cyrillic: "I HAVE NEVER BEEN TO A FUNERAL."

I imagined what it might be like. Would we dress in black? Would Nikola be there, and were we supposed to talk to him, or hug him? Would his status as classroom sex pest be forgotten?

I wouldn't get to find out, since my parents decided that I wasn't allowed to go.

"But we light candles for people who died in Croatia . . ." I said, confused.

My dad explained that Nikola's father was a "Tiger," one of the volunteer members of Arkan's small and ruthless paramilitary force. The candles we lit were for the civilians who were murdered *by* people like Nikola's dad, he told me.

Oh.

Again, I was faced with just how much I didn't really understand. My brain was full of contradictory feelings as I again tried to sort out the good people from the bad, to work out who were the ones we mourned and who were the ones whose deaths we quietly ignored.

So we were still friends with Mira's parents who supported Milošević, but we couldn't go to the funeral of a paramilitary "Tiger"?

"That's right," Dad said, adding that there was a difference between conscripts, like my cousins would have been, and the volunteer nationalists, who put their hands up to go to war. "Those are the people who we cannot support." Were we happy Nikola's dad had died? I ventured. "No," Dad said, and my mother added, "Imagine what it's like for poor Nikola losing a father." "We support peace," Dad added. "We don't think anyone should die." "Even assholes," my mother threw in.

"As I said," I wrote in my diary later that night, "I've never been to a funeral before, and it's not something I want to do anyway." I didn't write about how guilty I now felt for having enjoyed Nikola's humping, when the whole time he had actually been the enemy.

As 1991 came to a close, Yugoslavia was officially at war. The Croatian War of Independence had begun. The thing my dad had feared three years earlier was finally happening. People were dying in Croatia, and the effects of the conflict were starting to touch Belgrade in different ways.

On a freezing day in January 1992, my parents were walking to the grocery store, discussing the political situation and the rising death count in Croatia. In eastern Croatia, ethnic cleansings had begun: whole populations of Croats were being driven out of some areas by Serbian nationalists, and Serbs were being driven out of others by Croats. At that point in time, things were going better for Milošević than for Croatia's Tuđman. The Serbian forces had taken Vukovar, and now controlled a third of Croatia.

Everyone was becoming poorer. My mother threw out her moth-eaten winter coat in the trash can in front of our building, only to see an older, respectable-looking lady wearing it on the street the next day. Hyperinflation was beginning, and whispering men in long coats sold deutsche marks to passersby in exchange for their quickly devaluing dinars. One day, my neighbor Mira and I bought a chocolate bar along with the milk her grandma sent us to buy, and when we returned home with it, she screamed at us that we were wasting money—and we felt ashamed and confused, having never been scolded for buying ourselves a cheap treat before.

Contemplating the situation as they walked, my parents paused in front of a store that sold luggage. "Our big red suitcase is broken," Dad ventured. He and my mother looked at each other, and without an argument, without a word, went in and bought a new suitcase. It was time to go, again.

Not long after, the army would start conscripting men my father's age, and some of them would still attempt to flee at the last minute, like our friend Boris, who walked out the back door as his army summons was delivered at the front, running to the neighbor's place in his slippers and getting a lift straight to the airport. Money soon became worthless. It got to the point where people would pass by trash containers full of dinars, and then eventually, the ridiculous 500-billion-dinar note was printed, and with it, you could buy a bundle of nothing. But we would be gone by then.

When I found out that we were returning to Australia, I wrote a series of full caps entries in my diary, hoping the large letters would help to emphasize my nine-year-old panic. As usual these days, I wrote in Serbian.

MY SISTER HAS AN EAR INFECTION (THE THIRD ONE SINCE WE CAME TO YUG). WE ARE GOING BACK TO AUSTRALIA (BECAUSE OF THE SITUATION NOT HER EAR).

My next diary entry says:

IN AUSTRALIA WE WILL BUY A HOUSE AND A DOG.

The house-and-dog scenario features prominently in the diary, in which I explain that if we manage to sell our apartment in Belgrade, we will likely be able to afford a two-story house in Melbourne (this was a fantasy that I firmly believed, choosing to remember Australia as even bigger and more luxurious than it was). The pages following the entry are full of maniacal drawings of houses (with neat scales of 1000:1 written beside them, as I'd been taught in my geography class with Ms. Danica), as well as drawings of various breeds of dogs. In the Cyrillic I'd spent so long learning and that I would soon have no use for anymore, I wrote:

I AM SO HAPPY AND ALSO *NOT* HAPPY TO GO TO AUSTRALIA. I ♥ AUSTRALIA AND I ♥ YUGOSLAVIA, BUT FOR DIFFERENT REASONS. I LOVE AUSTRALIA BECAUSE IT IS BASICALLY A HEAVEN-COUNTRY. THERE IS A LOT OF GREENERY, THE RELAXED SCHOOLING SYSTEM IS *SUPER* AND I AM HARDLY EVER BORED THERE.

I LOVE YUGOSLAVIA BECAUSE MY FAMILY IS HERE, MY FRIENDS AND BECAUSE *THIS* IS WHERE I WAS BORN, AND I AM SAD IF WE LEAVE AND THERE IS WAR. I WILL BE SAD FOR ALL OF THE PEOPLE HERE, "MY" PEOPLE.

My dad's workplace was experiencing mass resignations. The bosses snapped up the coveted visas to America, which were harder to get. The younger employees grabbed visas to Australia or Canada. For those going to Melbourne, my dad said, "I'll see you there," except we had to jump a few hurdles before we could return.

In order to get his old job back, my dad was told he'd have to do some time in the town of Whyalla, where his employer BHP's mine was situated and the computer systems needed updating. So in February 1992, my dad got on a plane bound for South Australia, where his Driza-Bone coat and his Akubra hat would be more at home than in Belgrade or even in Melbourne. He would find us a place, and we would follow, just like before.

The day after he left, as I trudged to the tram stop in the snow, a kid on the street said, "Hey, are you in that TV show, *Broom Without a*

Handle?" I was too flabbergasted to utter a casual "Yeah, that's me," as I had practiced a million times, so I just squeaked "It is me," thinking it was just my luck to be leaving right as my glory days were starting.

A few weeks later, it was the three of us off to the airport again: my mother, Natalija, and me. Four years earlier, we had sat in a taxi crying, and now we were sitting in a taxi crying again. Natalija, who had just turned four, was too little to understand what was going on, but she cried nonetheless, in sympathy with my mother and me. I clutched my backpack, which contained letters from my friends at school decorated with stickers and drawings of koalas and full of promises that we'd stay close forever, with multiple, earnest exclamation marks. *Goodbye my friends,* I thought, trying not to cry, but to smile gently and beatifically, channeling the scene in which my beloved fictional Winnetou, the Apache chief, is dying, when he remains calm and strong. Also in my backpack was an English-language copy of *Wuthering Heights,* from my aunt and uncle, a reminder of their home where I'd felt so comfortable, a grown-up story from their bookshelf that I could take with me. It was back to the English-speaking world for us. *My English will be a little shaky after two years away,* I thought. And then I wondered if my Serbian would start to suffer if I would only be speaking it to my family. I promised to myself that I would keep writing in Cyrillic in my diary, and I now wished my uncle and aunt had given me the Serbian translation of *Wuthering Heights.* "I won't forget you," I whispered to my city, as I looked outside at the gray streets.

I opened the window and stuck my head out into the freezing cold, like a woman I'd seen on TV. I imagined my hair wildly flying out the side of the car, the people behind us getting a glimpse of my departing form. "Goodbye, Belgrade, my home," I wanted to say, with my hair whipping out the window like a flag. My mother stopped crying to tell me that I must always ask the driver if I want to open the window, and embarrassed, I retracted my head and rolled the window up.

On the plane, we continued crying. We were going to be migrants again, stretching ourselves painfully across continents once more. Separated from our loved ones by oceans and the prohibitive cost of a plane ticket, we would be left to face our tragedies alone, and we would leave our loved ones to face theirs. My mother had pushed for a return to Belgrade but she'd seen for herself that it wasn't a place she wanted to bring up her kids. Her husband, she could now admit, was right. She would say to her friends later that leaving Belgrade for the second time felt like having a cold breath on our necks—because she felt the chill of the horrors to come.

We took off, leaving the fading lights of the city. Natalija read her little books and complained about her ear pain, while I read the letters from my friends and examined each of the precious stickers they'd decorated the pages with. I rubbed the stickers anxiously, worried they'd peel off, and tried not to think about the prospect of having to make new friends again. We were off to Whyalla: another unknown, where the only familiar sight would be my dad's open arms.

5

The Asshole's Asshole

As we would soon discover, if Australia was the asshole of the world, Whyalla, South Australia, was the asshole's asshole. The state of South Australia is largely empty of people—and two thirds of the small population lives in the state capital, Adelaide. "This place," as one of my dad's work colleagues put it on his first day, "is a hole."

A full four hours' drive from Adelaide, our new home was a town known for its steel factory, which was owned by my dad's employer, BHP. And that's where his bosses sent him now, as "punishment," he said, for having quit the first time to take us back to Yugoslavia. He could get his old Melbourne job back—in about a year, just as soon as he finished the software project at the factory in the middle of nowhere.

I imagined my dad as Cinderella, scrubbing floors so he could go to the ball. But actually, instead of scrubbing floors, he drove down a highway, where every now and then he saw the carcass of a kangaroo that had been hit by a car, or glanced at the feral camels—creatures that had been brought to Australia by Afghan traders back before there was a railway system. The camels, now wild, roamed the outback, eating precious plants and making a nuisance of themselves, one of the only species able to survive the climate.

My dad drew inspiration from their survival against the inhospitable environment, thinking that if they could manage, we could, too. As he pulled up at the factory, my dad remembered his birthplace, the mining town of Bor, and considered how strange it was that he had ended up here, in regional Australia. He went into the factory, walking past the steelworkers and into an air-conditioned office. Thankfully, the reality was that he could work as a programmer anywhere in the world, and soon he'd be gone from Whyalla, unlike the laborers who toiled around him. He counted his lucky stars, thinking about the hard life he might have faced if he hadn't gone to school, and about the war he'd be fighting in now had he not scrambled across the world on the back of his degree.

My mother had criticized Melbourne's suburbs for being dead, and as she looked at our new place, she was too dumbfounded to even make a scathing comment. Our new house was at the end of a bare street, sparsely populated with other flimsy, low-roofed homes, and beyond it was "the bush"—essentially, scrub. Dad had warned us the house was "kind of crappy," and I had already prepared what I was going to say when we arrived, using a line stolen from a Baby-Sitters Club scene where the heroines find themselves in a shitty place and make the best of it. When my mother, sister, and I walked up the creaky porch steps and into the house, a linoleum-floored, moist-smelling, flimsy shack, I put my hands on my hips, looking around. "It's small," I said as planned, "small—but cute." I'd hoped my parents would be cheered by my rehearsed enthusiasm, but they weren't paying attention. My mother was saying "oh my god" and walking around the house in disbelief, the linoleum emitting loud hollow sounds with each of her steps, as if she were a giant making the earth quake.

Meanwhile, Dad led us to the Formica kitchen table, in the middle of which sat a little house made of chocolate. A guy at his work built chocolate structures as a hobby, and Dad had commissioned this especially, to greet us in our new home. The chocolate house had a large slanted roof, and big square windows, unlike the house we were in, which was flat-roofed, small-windowed, and dark. At Dad's encouragement, I carefully snapped off the door and put it in my mouth. The chocolate was rock-hard, and when I managed to get my teeth through it, it was chalky, but I told him it was delicious.

Even when the rest of the family gave up on the chocolate, agreeing it was disgusting, I stuck to my story, determined to eat it. I couldn't handle the thought of Dad's gift going in the trash. To see him smile proudly, I would have eaten the whole house in one sitting, but my mother took it away before I could choke down even half of the roof.

The ground around our place was a red-brown, pebbled terrain, with only the most resilient spiky grass and bushes jutting out of it, tough plants that could live with barely any water and heat that got up to 120 degrees Fahrenheit in the summer. The street was sparsely populated, with replicas of our low-ceilinged, wooden house painted in a thick, matte reddish-brown, as if to blend into the desolate surrounds. The window in the room Natalija and I shared looked onto the backyard, which was a patch of red earth. There were anthills rising up all over it like pimples, and in the middle of the ant kingdom was a large water tank. Nature was closer to us than ever before, and came in the form of giant, biting ants that attacked anyone who set foot in the backyard, sinking their pincers into exposed toes or feasting on bare legs. Mrs. Melville, my barefoot teacher from Melbourne, would not do well here, I thought to myself.

In our kitchen, we discovered a redback spider, which could muster enough venom to kill a small child. Once the spider was dead, courtesy of my mother's shoe, I thought of poor Natalija, who, in my opinion, had dodged yet another bullet. Yes, she had survived Belgrade without being kidnapped, but now, here she was, four years old and just the right weight to be killed by a redback, or a brown snake—one of the most dangerous serpents in the world, which also called South Australia home.

On our first night in Whyalla, Natalija was not contemplating the potential of her untimely end, as I was. Instead, she pointed through the small window of our new bedroom and shouted, "Look, it's the moon—my friend!" I was touched by my sister's optimism, her willingness to count a celestial body as a personal friend. Older and wiser, I knew that a moon was no help when you were the weird new kid, and soon I'd be starting at the local school.

My mood was lifted that night by the novelty of our new bunk beds, and I climbed up the ladder, turned on the lamp Dad had got me, and took out *Wuthering Heights*, forgetting for a moment the loneliness that was to come. Jet-lagged, I read for hours, wondering if I could ever love the creepy landscape outside my own window in the way Heathcliff and Catherine loved the moors. Probably not, I decided, as I climbed down the ladder to go to the bathroom, creaking along the flimsy floor, the eerie light of the moon filling this uncanny new house full of our familiar things, yet completely alien.

Whyalla was a workers' town; cheap to live in, and ethnically diverse: our neighbors were Indian, German, and Turkish. We were, though, the only Yugoslavians in town. Now we were isolated from our family in Yugoslavia, where the political situation was getting worse, and far from Melbourne, where we at least had some friends. I was far from the day-to-day routines of Belgrade, which were occurring without me, and I felt in some ways like I was dead—obliterated from that place without a trace. Aunt Mila would still watch films, Nemanja would carry on being handsome, Jasna would continue to be the most popular girl, Nikola would mourn the death of his father, the people would go to protests, kids would play—I just wouldn't be there any-more. Right now, as South Australia sweltered, the snow was melting in Belgrade, in the yard where my dad had helped me build a snow-man (whose breasts I'd carefully molded, eager to show that not all snowmen were men)—she was now slush, and we weren't even there to mourn her passing.

Would my school friends talk about me, and remember me as that girl who was here for a while and then left again? Would Natalija and I be reduced to those framed images in our grandmas' apartments, to short sentences describing us—"Sofija likes to read," "Natalija has a sunny personality"? Would our idiosyncrasies fade, leaving us to be-come "the granddaughters from Australia" once again, frozen in the fake smiles we put on for photos, when really we were still living and breathing in Whyalla, like some desert ghosts?

I would have to make friends here, and the prospect of being new again sat heavy in my stomach. As for my Melbourne friends, whom I would see as soon as we escaped Whyalla—did we even have anything in common anymore? Alicia and I had spent most of our time together doing little-girl things—jumping on her trampoline, tracing pictures of lions from books because they were Alicia's favorite animal and she never wanted to draw dogs, like I did. Alicia knew the old me—before I'd read many books, before I could write in Cyrillic, before I liked to think of myself as a peace activist, before my Australian accent got warped by my uncle's British English. She wouldn't know the names of Serbia's opposition leaders, or about Smoki peanut snacks, about war, or even about snow. The only people who somewhat understood what it was like to be me at this particular moment were my parents and Natalija. But there were vast chasms between us too, each of us preoc-cupied with our own issues.

For my part, I was concerned with the freakish things my body was starting to do, ahead of most kids my age. Like the stretch marks that appeared on my thighs and the little fat boobs that were starting to show on my nine-year-old body. One day, I noticed a dark hair growing between my legs. I knew what this meant thanks to the well-thumbed Serbian translation of the classic sex-ed book *What's Happening to Me?* which I had frequently consulted: I was going through puberty. I felt sad for my parents, who, I imagined, would be distressed. Dad would wipe a tear from his eye and say, "My little girl's growing up," like a TV dad. If he said this, I decided I'd put my arm around him and say, "I'm still your little girl," though technically, I believed that the pube had opened a gateway to adulthood, romance, and sophistication.

I decided to break it to them lightly, using a joke appropriated from a television program we'd been watching every night, for lack of other things to do in Whyalla. That evening, once Natalija was asleep, I emerged from the bedroom nonchalantly, leaned on the door frame, and said, "Well, as Rose from *The Golden Girls* would say, 'I never thought I'd grow a hair there!'" while pointing in the direction of my crotch. My parents, jolted from their conversation, stared at me for a few seconds with raised eyebrows, getting their heads around what I was saying. My mother smiled before telling me this was a normal part of growing up, and that I should go back to bed. She added, "There will be more! And under your armpits, too," and Dad said, "You don't have to tell us about each one!" As I climbed the ladder to my bunk, I heard them laughing—and I imagined less callous, more attractive TV actors taking their place as my parents.

Meanwhile, Natalija became interested in drawing. She worked with her hair tied in a palm-tree style, her cheeks ruddy, her eyes focused on her works, her chubby bare feet swinging from the porch, delectably out of reach of the ant lords. She gave her drawings to our mother, who surveyed them with concern, then filed them away, like she did with the pictures of her traumatized child clients. Looking over my sister's shoulder, I tried to interpret the drawings, based on the knowledge my mother had previously shared with me, or that I'd overheard. Troubled kids drew pictures of blood and guts, or sometimes, monstrous suns burning people below. Parents who were abusive in real life were often depicted with oversized, menacing hands. Natalija's drawings were different. They were of houses, some of which had wheels, while others had wings. The folder in which her drawings were stored was labeled in my mother's handwriting: "The child who befriended the moon (lack of permanence in early childhood)." My mother planned to write a thesis on children like my sister who moved around a lot, who had trouble working out where their home was. She talked about writing something and getting it published, but more often than not, she'd just look through the folder of portable houses, the quotes from Natalija about being friends with the moon, sigh, and put the folder away again. She was feeling low again, and the thought of exploring her daughter's psychological issues made her even more depressed.

But unlike during our stint in Melbourne, she would not be a stay-at-home mom. A few weeks after we arrived, my mother got her first job in Australia. As Slobodan Milošević's reputation grew worse globally, Yugoslavia's standing also became flimsier, and many people were struggling to have their Yugoslavian degrees recognized. But, because she'd already secured her position in the Australian Psychological Society, my mother had no problem getting a job—at the public hospital in Whyalla, where she was hired as a children's counselor.

Every day, she boarded an empty bus that stopped in front of our place. It took her through the bare streets of Whyalla and onto the highway, past auto repair stores, and delivered her, often still the only passenger, to the front of the hospital.

When she came home from the hospital, along this same lonely route, she would tell my father that there was more familial abuse here than she'd ever seen before, and that she wished we were back home.

Inevitably, my father would say something like: "Are you forgetting that your precious Yugoslavia is an experiment that failed?!" My mother would shout that there were still some good things about that place, she would assert that it was her home, she would shout that she was lonely, and inevitably she'd start crying. The evening would often end with Dad reading in his room, and my mother watching *Twin Peaks*—as if living in a creepy small town while people murdered one another back home wasn't enough; she had to watch a TV show about a creepy small town in which people murdered one another right there. I would often fall asleep to *Twin Peaks'* haunting, jazzy soundtrack and the smell of her cigarette smoke.

I was enrolled at the local primary school, in a class of sixty kids, ranging from grades three to six. There were three teachers to handle the high volume of children (though one quit after my first week, because, according to the other children, she had won a Mercedes in a raffle, sold it, and was now rich). I was adopted by a group of girls who had known one another since birth—their parents went to the Aussie rocker Jimmy Barnes's concerts together—and these girls all listened to Jimmy Barnes's kids' band, the Tin Lids, which I pretended to be into, too. In many ways, the setup was familiar: children sat on the carpeted floor, the classroom was colorful, and the work was easy—after my grueling time in a Belgrade school, I was well ahead in math and science. Kids raised their hands all the time, and even the kids who gave the wrong answers, or weren't good at their work, who weren't "talented" as Ms. Danica might have put it, were praised.

Natalija was enrolled in the kindergarten class attached to my school, and when my mother and I dropped her off one day, we spied through the window, to see how she was settling in. Natalija, with her palm-tree hairstyle, sat confused in a circle of small children and a sunburned, matronly teacher. All the kids except Natalija were familiar with the board game they were playing, which involved shouting names of farm animals. Every now and again, Natalija would echo something one of the other kids said—"Pig!" "Moo!"—not sure of the rules exactly. Nevertheless, the teacher lavished praise on her. "*Very good,* Natalija," she said, "this chicken belongs to you!" And she grandly handed my sister a card with a chicken on it, which Natalija graciously accepted, pleased with herself. My mother chuckled as we walked away, saying something about a land of unconditional praise. From then on, every now and then, my mother would say to my dad "Very good, Lola, this chicken belongs to you!" when he did something seemingly simple, like taking out the trash, and my parents would laugh. They couldn't help but be charmed by a system that rewarded everyone, but they'd also complain about the incompetence of their colleagues and blame it on the Aussie system, or they'd hear about just how many sports and cooking classes I did compared to math or science and they'd say, "Well, what do you expect in this country?"

Not long after the emergence of the fledgling pubic hair, I woke with a brownish substance on my underpants, confirming that I was destined to always be the weirdo. At nine, I was the first kid in my class who got my period.

Wearing the gigantic pad my mother provided me with, I felt like a clandestine cowboy. I stood around uncomfortably with the girls at lunchtime, in the heat of a Whyalla summer, feeling like an impostor both because of my contrived, Tin-Lid-loving personality and the hidden period. I looked over at the foursquare court where an attractive, blond, spiky-haired boy called William was playing with his friends. Jessica told us that William's dad, who lived in Coober Pedy, six hours' drive north of us, had found a black opal when he was renovating his bathroom. Coober Pedy, I knew by then, was a mining town, known for its underground homes—people escaping the heat by building burrow-like lodgings in the earth. In fact, there was even a Serbian Orthodox church underground, built by the growing community of ex-Yugos hoping to strike it rich in the mines.

As I was listening to the girls talk about the difference between regular opals and the more expensive black kind, the ball bounced from the foursquare court toward us. Never sporty, but always keen to make contact with a boy I liked, I picked the ball up and tried to toss it casually back to William, but instead, with some freakish new period-power that *What's Happening to Me?* never mentioned, I threw it hard and whacked him in the chest. His blue eyes grew wide, and he resembled a deranged child James Dean. He screamed, and ran toward me, and for a shocked second, I found myself thinking: *William is the type of child my mother would be interested in, whose drawings she would store in a special folder.*

"What the fuck did you do that for?!" he screamed and, before I had a chance to process that he'd said the F word, which was against school rules, he pushed me in the chest, causing my new boobs to hurt. Next, he had knocked me to the concrete and was pinning me down by the throat, his face right up against mine. Kids started howling with excitement. Up until that moment, I had never been in a fight, but I had received some basic training. My mother sometimes encouraged Natalija and me to scream into a pillow, as loud as we could, to get out any anger we had inside. She also got us to play a verbal game that was meant to teach us to stand up to bullying or abuse. She would say "yes" and we would forcefully say "no" back at her, and the more insistent she got, the more insistent *we* got, until we were screaming it at the end: "NO!" Which is what I shouted now as I kicked William in the balls, and he jumped back reeling, cupping himself and rolling on the ground. I stood up, disheveled, red in the face, my pad slightly slipped off to the side, but still intact. I'd fended off a tough kid. For the rest of the day, I felt the adrenaline running through me. Yes, I was new, I was foreign, I had my period, but William wasn't my first bully. I wasn't a little girl feeding farm animals through a fence and crying anymore. It occurred to me for the first time that I might be a tough kid, too. William was punished, and for the rest of the day, the girls stood protectively around me, in the electrified way kids gather after a drama.

It was 1992 and my parents had somehow found a morning Serbian-language radio program. Now, like in Belgrade, every morning we were jolted from sleep by bad news. The six-republic-strong Yugoslavia I'd been born into was decreasing in size, and the republics that now referred to themselves as Yugoslavia were just Serbia and Montenegro. Slovenia and Macedonia had gained independence, Slovenia with its brief war, and Macedonia managing to leave after a referendum, without casualties. The war for independence in Croatia was still in motion, but recently, and as predicted by my parents and their friends back home, the republic on every news announcer's lips was Bosnia, home to Bosnian Muslims, Croats, and Serbs, in roughly equal numbers. Bosnia had declared its independence, which triggered a war with the Bosnian Serbs. The capital, Sarajevo, the most diverse city in Yugoslavia, was soon occupied by rival militias, each with their own nationalist agenda.

Every night after the news, my parents yelled at each other in an intense way that might have been disturbing to onlookers. But strangely, the people least traumatized by their arguments were my parents themselves. They experienced the screaming matches as a sort of cleansing, intellectual debate. When she shouted at my dad, my mother didn't feel like she was attacking him personally. She was yelling into the abyss, and exploring various sides of an argument. Thus, they challenged each other's opinions, and explored truths that were hard to swallow.

When my mother was feeling ambivalent about her own Serbian identity, instead of stewing on it, she would scream at my father, accusing him of being anti-Serbian: through him, she was attacking the part of herself that was uncertain. My father would then jump to defend this anti-Serbian stance, which he would embrace for the sake of the argument. Often, when my dad was in a political discussion with someone else, he would appropriate one of my mother's points that he had vehemently opposed in a previous argument, as if this was completely normal.

Though their fights were unpleasant for me and Natalija, causing us to shut ourselves in our room, they were my parents' way of venting. They ranted and raved at each other, the equivalent of screaming into a pillow, bemoaning the miserable piece of land that we came from, which seemed doomed to war after war.

Based on my parents' heated conversations, which carried through our tiny house so easily I didn't even strain to eavesdrop, I reasoned that Yugoslavia would soon be destroyed—in my mind I saw scorched earth where the land had once been, gone and along with it our language, and the entire population. On the inside cover of my diary, in a careful cursive, I wrote a riddle in English:

> If when I die someone finds this diary, it is written in XXXX so to read it you will have to find some-one who speaks XXXX. Please do not think that it is spooky to read a dead woman's diary because I will not haunt you or anything like that. P.S. You will find out what XXXX means on the other side of April showers.

I imagined a girl from the future discovering my diary in an attic. If she solved my genius riddle, the future girl would realize that "April showers" was the poem on the back cover of the diary, and that I'd glued a page to the inside cover that, when peeled back, revealed the following note:

> Dear Finder,
>
> You are very clever. My name is Sofia (Sofija in my language) Stefanović. I am writing this in the year 1992. It is raining outside. This is spooky because you are reading this when I am dead! You probably have much more advanced technology.
>
> Yours sincearly,
> S Stefanović
>
> PS XXXX means Yugoslavian

I pictured the future girl musing to herself, "Yu-go-slavia—what *is* this place?" She'd go to an ancient library, eventually discovering that Yugoslavia was a land that once existed—like Atlantis, or Lemuria—whose people had all died in a bloody war. The language and customs were destroyed, and there was nothing left. She would realize I was someone who got out, and then lived out the rest of her days in Australia, cherishing the old language in this very diary. The future girl would learn the language and stay up late in the evenings, with my diary before her, savoring each word she translated, wondering about this girl, this Sofija. *Was she beautiful?* the future girl would muse. *Did she find love?* she would ask. "Yes," I whispered, imagining my ideal future. "And she became a famous film writer-actor-director."

In reality, the future girl would probably feel swindled, having learned an entire lost language only to find that the secret musings contained in the diary were mainly complaints about other children at school and my worries that Natalija would be "spoiled" by my parents' permissive upbringing. But I didn't consider the boring contents of the diary then. Instead, with a mix of sadness for the future of Yugoslavia, and egotism about the prospect of becoming a beloved ghost, I carefully signed my name at the bottom of the note, and stuck the last page of the book down on top of it.

Meanwhile, back in the very country I was romanticizing, Serbs were taking control of parts of Bosnia, hoping they could section them off, in the way they had tried to take parts of Croatia. Croats were also after Bosnian land, wanting to augment their own nearly independent state. It was at this time that Bosnia's leadership called for the international community to send in peacekeeping forces—assistance that did not come.

Sarajevo had become a war zone, with Bosnian Serb forces attacking it, and locals, including soldiers loyal to Muslim president Alija Izetbegović, criminal gangs, and laypeople defending it.

We made phone calls to Aunt Mila and my grandmothers, who were delayed voices on the telephone, their quick political summaries punctuated by the sound of cigarette smoke being inhaled and exhaled. The Milošević-controlled Serbian television programs downplayed the siege of Sarajevo, airing photographs of the city from peaceful times, intentionally hiding the actual havoc from the population, so that the bloodshed was not apparent to Milošević's potential voters.

In Belgrade, where the population was predominantly Serbian, there was no fighting. Our family and friends were feeling the effects of war through poverty and sanctions and embargoes from the rest of the world, which disapproved of what it saw as Milošević-supported violence in Croatia and Bosnia. People in Serbia stopped driving cars because they couldn't afford gas, homes went without heating, hospitals lacked medicine, and by 1993, about half of the people would be living at or below the poverty line. There was also the rise in corruption. War profiteers were becoming the most powerful people in Serbia, rich from looting in the war zones and especially from smuggling into the country goods that were scarce—cigarettes, alcohol, gas, coffee, and cosmetics—and selling them on the black market.

As I watched the atrocities play out on the TV, I was pretty sure we came from the most horrible place on earth. Yugoslavia was self-destructing—and it was represented on the news by explosions and guns. I could understand the words of the people screaming in the background, about dead loved ones and destroyed homes, in Bosnian dialect, as English-language voice-overs talked about the deaths and ethnic cleansing. Here in Australia, where people had previously just filed us away in the "foreign" or "wog" categories in their minds, we were now from a place they'd heard about—a place they'd seen on TV. If we said we were from Yugoslavia, people thought we were from the war zones, and we'd have to say, "No, we are from Serbia, there's no fighting there." And then, people would reply, "Oh, you're the bad guys."

I wanted to respond, "No, my family opposes the war, and they are against Milošević, that's the whole reason we left." But, just like me only a few years earlier, people often had mental space only for "good guys" and "bad guys." The intricacies of our messy homeland, with all the ethnic groups, and all the pockets of fighting, all the leaders, were hard work to understand, and even harder to explain. I became embarrassed to talk about where I was from.

For the first couple of months in Whyalla, I walked the same way to school, feeding my lunch to a dog that was owned by a man who slept on a deck chair and drank beer. I casually mentioned this ritual to my mother one day as I was scoffing schnitzels after school, and she banned me from walking down that street, shattering my dreams that we could adopt the dog—whose owner called him simply "Dog"—and that I would become the lead in my own kid-meets-dog buddy story.

The next day, my mother made me walk a different way to school, one that took me past a large wall on which I saw some graffiti I didn't understand. When I got home, I asked my mother what "Piss on the Abos" meant. She wasn't sure. "Piss on" was obvious, but "Abos" was a new word, and one we couldn't find in the dictionary. Later, my dad explained that it was derogatory slang for "Aboriginal." He said the graffiti was written by racists.

We'd never learned about Indigenous history at school. I had never met an Aboriginal person. Later I learned that many Aboriginal people had been murdered or displaced during colonization and beyond. The land had been declared "*terra nullius*," "nobody's land," by the British who chose not to recognize the traditional owners who had inhabited the land for over fifty thousand years before European settlement.

Seeing the graffiti was the first time I understood that my homeland wasn't the only place with blood on its hands. Australia, which had seemed to me so clean and fresh, like the chewing gum ad I adored, also had filth beneath its surface. I would later learn about the "Stolen Generations" of Aboriginal children who were forcefully removed from their mothers and placed with white families, cleaved from their culture and history. I would learn as a teenager that the government had refused to issue an apology to the Stolen Generations, and that to this day, Aboriginal people and their cultures suffer from the wrongs done to them in the past, into the present.

These early experiences began shaping the beliefs I came to later on, that wars and oppression don't end when the acts of violence stop; so that on a random day in Whyalla, someone will write a racist remark on a wall in giant letters, in an act of hatred that stretches back for generations, continuing the cycle of violence and degradation. From then on, whenever I passed the graffitied wall, I walked as fast as I could lest an Aboriginal person drive by and see me next to it and associate my white schoolgirl form with the hateful words.

Three months ahead of schedule, my dad finished his work at the factory. We had been there for nine months, and would be leaving Whyalla the day after my school's end-of-year talent show, also known as my last hurrah. I declined to participate in the synchronized dance the other girls were planning, opting instead for a solo performance. If I was going to be leaving this place forever, I might as well go out with a bang.

My version of "a bang" was to lip-sync the popular standard "Dream a Little Dream of Me," as sung by Mama Cass Elliot. I was obsessed with Elliot—who was rumored to have been unhappy in love, and tragically died young from an obesity-related heart attack. Up there onstage by myself, I was wearing an oxblood velour tracksuit from Belgrade, with diamantés sparkling on the front—an iconic image to go with the iconic lyrics, I thought. I wished parents had been invited to the show so that I could have an even bigger audience, but I had to settle for just the students and teachers.

I fake-crooned the romantic lyrics, shifting from one foot to the other, behind the mic, which was too high and obscured most of my face. My performance was full of emotion, tears in my eyes from nerves and the thrill of being onstage at the culmination of my time in this strange new place, but to everyone not sitting in the front row, it appeared as if I was just standing there while a slow song played over the stereo.

"Night breezes seem to whisper 'I love you,'" Mama Cass sang, and my voice, breaking out of lip-sync mode, accidentally boomed out the "I love you." The kids didn't throw their hands in the air, or link arms. They didn't sing along, like I'd dreamed, which would have prompted me to take the mic off the stand and walk to the edge of the stage, bending down, still lip-syncing, holding my hand out for people to touch, some of them shouting over the music "Don't leave!"

About fifteen seconds into my performance, one of the teachers banged a gong and people cheered. I didn't know that the gong was meant to send bad performers offstage, so I just kept standing there mouthing the words until someone shouted, "Get off!"

As the music kept playing, I stepped away from the mic, leaving the stage in my blood-red tracksuit, Mama Cass's voice singing on.

I couldn't bring myself to look at any of the other kids for the rest of the talent show, as they cheered for the dancing girls, and the acts continued uninterrupted by any soundings of the gong. This was certainly not a "this chicken belongs to you" scenario in which I was praised just for being there. The tables had turned, and I felt that my subtle performance was ignored in favor of prepubescent girls in bikini tops. No one seemed to care about my feelings, and I was reminded that school environments are cruel, no matter if you're sitting on the floor or at a little desk. "I cannot wait to leave this provincial shithole," I said to myself in Serbian, channeling my mother.

The next day, after I'd told my parents about my humiliation and they acted appropriately outraged (calling everyone at the school "fools" for missing the artistry of my piece), my family started the twelve-hour drive to Melbourne with a euphoric rendition of our made-up song "*Why, why, why, WHY-ALLA!*" to the tune of "Delilah." As we drove through the wine-growing regions of South Australia, heading toward more temperate Victoria, we talked about all the things we wouldn't miss about Whyalla: "The Pizza Hut!" my mother said, recalling one of the town's only attractions. "The steel factory!" Dad said. "The dick-heads at school!" I said, and didn't get reprimanded, because my parents really didn't care if I swore or not. We watched the countryside zip past us, taking us farther from Whyalla.

Eventually we started reflecting on our nomadic life, and on the funny things that had happened over the years. Dad recalled an exchange with one of his BHP colleagues in Melbourne who, seeing a framed reproduction of the *Mona Lisa* in his office, asked if Dad had painted the woman himself. I recounted a memory from Belgrade, when we'd bought a tiny blown-glass elephant family on a snowy night as we walked home. "What happened to those elephants?" my mother asked, and we tried to remember which relative was keeping them for us. Suddenly, out of character, Natalija shouted, "Shut up! Stop talking about all these memories!" and she started to cry. "All of you always remember things, and the only thing I remember from before is a green door! That's all, just a green door! I don't remember anything else about our life!"

My mother said this was a great memory—the green door was the entrance to our building on the Boulevard of Revolution, our home in Belgrade. Dad comforted her by saying she was only a baby when these memories happened, assuring Natalija that there would be plenty of new things to remember in the future. I realized then that my sister had enjoyed being in Whyalla, and that she didn't like being in a car, off to some place new again.

My mother looked thoughtfully out the window, considering how this outburst tied in with Natalija's fantasy world, where we had a house on wheels, where we didn't have to keep saying goodbye. We stopped talking about the things that had passed, and I kept to myself my suspicion that four-yer-old Natalija didn't really remember the green door in Belgrade. I suspected that her memory of it came not from the real thing, but from the photos we looked at, my parents and I touching the images like precious objects, while little Natalija just sat there staring at the photos, trying to remember, struggling to be part of our story.

Instead of returning to the suburbs of Melbourne, we found ourselves in the beautiful, bustling neighborhood of Carlton, right near the center of town. Dad's work had provided us with a furnished apartment while we sorted out our living situation, and it was the most luxurious place I'd ever stayed. There were soft towels and thick carpets, and whenever we walked in or out of the building's sliding doors, I looked around, hoping someone would be watching us enviously.

On our first evening, we went for a walk, and saw that Melbourne had a side we'd never appreciated from the suburbs. There were people on the streets, packed restaurants, stores open past 5:00 p.m., trams, students, dogs. We walked down Lygon Street, Melbourne's Little Italy, where loud Italian men cajoled passersby to come try the spaghetti, and we did. It was the best spaghetti marinara my mother had ever had, she said, while my dad, sister, and I devoured our fettuccine carbonaras. We stopped at a music store after dinner, and as I savored a maple-walnut ice cream from the New Zealand ice cream parlor, Dad said I could have any CD I wanted. I chose Madonna's *Immaculate Collection*.

Later that night, in my own room that I didn't share with Natalija for once, I got into my fancy bed, which, instead of the mismatched bedding and old blankets I was used to, had a top sheet that smelled floral, tucked so tightly that I squeezed myself into it like a letter in an envelope. I stayed up looking at the CD itself, a shiny silver disc with light blue polka dots. We didn't have a hi-fi yet, so I treated the disc like a precious object, and the lyrics to the songs were printed in a booklet which I examined closely from my cozy spot, excited about the adult content of the songs ("Like a Virgin"!). I fell asleep imagining: What if this was our life now? What if I was now a fancy, romantic girl, like Estella in *Great Expectations*, or Milady in *The Three Musketeers*, or Cathy in *Wuthering Heights*? With my head on the softest pillow on earth, I lay in the center of the bed, stretching my arms and legs out to occupy the entire twin mattress with my now ten-year-old form. I didn't dwell on Yugoslavia or my family, I didn't spare a thought for Whyalla, and I didn't think about starting school again in a few weeks, after summer vacation was over. I was just a girl, in a plush bed, with not a care in the world.

Within two weeks, we found an apartment to rent, in the same suburban area where we'd lived before. It wasn't a house, I noted, but we were on the lookout for one to buy, and I would sit between my parents on the couch excited, as they flipped through real estate listings.

My mother got a job as a psychologist at Health and Human Services, where she counseled abused children under the age of five. Grandma Xenia dipped into her savings once again and came to stay with us, while I went back to Bentleigh West. My old friends Alicia and Cara were ready to welcome me with open arms, but then, observing the new me, they immediately told me I needed to go on a diet, as I was now not only a head taller than them but also, in their opinion, "chubby." To demonstrate their point, the three of us squatted and I was dismayed to see that my thighs were indeed the thickest, curving out from my knees. They referred me to *Girlfriend* magazine, which featured thin young women, and when I told them about my period, my weight was forgotten, and we all pored over the articles discussing periods, my friends in awe of my early admittance into adulthood.

Natalija started at the school, too: she was now five, the same age as I had been when we first came to Australia. But instead of being scared like me, she was audacious, unafraid to approach us in the big-kid part of the playground. When my friends demanded we stop speaking Serbian to each other—"You are in Australia! You have to speak *English*!" Cara said—I was the one who obeyed, shushing my sister unless she spoke to me in English.

My bold little sister even led a raid of the candy jar in her classroom, stealing the candy that was meant as a treat for good behavior. As usual, I was afraid that Natalija would fall prey to something terrible; in this case, I feared she was headed toward a life of crime. I couldn't abide my sister becoming a thief, so I went to the staff room during lunchtime and gave her up. That is how desperate I was to toe the line, terrified that people would think badly of me or my family, forever marked by that incident with my mother—the stolen lollipop and the smack across the face, the fear that someone would say, "Look at that ethnic, stealing from us." So, due to me being a snitch, Natalija was given her first reprimand, and forced to return the Jelly Babies she had secreted in her little schoolbag.

As the troubles back home intensified, more people were leaving Yugoslavia and coming to Melbourne, and our diaspora community was growing by the day. Those from Serbia came on professional visas if they could; those from warring Croatia and Bosnia came as refugees. We found ourselves at Yugo parties every weekend, explaining to people from Belgrade, Zagreb, or Mostar that Vegemite was pretty delicious once you got used to it. Among the new arrivals were Tamara and Neboysha, the artists my parents had met at the Belgrade protests, in the bathroom of the Hotel Majestic. My mother became a huge admirer of

Neboysha's work, which included alchemical symbols, and figures with third eyes and many heads. Finally, she felt like some of "her" people were coming to Australia.

Soon, my dad's best friend, Darko, and his family would come over, too. Darko and Dad had been friends since they were both five-year-olds new to Belgrade, bonding because the Belgrade kids made fun of both Darko's Bosnian accent and my dad's rural one from the mining town of Bor, where he was born. I liked this story—that my dad had been a new kid once just like I always was—and I wondered if I would make a friend for life in the way he had.

One day, some refugees from Bosnia came to our place. The parents went to the living room with my mother, while Dad tactfully went to work at his computer in another room, indicating that this was more of a professional visit than a personal one. My mother told me in advance that the daughter of this family had a tic from the war, which meant that she kept blinking, but that I was not to comment on this. The girl with the tic and I sat in my room, drawing on large pieces of paper, decorating our creations with sparkly stickers that had been bought for the occasion, while our parents talked in the next room. We heard the girl's mom crying, but neither of us commented. The girl blinked every few seconds, hard, her whole face grimacing, and I pretended not to notice, though I was certain I was blinking more frequently too, her blinking affecting me the way a yawn is contagious. After they left, I asked my mother why people have tics, and she said that they can come from trauma, and reminded us how lucky we were that we never had to listen to bombs falling near our beds at night. The next time there was a news report on Sarajevo, I looked at the bombed-out buildings and reminded myself that there might have been children sleeping inside.

Our three-room apartment was about to accommodate not only our family and visiting Grandma Xenia but also Dad's friend Darko and

his wife and son, who would stay with us while they looked for a place. Despite the sudden crowd, my parents kept an important promise they had made to me, now that we were in Melbourne again. Finally we were here to stay, which meant we were getting a dog.

Dante was a miniature dachshund, like the dog on the golden charm my mother wore, and he was nearly as small as a trinket. In the car, Grandma Xenia held him in the palm of her hand all the way home from the breeder, while my sister and I cooed at him. When we got home the two of us fed him slices of cheese, kissed him, and passed him to each other until he vomited.

While Darko and his family were staying with us, the news reported a breaking story from Mostar, in Bosnia, where Darko was born. *Most* means "bridge" in our language, and Mostar was named after the defenders of the beautiful stone bridge, who stood guarding it in medieval times. According to the news, it had been shelled around sixty times by the Croatian army, which was fighting the Bosnian Muslim army for control of the city. On our television screen, the old bridge collapsed, as the adults all held their hands up to their mouths in shock.

When summer vacation was over, and our houseguests finally moved out of our place, Darko's son, Vuki, started at my school. At the assembly at the end of the week, a teacher made Vuki stand up in front of the whole school so he could introduce him. "Vuki is a child from Bosnia," he solemnly told the students. "You may have seen the footage on television: Bosnia is a war zone. Please make Vuki feel welcome and safe in his new environment." I was annoyed, not only because I'd never received such special treatment, but also because Vuki wasn't from Bosnia, he was from Belgrade, Serbia. His father was born in Bosnia, but that wasn't the same thing. *Lucky Vuki doesn't speak English yet,* I thought, as he stood in front of the school, slightly baffled as everyone clapped.

After this awkward introduction to Vuki, my fifth grade class stood

up to perform a song for the entire school, Michael Jackson's recent hit, "Heal the World." Even though I knew that Vuki wasn't from Bosnia, and I found him slightly annoying and childish, I found myself looking in his direction as we sang. He was sitting on the floor with his new third grade classmates, wearing jeans instead of the prescribed school uniform, looking around confused as I'd done when I first came here. I imagined he was scared, just as I had been. Other kids whispered to one another, and he sat among them, friendless. I thought of the little girl with the tic, Vuki, and me, and I found myself sobbing out "Heal the World" with genuine emotion.

When I was twelve, just before I entered high school, my mother, Grandma Xenia, and I started attending house auctions. My parents had sold our Belgrade apartment for a small sum, and with their wages, now we had enough money to get a mortgage and buy a house of our own. Dad didn't go with us to the auctions because, according to him, my mother and grandmother picked places that were out of our budget, and we would only be disappointed. So we went along and just watched, imagining one day bidding. On a sunny spring day, we attended an auction in the backyard of a lovely suburban 1950s brick house. We leaned against the blond brick and breathed in the jasmine that was creeping down the side of the house. The auctioneer stood by an avocado tree, and my mother held Dante's leash as he let out a puppyish yap every now and then. Grandma Xenia was holding a few bags from Bentleigh market, where she snagged secondhand bargains every week.

The bidding began, then not long after, it stopped. The desired price had not been reached, and therefore, the house was still on the market. "Let's get it!" my mother yelped.

We drove home, where Natalija and Dad were playing their favorite game, "Mom and baby." Six-year-old Natalija pretended to be an overanxious, demanding mother, and Dad pretended to be an idiotic baby.

Natalija would order him with zeal to do something, he'd get it terribly wrong, and she would laugh like crazy. When we arrived, Natalija was squashed on the couch under a blanket, Dad sitting on top of her, pretending he had no idea where his "mama" was. "I'm here, you stupid baby, I'm *here*!" she squealed from under the blanket, laughing so hard I worried she would pee herself.

With our boundless enthusiasm, our description of its roominess, the gorgeous yard, and the bargain price, we managed to convince Dad, and that afternoon, my parents contacted the real estate agent and put in their offer for the house. A few days later, the paperwork was done, and our family had a house and a mortgage. The stars had aligned, and the dream sketches in my diary became a reality. We had a proper house and a dog. And even more exciting, the house was just within the McKinnon High School zone, which meant that in a few months, I'd be going there with my friend Alicia, who was also in the zone. For once I wouldn't be friendless at a new school.

In my excitement about high school, the world news eventually became something I could tune out. The war, it seemed, would go on forever; for all the protesting my parents' friends were doing back in Belgrade, and for all the debates and discussions that kept going, it would never stop. The radio switching on in the morning became like a distracting soundtrack in the background, a niggling in the back of my mind, the words going in one ear and out the other on purpose. I repressed the war, and in some ways it worked. This was just another thing my parents were into—like playing cards, or going to the hardware store—that didn't concern me, I told myself. I was about to enter a new phase of my life: being a suburban teenager. I couldn't think of anything more wonderfully normal. And it was, until it became a nightmare.

6

The Tempest

When I was twelve, a week before I was to start high school, we came home from buying my school supplies to discover that Dante (now a fully grown but still very small dog) had pulled down the new living room curtains and shredded them into ribbons, in protest for being left alone. Dad chased him down and kicked him, and in unison with our little dog, my mother, sister, and I yelped. Dad's anger wasn't a surprise—both my parents had tempers—but it was usually confined to yelling (at each other, and less frequently, at us). So my heart started beating rapidly as we watched Dante run behind the couch because Dad had booted him, as my mother shouted, "You could have broken his ribs!" While we crowded around Dante, Dad shouted about the price of the curtains, how we weren't rich, how this dog was ruining his home, and as he shouted, he stalked up and down the room. As this scene was unfolding, I kept thinking about more pleasant ones instead, like how Dad would pick Dante up and lift him into the air saying, "Look, it's Laika, the first dog in space!" And undaunted by the great height, Dante would wag his shoelace-thin tail.

When we looked back on it later, we realized that kicking our little dog in the ribs wasn't the first out-of-character thing we had witnessed Dad do. He had been rude to our family friend Lina at her own birthday party a week before. She'd made a dumb comment, and Dad had called her a moron. My parents called people morons all the time, so the sentiment wasn't unusual, but they did it behind people's backs, and this was said point-blank with venom. My mother apologized to the hosts, saying that Dad had had too much to drink (though actually, he'd only had one beer), while Dad, Natalija, and I waited in the car. Something was up with Dad, but I didn't think much of it at the time.

On the first day of high school, Alicia and I stood around the front entrance in our ugly new uniforms, big blue dresses that belonged not to 1995 but to the olden days, when women wore belted frocks, long socks, and shiny black shoes. That first morning, we tried to contain our excitement, looking furtively at the other students entering the school grounds, the older kids with their navy school sweaters stretched painfully into a grunge aesthetic, some of them sticking their thumbs through a hole they'd poked in the cuff. Watching those cool students, I thought of when Grandma Xenia and I once walked past a guy wearing a massive nineties sweater, the sleeves of which hung past his hands, and she said without a trace of irony, "Look at that poor young man, he's lost his hands. Maybe he was a soldier."

Alicia and I stared at certain girls who exuded style despite having the exact same uniforms as we did, and breathlessly muttered "he's hot" as we ogled teenaged boys in gray shorts and white shirts and tried to keep our hormones in check. Alicia was still slight, athletic, period-less, a better match than I was for the boys who hadn't had their growth spurts yet, and every now and then they looked over in her direction. She shrugged like she didn't care but still got me to check her braces for any stray bits of food.

I overheard some kids making fun of a boy called Al Chan because he shared a bedroom with his grandma and the floors in his house were falling apart. "Your family is *so povo,*" a boy said, and I thought about what my dad (who hated it when people said "seeya" instead of "see you") would think of that butchering of the English language. I imagined him correcting the bullies: "You should say, 'Your family is so impoverished.'"

What would these high school kids think of my place? My mother loved contemporary art, and some of the paintings on our walls were disturbing, like the one of headless naked corpses flying through the air, their legs akimbo and assholes and penises on display, or that topless portrait of my aunt a Belgrade artist had done when she was in college. Also, my mother continued to smoke inside, despite the fact that I'd recently been bombarding her with literature on lung cancer. But while in primary school I was embarrassed my mother didn't watch morning television shows like other kids' moms, I was now proud that both my parents worked. In Belgrade, my friends' moms had jobs, and I started saying things like, "Why do so many women in Australia stay home, and men get to work?" to my Australian friends.

There were parts of my culture that I was proud of, thanks to my parents. In response to people talking to them like they were children because they had accents, my parents would say later, "These dumb Aussies don't even speak any other languages," or "What a pathetic schooling system, you don't even read the classics! Back in Yugoslavia, *War and Peace* was required reading for students aged fourteen!" So, whenever I felt small at an all-Aussie gathering, I secretly repeated the things my parents said, to make myself feel big again. I kept *War and Peace* on my shelf, ready to read it as soon as I turned fourteen, so I could feel privately better than Aussies. Despite all this, on the first day of school, I didn't want to be lumped in with Al Chan for having a "weird" house, and be labeled a freak like a boy called Gary (who didn't get his McKinnon uniform in time and showed up in a purple sweat suit, destined to be called Grimace, after the McDonald's character, forever more).

I wished our house was tidy, and that we had "shopping days" like my friends did, when the whole family went to the supermarket for the week's groceries, instead of running to get stuff at the last minute. I wanted our family to have a "pizza night" or "Chinese night" or designate one night a week when Natalija and I would commandeer the kitchen and make some adorable meal that our parents would lovingly eat, even though it was a bit gross. I wanted to be like a kid on television shows, and I resented my parents for not wanting the same. Basically, I wanted a G-rated home life, while in reality—with the coarse language, adult themes, and the violent war content my parents were obsessed with—it was more likely rated R.

"Why does your mom just honk when she comes to pick you up, instead of coming in and talking to my mom? It's rude," my friend Cara once said in primary school. When I repeated this to my mother, she said, "I work all day, I don't have time. And even if I did, I don't give a fuck about talking to Cara's boring mother." I considered translating and passing this on to Cara (minus the cursing which sounded worse in English than it did in Serbian) and then decided against it. Though I was slightly thrilled by my mother's audacity, I was also embarrassed by her attitude.

High school was my chance to reinvent myself. I knew I had a foreign name and that I was never going to pass as an Aussie kid. But I was determined to do well in school so I could become something—a writer or a director, or an actor. Never again would I be that foreign girl who cried endlessly in class. *I* was reading *Lord of the Flies*, which was the prescribed text for year ten students, even though I was only in year seven. Like my dad, I wrote little notes in the margin in faint pencil. I was excited to form my own small opinions, feeling my confidence rise, as I annotated the book with my observations.

When we were assigned classes, I was separated from Alicia. Alicia had always been able to gather crowds around her through primary school, where she was the boss of games like "Goblins and Girls," and the orchestrator of themed parties that the whole school talked about for months. Now she would walk right into a new classroom and command it, and my plan to ride in the slipstream of her cool was thwarted. Fighting panic, I went to my new class and sat down next to a girl with silky hair and dark eyeliner, hoping she might take me under her wing. She introduced herself:

"My name's Toto, and if you make fun of my name, I'll bash the shit out of you."

If anyone gave her shit, she continued, her older brother and his Italian friends would also bash the shit out of them. I was magnetized by her attitude, the relaxed way she threw around threats and curses, and I was suddenly eager to introduce "shit" into my vocabulary though I had avoided it until now because it was against school rules. What a baby I had been, following school rules! Why did I think cursing was only acceptable in Serbian and that English was too pristine? *Yes, I decided, "shit" will be replacing my current repertoire of "shivers" and "fudge."* Of course, I would also have to learn to apply makeup, pronto, if I wanted to ooze Toto's level of cool.

On that first day, our English teacher, Mrs. Reynolds, made us introduce ourselves with our name and an alliterative descriptor— "Awesome Adam," "Truthful Tien," "Radical Regina," and so on. In all my excitement, and thrilled by Toto, the only adjectives I could think of that started with "S" were "Sexy," and "Shit-hot," words that would have put me squarely in creep territory. Lucky for me, I was given a bit more time to think because a boy with a rat's tail haircut had somehow missed the rules of the game (even after half the class had done it) and introduced himself, in a breaking voice as, "um . . . I dunno, Funny Alex." The classroom burst into hysterics, and I laughed the loudest. Exchanging elated looks with my new classmates, I dreamed about the jokes we'd share in the years to come. When it was my turn, I slipped in a cool "Scintillating Sofija," to which Mrs. Reynolds said "good word," and I shrugged modestly.

Mrs. Reynolds asked us to take out our assigned reading materials. As I privately rejoiced that we were getting into books already, Toto muttered "boring" under her breath. Just as I was glancing around the room to pick out who was going to be my best friend—probably the beautiful Asian girl whose copy of *Goodnight Mister Tom* was already well thumbed and full of notes—there was a knock at the door and an elderly teacher with a silver bob walked in. "I'm here to pick up the English as a second language students. John? Irena? Sofija?" John and Irena stood up. In shock, I sat there for a few seconds, then I stood up too, dazed.

Before I knew it, I was trudging along behind Mrs. Anderson next to Nigerian John and Russian Irena, feeling nauseous. At the end of last year I'd been told that I'd placed out of ESL. To my delight, they said I was the best English student in the *regular* English class. One of the reasons I'd studied English so fiercely was precisely so I didn't have to stand dumbly, like some kid fresh from overseas, crying like the baby I used to be. And today especially, I had planned to dazzle Mrs. Reynolds, casually mentioning I'd been reading *Lord of the Flies*. I was going to stake my claim fast, establish my position as top student, and become the queen of English. How could I accomplish any of that from a stupid ESL class?

In Mrs. Anderson's classroom, we took our seats among other ethnic kids who had been plucked from regular English classes. She asked us a question and then said slowly, "If you understand, please put your hand in the air." Everyone raised a hand, except for Anastasia, a newly arrived Russian whose perfume enveloped us all. Irena whispered to her, and Anastasia put her hand in the air, giggling.

I kept my hand up.

"I will have you know," I said, formally, intending to wow Mrs. Anderson with my articulate English, to give a speech that would put her back in her place, get an apology out of her for dragging me to this class. Then I felt tears rise to my eyes. "I will have you know that I have been reading *Lord of the Flies*, by William Golding, which is a year *ten* text!" I squawked, trying to steady my voice, blink away the tears. "I shouldn't be here!" I said, and then the sobs burst forth, the tears, all the exposure I thought I'd left behind in primary school. The whole class was looking at me.

Mrs. Anderson suggested I might like to go to the bathroom, and miserably, I complied, remembering the other time I'd run to the restroom distraught, back in French kindergarten, just before my heart was broken for the first time. Now, I watched my puffy, snotty, heaving face in the mirror, gasping "why" dramatically in Serbian to myself like I was a young child again, as my already large nose became larger, my small eyes ever smaller. When I returned to class feeling defeated, looking like an ESL Elephant Man, all the students were writing quietly in their notebooks, under the title "About Me," except for one boy, who I noticed was drawing a large, detailed penis, complete with pubic hair and elaborate shading.

I was about to take my seat among the other foreigners when Mrs. Anderson said: "You can go back to regular English class." Even though it had been not through an eloquent speech but an infantile breakdown, I had gotten what I wanted. I slipped back into class next to Toto, muttering, "That teacher just made a shitty mistake taking me to the wrong class, and then I had a hay fever attack!"

Though I'd managed to extricate myself from the ESL crowd at school, there were lots of new ex-Yugo kids popping into my social life (which, at thirteen, still involved trudging along to family friends' places with my parents) as the diaspora continued to grow. Most of these ex-Yugo kids lived even farther from the city than us: in the outer suburbs, hanging around Dandenong Market, or smoking cigarettes in the parking lot behind the Serbian church in St. Albans. The new ex-Yugos didn't come here on professional visas, like my family had, but on refugee visas from Bosnia, escaping conflict. Some of them had spent time in refugee camps, had temporarily lived in Austria or Germany before making their way here. I was glad these kids weren't at my school, where I'd have to babysit them. I didn't want to be the translator, the "local" showing new arrivals around. I felt I finally had the things I wanted: a house, a dog, and the academic, social, and romantic possibilities of high school life. I wanted for once to be an insider, and, though I'd never say it out loud, I didn't want some refugee kids with facial tics ruining that for me.

I was, of course, still not going to be mistaken for a straight-up Aussie. Even among us immigrants at school, it seemed there were a bunch of different ways to "be ethnic." Some kids in my school were what I considered "extreme" ethnics: like Irena and Anastasia, the Russian kids who had recently emigrated, and spoke Russian to each other all day. They had their own fashion sensibility. While the rest of us were embracing the ripped jeans and big sweaters of grunge when we were out of school uniform, they would wear tight pants and grow their nails really long, manicure them beautifully, and then pierce them with a diamond stud that dangled off the fingernail. They listened to music from Russia, and they had Russian boyfriends who didn't go to our school.

Then there were the kids who formed "Aussie-ethnic" cliques, like "the Greeks," for example. These were kids who were born here, to immigrant parents, and had formed a whole new cultural group specific to their idiosyncratic circumstances. Some of these kids had never been back to the "mother country," but they still identified with their roots, or at least identified with others who were second-generation immigrants with the same backgrounds. They spoke their own versions of English, with their own slang, and their own peculiar accents. They knew no other home apart from Australia, but within Australia, they were part of a proud minority. A local gang would tag "3166 wogs" on the train stations, combining the postal code of their neighborhood with the derogatory term they'd reclaimed—they called themselves the Oakleigh Wogs.

"Wogs rule, Skips pull" they would write inside the train carriages. "Skip" or "Skippy" was an attempt at a disparaging term for white Anglo Aussies, appropriated from the long-running TV show *Skippy the Kangaroo*, while "pull" was a reference to masturbation. To me, the Oakleigh Wogs seemed a bit like Robin Hood, or the Australian outlaw Ned Kelly, who went against the establishment, who wore their underdog status proudly. I liked that they were saying "fuck you" to the powers that be, and I imagined incensed Aussie train employees scrubbing the graffiti, while the wogs on the train, me included, smiled just a little to ourselves.

Of course, I identified with immigrants more than I did with Aussies. Privately, my heart went out to the ESL kids—because I was really one of them. They'd never mentioned my tearful outburst, even though it had been predicated on the disgust I felt at being slotted into an inferior class (in both senses of the term) with them, and I felt embarrassed. But still, I wanted to cut ties with my blood; I wanted to shed my national identity and live the unencumbered life of a "Kylie" or a "Samantha" who didn't have to subject herself to all sorts of associations she had no control over every time she introduced herself. I didn't enjoy having to link myself to Serbia every time I made a new acquaintance and I thought, *All my friends in Serbia don't have to talk about being Serbian every day, they're not "the Serbian girl in class 7F," they're just normal.*

Even though I was further from my birthplace than ever before, forgetting little details about Belgrade, slipping in English terms into my conversations at home, I was the most Serbian person the Aussies in my life knew—the only Serbs other than me were those on television—and they didn't look good.

In those days, my parents argued a lot, mainly about what was going on back home. Fundamentally, they shared a worldview: they both wanted the war to end, even if it meant that Yugoslavia would no longer exist. But every day, there were new atrocities, and they were getting mixed reports about what was actually going on. They weighed up the information, from the news, the radio, and our relatives and then argued as they tried to make sense of it. On the Australian news, the Serbs were, as usual, portrayed as the oppressors and murderers. And even though there *were* plenty of Serbian bad guys (some of them later being tried as war criminals), my parents (especially my mother) were pissed that the Australian news didn't *also* show the other side: that Bosnian Serb civilians were being killed and driven out of villages, too. And there were plenty of Serbs who opposed the war—like us, and there was the opposition movement in Serbia—that never got any airtime. There were perpetrators and victims on all sides.

My mother started seeing media manipulation in all news reports, and my dad sometimes agreed, though other times he called her paranoid, or teased her about being a Serbian nationalist. "I never, ever called myself a Serb, I was always a Yugoslavian, until I came here and saw how they represent us in the news!" my mother shouted, suddenly patriotic. She hated that the news was so black-and-white. Slobodan Milošević was seen as the butcher behind it all, and the media aligned the Serbian people with his image. But how culpable was he? How much control did he really have over the Bosnian Serb army, which was led by local generals?

"Humans are *all* swine, once you scratch below the surface!" she yelled. "And we come from a fucked-up place where every fifty years there's a war, and our swinishness comes out!" Her shouting was directed at my father, but really she was yelling at the army generals, at the soldiers on the ground, at the psychopathic paramilitary raping and murdering, at the Western media who were against us. She yelled at the world, demanding for it to see us *all* as swine and *all* as victims. Bosnian Muslims, Serbs, and Croats were losing their homes and their lives at one another's hands, and, depressed, my parents watched each night, trying to make sense of it all. Every now and then, Dad would take his glasses off and put his head in his hands, saying he was tired of it all, and my mother would look at him, slightly surprised, not used to being alone with her rage.

I wanted out. I didn't want to hear the horrible stories. I reasoned that whereas my panicky parents, with their accents, and their insistence Belgrade was their "real home" were inextricably welded to ex-Yugoslavia, and were therefore stuck with the diaspora community, I was not. I could become friends with kids who were not bound to me by ethnicity, but in other ways, ways that could be even more meaningful. I had the opportunity to reach further. I resolved to make friends with those who had a connection to my *soul*, people who liked to read, who were artsy, cynical, intelligent, and whose conversations were not exclusively about the war in Yugoslavia. One person who I was keen to connect to was Harry, a dark-haired kid from Alicia's music class, who read even more than I did, and who I could talk to about such pressing issues as dating, books, and cigarettes.

I talked to Harry on the phone every day, and dreamed about dating him. Sometimes he cleaned his aquarium while we talked, and when there was a lull in the conversation, I heard splashing noises from his end, while I observed myself in the mirror checking to see what I look like when I laughed, or kissing my reflection passionately, hoping to prepare myself for "the real thing" one day. Luckily, if while I was talking to Harry my parents yelled at my sister to get the fuck out of the living room when the news was on, I could pretend that that was just my folks calling Natalija for dinner, since Harry didn't understand Serbian. Harry and I gossiped about who had got with who, casually using words we'd just picked up, like "pashing" for kissing. I don't think we ever talked about the war in Yugoslavia, but if we did, I would have brushed it off, as if it was no big deal. I'd pretend I wasn't aware of the intricacies, even though they filled my home and ears in the hours I wasn't at school. What was important was the microcosm of McKinnon High School, where certain kids were smoking weed, others were pashing and possibly more, and that is what we talked about, ceaselessly.

It was during one of these conversations that I casually said, "We talk on the phone so much! We should probably go out?" and then I laughed like it was a joke, though actually, I felt as if my heart had come out of my chest, through my mouth, and was now being squeezed through the little holes in the phone speaker, like meat going through a mincer. "Nah," Harry said, "I think we should just be great friends." I pretended like I didn't care one way or the other—going out with him, not going out with him, no big deal, I chuckled, hoping it wouldn't sound hollow, like the pretend laugh of someone who had finally gathered some guts and now felt like those same guts were being shoved back down her throat. But friends it would be.

One sunny afternoon, I was engaged in a new activity—applying eye liner in the school bathroom—when, over the PA system, it was announced that there would be auditions for Shakespeare's *The Tempest*. The drama department welcomed all students to audition, so even as a lowly year-seven, I would have the opportunity to try out for the romantic lead: Miranda. Landing a part in the school play would be the perfect way to wrap up my first year of high school. I felt my courage rise, hope rearing its excited little head, my Disney princess dreams resurrected once again.

I imagined myself going into the audition, delivering my lines, somewhat hesitantly at first, but then allowing the passion of the scene to overcome me. When I finished the powerful piece, the drama teacher, Mr. Fisher, would stare at me for a few seconds inscrutably. Then he'd say, "You may go." I'd turn, eyes downcast, and as I got to the door he'd call, "One more thing." I'd spin back around. "You've got the part. Welcome aboard, Miranda." And, like in the movies, I'd leap into the air, whooping with abandon, because suddenly, I'd be queen of the school.

With trembling hands I brought home the photocopied sheet of paper that contained the audition piece for Miranda, my confidence somewhat depleted once I'd actually read the thing. For one, I couldn't understand the complicated Shakespearian language. As I stared at the nonsensical lines (*"The sky, it seems, would pour down stinking pitch / But that the sea, mounting to th' welkin's cheek / Dashes the fire out"*) I zoned out. "What the shit is a welkin?" I practiced how I would say it on the phone to Harry, trying to recoup the cool I had lost at the horror-themed party at Alicia's the week before. I'd zealously coated myself in zombie makeup and then had to sit on Alicia's mom's couch on top of a towel so I wouldn't smear it with body paint. Looking like a creep, I watched thirteen-year-old couples slow-dancing stiffly to R.E.M.'s "Everybody Hurts," and worst of all, I had to witness Harry touch tongues with Toto during spin the bottle. The bottle didn't land on me, so I'd sat there, my hideous makeup hiding the hope draining from my unkissed face. My childish excitement at dressing up had made me look like a fool next to Toto, who was ingeniously dressed as a vampire's victim in a tight top and baggy jeans, with two tiny red marks on her neck. As she hung her arms loosely around Harry's neck and leaned her head against his chest during a slow dance, I thought, *She looks like an adult woman in a film.*

After I'd spent hours memorizing the monologue, Dad came home and I recited it to him in a confused rush. Even though he seemed exhausted, his inner nerd was activated, and he insisted we look up each of the things we didn't understand in a massive annotated Shakespeare book he had. He loved the English language, and Shakespearean English was a particularly juicy challenge. This was unlike my mother, who saw our adopted language as the enemy, out to trick us with stupid spellings and nonsense phrases. ("Kevin Costner—*why* a K and a C, when they make the same sound!?" And: "Why would a woodwind instrument be called such a stupid thing? A recorder is something that records, damn it!")

Dad and I examined this monologue, in which, I eventually understood, Miranda was imploring her father, Prospero, to stop the storm he'd conjured with his magical powers, because it was causing a shipwreck off the coast of their island home.

"If by your art, my dearest father," I recited in a singsong voice.

"If," Dad interrupted me, putting a hand to his heart, "by your *art*"—he looked heavenward, dramatically illustrating which words needed emphasis—"my *dearest* father . . . you have put the wild waters in this roar, *allay* them."

In Belgrade, Dad had been the star of his college production of *Romeo and Juliet*—a reprieve from his engineering course. The photos from that play show him at nineteen, a Romeo with thick seventies sideburns and a delighted, almost maniacal smile, revealing his white teeth. I knew this gleeful expression of my dad's; I'd seen it at various times. Like when he did a headstand in front of his friends, just to prove he could do it, or whenever he won a game of cards.

It was clear from the photos, and from the way he read the lines, that my dad still loved the arts. Knowing that literature wasn't practical to study, he'd gone into engineering instead. Thinking about those delighted photos of Dad as Romeo made me wonder where we'd be if he'd followed his passion. Would we have managed to get a visa for Australia?

At thirty-nine, Dad's face was leaner than in the photos from his acting days; his blue eyes seemed smaller behind his glasses. And as we practiced the monologue, I noted that Dad's skin, normally pale, was looking especially dark, almost as if a yellow glow was emanating from inside him.

Dad looked at his watch and jumped up. It was, of course, time for *SBS World News*, which meant our *Tempest* session was over. He turned the TV on full blast, and like Pavlov's dog responding to a treat, my mother ended the phone conversation she was having with Aunt Mila, leaving the cordless phone on the bed and rushing to the screen. I put the phone on its cradle to charge, hoping it would fill with enough juice so I could talk to Harry.

We all sat silently in front of the television as usual, our faces glowing blue by the light from the set. I sat closest to the phone, because if it rang, it would definitely be for me—no ex-Yugoslavian in their right mind would make a phone call during *SBS World News*, and there'd be hell to pay if my parents missed a single word of the broadcast because of the phone ringing.

Croatia was up first, which was unusual, as these days Bosnia was the most war-torn. What we didn't know, as we watched the screen, was that this was the final battle in the Croatian war, "Operation Storm," a major Croatian offensive against the Serbs. My mother said "See!?" to no one in particular as we watched local Serbs being driven out, and my dad snapped "Shut up!" so he could hear the report.

The camera followed a truck loaded with people, and it zoomed in on an old lady, her daughter, and small granddaughter. The old lady was crying, as the truck rolled past some soldiers who held their machine guns in the air in a celebratory gesture. In the shaky footage, the daughter comforted the old lady, who used a clenched fist to wipe away tears, clutching a cheap leather bag. My mother cried as we watched, as she often did. I looked at the old lady, with her short haircut, her old clothes, and the bag she held to her, and I imagined her buying that bag, at the market, in better times, when Serbs and Croats mingled with one another, bargaining. I considered if these people leaving their home would end up here, in our diaspora.

And then the report was over. The anchor started talking about Afghanistan and my mother turned the volume down, as if these people in Afghanistan, also being blown up and fleeing, were not important. "Each to their own tragedy," I imagine she would have said if challenged. There's a difference between seeing strangers suffering, and seeing people who are speaking your language.

The tension seemed to shift from the screen into the room, and I knew what came next: my parents arguing about what they'd just seen.

Their arguments were getting nastier; their patience with each other was shorter, and sometimes they looked at each other with a kind of bemused distaste, both of them apparently wondering how they had ended up here, and why they were stuck with each other. Now I was older, I could tell that their arguments were bad, that, with their name calling, they weren't just lively debate partners, but people who found each other increasingly annoying.

They never mentioned a separation, though. Here, far from home, where they were foreign, it was a frightening concept, more frightening than staying together, snapping at each other like dogs in a cage.

"Let's go play Nintendo," I said, in a sudden burst of compassion for my sister, who, like me, had to listen to this every day. Her hair was in a short, boyish cut, which she had insisted on getting soon after I got my short cut. She didn't know that I, in turn, had copied it from Winona Ryder—a person who looked good with a pixie cut thanks to her superior bone structure and shiny locks, unlike me, with my angular, pointy features and brushlike hair. The cut didn't work on either me or my sister, and as she jumped to her feet, touchingly delighted that I agreed to play with her, she looked like a smaller, sillier version of me, a living testament to all the ways I'd failed. We left our parents to their fighting.

"Would you like to be Princess?" Natalija asked me respectfully once we were in her room, ready to play our video game. Nobody looked at me the way my sister did: she was the only person in the world who thought I was all-knowing, beautiful, and magical. In typical older sibling style, I appreciated her when I needed it, and I ignored her the rest of the time. Now I settled in front of the screen and picked up the controller, as Natalija did a butt-shaking dance, which I encouraged by wiggling my head and shoulders, flaring my nostrils comically, and singing along to the *Mario Kart* theme music in a way I did when my friends weren't around and I could afford to be childish. Harry was probably talking to Toto right now. My sister picked up her controller, as I scrolled past Princess and chose Bowser, the scaliest monster of *Mario Kart*.

The morning of *The Tempest* audition, I got in the car to find Natalija murmuring to herself, preparing for a stupid joke.

"If by your *fart* my dearest father!" she said, misquoting my lines and guffawing. But I was not in a friendly mood. Today was possibly the most important day of my high school life, and of course a stupid eight-year-old wouldn't have the sophistication to appreciate that.

To ignore her, I looked out the window. In the front seats were both of my parents—we had a whole-family doctor's appointment before school and work. The doctor thought Dad might have hepatitis so the rest of us needed to be vaccinated. Even though it felt like a little-kid thing to do, I'd made a card for my dad, trying to make light of something troubling. I drew a cartoon of him as a superhero, with his yellow skin, his bushy beard, and a red cape. A banner declared that he was "Hepatitis Lolitis." He had laughed and put it on the table next to his bed, beside a neat stack of books.

In the clinic he was taken away for a scan, and our GP, Dr. Kearney, asked my mother, sister, and me to bare the top of a butt cheek for a painful injection. As we were walking out to the parking lot after the appointment, all of a sudden the world went slippery and black.

The next thing I knew, Dr. Kearney was looming over me, commanding, "Hold them up!" I was flat on my back, splayed out in all my ridiculousness. I looked up at my mother's plump face with her concerned eyes and high, arched eyebrows. I saw my dad's yellowish face with his light brown beard and his big glasses, his blue eyes squinting at me. Each of them was grasping one of my shiny black school shoes. They looked funny from this angle, my parents, the people who saw me as a baby even now, despite my awkward adolescence. I was reminded of my legs, which I hadn't started shaving yet, covered in blond fluff, the cellulite distributed around each thigh, displayed for all to see. My pink cotton underpants, which my mother got from Target, were undoubtedly revealing some pubic hair out the side. I tried to sit up, but Dr. Kearney wouldn't let me. "You're going to stay down there for a few minutes. You fainted from the injection." Though I'd always been interested in fainting, like a waif in a book or film, the reality was less dignified than I'd imagined: I was more upside-down cockroach than pallid heroine.

My sister looked at me, impressed, while people peered through the windows of the waiting room. What were the chances, I wondered, that some kids from my school were being carpooled down this very street, and that they'd look out and see me and then say to each other: "Did you see that girl Sofija lying on the ground on Jasper Road with her legs in the air? What a loser." I remembered the attractive girls on the netball courts, with their cute boyish bodies like Winona Ryder, and their lean, muscular legs. I freed my terrible legs from my parents' grasp and sat up.

The school day passed in an awkward blur. I was distracted by the humiliation I'd had to endure in the morning, and nervous about the one I might have to endure soon, as the Shakespeare audition neared. At lunchtime, I found myself in front of bald Mr. Fisher, who looked at me unmoved as I shakily recited the lines I'd so carefully prepared with my dad. I tried to imagine Mr. Fisher not as a portly drama teacher, in a hall smelling of teenaged sweat, but as a powerful wizard on a desert island, whipping the weather up into a frenzy. "If by your art," I said, closing my eyes, putting my hand up to my heart, "my *dearest* father, you have put the wild waters in this roar, *allay* them . . ."

At the end of the day, looking at the long list of names on the corkboard outside the staff room, I saw that the lead role of Miranda had gone to Sally Martins in year ten. She was an older girl, someone who was much more capable of playing a romantic lead than I was. I knew nothing about romance, except that I wanted to be in one.

I continued to scan the column of names, and was shocked to find one that stuck out, stretching the Excel spreadsheet column just a bit wider. Yes, among the Sally Martinses, the Serbian "vić" of my own name was defiantly sticking out. "Iris, goddess of the rainbow," it said beside it. "Goddess," I whispered to myself, my breath catching.

As I slowly walked home, I remembered the stupid drama exercise in Ms. Danica's class where Jasna had played the princess and I'd been ignored. *How the tables have turned,* I thought. It had been decided—by a *teacher* no less!—that I would play a goddess. Who needs a princess's throne when you can be steeped in magical, mysterious grace? *After all, I wasn't named after the* princess *of wisdom, but the* goddess *of wisdom,* I thought, tossing the idea around in my mind. I was exotic, and full of secret knowledge. *Goddess.* Gods aren't bound by nationality, or wealth; they can travel across the seas without having to save for a ticket, they have the power to make people safe, to make the world a better place.

While I was having these lofty thoughts, I walked home, past Dr. Kearney's office, where my parents, unbeknownst to me, were being given some news that made them both silent for once.

They sat in the clinic staring at Dr. Kearney and trying to process her words. Dad's ultrasound showed a mass on his liver. The reason his skin was yellow was not hepatitis but because of the bile spilling into his bloodstream, from a liver so riddled with cancer, it couldn't function.

7

The Tragedy Competition

All at once, we were a family who knew a lot about livers. In the way my parents had watched the news obsessively and talked ceaselessly about the war, they now analyzed ultrasounds and frequently spoke to doctors, as if gathering information could give them some control over something that was uncontrollable. But they were helpless, and their knowledge was useless, and they should have learned that from the war, which twisted and turned and kept going no matter how much they willed it to stop.

Dad's surgery was scheduled a week after his diagnosis, so he took sick leave to prepare, while my mother continued to work at Health and Human Services. My parents agreed that she might end up being the only breadwinner, and shouldn't take time off. I looked after Natalija when we got home from school, which meant playing Nintendo for hours every evening.

At school, I felt my newly won status as "just another kid" revert to "freak" all over again. None of the other kids had a dad who was sick, who was about to have an operation, who might die. Most liver cancers are related to alcoholism, but the sort Dad had wasn't, and I felt myself rushing to explain that. "My dad has cancer of the liver. But he's not an alcoholic!" I assumed people would look down on him if they thought his cancer was a result of addiction. I hated myself for caring what people thought, but I couldn't help but be relieved he didn't have a more embarrassing cancer—as we had discovered in our health education class, several of the boys in my class couldn't even hear the word "testicle" without tears of laughter streaming down their faces.

Dad needed to have a large part of his liver removed to save his life from the aggressive disease, and only two surgeons in the country could perform the tricky operation. One of them happened to be in Melbourne. "You were right, for insisting we come to Australia," my mother said to Dad, who was so unaccustomed to her agreeing with him, he must have thought he was hallucinating—something that had, along with his erratic moods, started happening because of his illness. But she was sincere: "Imagine if this had happened in Belgrade?" Dad's work health insurance meant he had access to the best facilities and treatment, and that he could take medical leave, while Serbia's economy was still struggling terribly. Picturing the hospital he might have ended up in back home gave my mother chills.

In the week between his diagnosis and the operation, my parents met with the famous surgeon, a detached man who ate Twisties cheese snacks during their meeting, both of my parents watching bewildered: those orange, salty fingers dipping in and out of a bag would soon be responsible for dad's life. Afterward, my mother tried to see the upside. "Surgeons are *supposed* to be psychopaths," she said, as if this was a known entrance requirement for the prestigious field of medicine. "How can someone who is normal open up a human and pick their way through the organs, blood, and bones?"

During the operation, Natalija, who didn't know exactly what was going on, was sent to a friend's house, while my mother and I sat with Dad's friend Darko in our living room, waiting for the phone to ring to tell us if he had survived. I played a montage in my head, remembering holding Dad's hand with the fingernails bitten down when I was small, and how I still liked to sit in his lap even though I was thirteen and too old to be a baby. We'd seen him before the operation, and, from his gurney, Dad smiled at me and said, "See you, kid," and those words kept repeating in my head as we sat there.

After eight hours, the surgeon called—the operation had lasted longer than expected, but they thought they'd got the cancer out.

The next day my mother drove to give the surgeon and his assistant gifts—pieces from her art collection. The Twisties surgeon accepted with amused indifference an abstract oil painting by a Yugoslavian artist; his assistant said he would hang the pastel work she gave him in his office. My mother prayed that those paintings hanging in their offices would signify the end of this chapter: a punctuation mark to conclude Dad's illness, and indicate a return to our normal lives.

Meanwhile, Dad was on a morphine drip in the ICU. From the drugs, he hallucinated and complained that the nurses were plotting against him, hissing that the doctors were talking about *shiptars*, using the derogatory term Slavs use for Albanians in Kosovo. My dad, who had always been antinationalist and levelheaded, who had chided my mother for being the paranoid one, was now saying things he would have been humiliated by in a lucid state. My mother visited Dad after work, and often Natalija and I went with her. To get to him, we drove from the suburbs through the city, past a massive billboard for the strip club Men's Gallery. It was the brightest thing we saw before the hospital, that billboard of three women in lingerie, and I stared at them each time we drove past, looking at their healthy bodies, in stark contrast to Dad's brittle one that we would shortly see. The flesh of these women's legs was firm, their breasts rounded—*norgs,* I thought. That's what the boys in my class would have called them.

When Dad came home from the hospital a few weeks later, he tried to regain his strength. One day he wanted to go for a walk, and I went with him, holding him under the arm. He was overdressed for the springtime weather in his beanie and coat. I saw my classmate Tom's mom in her car waiting at the light as we stood at the crossing. Dad, in his getup, with his thin face; me, holding him steady, gripping his hand. Tom's mom probably thought Dad was drunk. Or she knew he was sick just by looking at him, like the old ladies in the supermarket who observed Dad in the produce aisle and whispered, one to the other, loud enough for me to hear: "It must be AIDS!"

Once he could walk around on his own, one morning Dad put on his suit and showed up at his office. When he got to his desk, he discovered his computer was gone. He just waited politely, as his embarrassed colleagues went about attempting to retrieve it, trying to hide their shock that he was back, when everyone had thought he was going to die. Dad made a joke or two, trying to remain dignified when he felt like a fool in his suit that was too big, and was exhausted from the effort of standing.

Though it seemed suddenly small in the scheme of things, *The Tempest* performance was nearing, and I looked forward to it. My costume was a green, flowy dress and a feathered headpiece, which I was particularly proud of. Natalija drew a family portrait in honor of the performance: skinny Dad, chubby Mom, little Natalija, and me—the largest character on the page, resembling a glorious green alien whose feathered headpiece stood up like antennae. We had a dress rehearsal at the amateur theater that had been rented by the school for the performance. Down in the backstage area, I adored being told what to do by busy older girls, who instructed me to hold still while they put "pancake" concealer on my face, and loads of makeup that I would keep on afterward because I thought it made me look beautiful. The actors were the stars, everyone fussed over us, and we waited importantly to be called to the stage from a speaker in the wall.

A boy named Andy played the mischievous sprite Ariel. I had never met someone flamboyantly gay before, so I was drawn to Andy, who would hug everyone, kiss us, and call us "darling." *Finally,* I thought— as I sat leaning my head on Andy's shoulder during a break, beside an older kid named Alon with long curly hair, who played Prospero—*I am among artists.*

As the youngest cast member, I longed for the other kids to take me under their wing—to recognize that I was young but mature, and include me in their social circle, as they joked and smoked after rehearsals, out of sight of the teachers. My social life was limited to looking after my sister while my parents focused on Dad's care, and school, which is where everything non-Dad-related happened. *The Tempest* was the best thing in my life, but I didn't want anyone to know it because it seemed pathetic, so I wasn't explicit in my desire to be part of the older kids' group. Mostly I just hung around, overeager, laughing at jokes, and planning clever lines to deliver ("I'd totally smoke, if I wasn't worried I'd get teeth like Mr. Fisher!") then chickening out at the last moment, remaining a smiling, yearning presence on the periphery of the group.

My family attended the performance, including Dad, who had transformed from Shakespeare authority to cancer patient in the months leading up to the show.

I stepped out onto the stage for my scene, wearing my green dress and feathered headpiece.

"Ceres, most bounteous lady!" I called, throwing one of my arms awkwardly out. I hadn't bothered to research what each word in my monologue meant because I hadn't wanted to do it without Dad— basically, I was a goddess, talking to another goddess about something

not really related to the plot. I delivered my lines fast, with a shake in my voice. But I was standing on the boards, and there were lights on my face, and even though I couldn't see the audience, I knew my family was there, and that Dad was looking at me and smiling.

When I stepped into the wings after my scene, I felt like I could collapse, like I'd been wearing a backpack full of rocks that had been unloaded that evening, my shoulders feeling floppy and loose. I high-fived my fellow goddesses backstage. "Great work, babe," we said to one another, as we waited for the final curtain when we'd be onstage again, to take our bows.

After the performance, the cast signed one another's show program, and for the rest of the year, I would often look at mine, rereading the things my peers had written on that day, when we had all hugged and cheered at our "wrap party," which was really just standing around in a classroom with some snacks and Mr. Fisher. When I asked him to sign my program, Alon had been eating a sausage roll, an Aussie delicacy of minced meat baked inside a flaky pastry. He put the pastry aside and left a thumbprint of ketchup on the program. "Sorry about that!" he wrote, with an arrow pointing to the stain, and I found this endlessly charming. I didn't even try to wipe it off. There was a note from Andy, with love hearts above the *i*'s. There was a note from Sally Martins who played Miranda. "Hope to work with you again soon!" she'd written, as if we were actual actors, working in "the biz."

The end-of-year holidays were spent quietly, Dad still recovering from surgery. There were bright moments, such as when Natalija burst into the living room on Christmas morning singing, wearing a tutu and reindeer ears, her hair unbrushed (parental attention had been lax thanks to Dad's illness, and her independence manifested in questionable hygiene and wardrobe choices). She jumped joyously on our mother, who observed that Natalija was not wearing underpants. "But Mama, it's *Christ-*

mas!" Natalija said, as if this was the one day of the year no one should be expected to wear underpants, and we all laughed.

After the holidays, a checkup revealed that Dad's cancer had come back. The specialist suggested that Dad might want to skip the hemato-therapy and chemotherapy treatments in exchange for a "better quality of life." Of course he would do the treatments, my mother said. Who cared about quality of life when we were trying to save him? My parents didn't realize that the specialist was implying that Dad was bound to die, and the treatments would make his last months painful, and foggy with medication. It might have been their imperfect English, or it might have been their denial, but my parents went for the treatment option rather than the "quality of life" option.

Every weekend, two of Dad's friends would come over to play the Eastern European card game preferans. My parents had met when Dad babysat my mother's nephews, though actually his version of babysit-ting the neighbors' kids was sending the boys to bed and inviting his friends over for preferans, and my mother would pop around to join the game. Now Dad's two well-meaning friends would come over to play a friendly game and distract him from his illness.

The three of them would sit around a table, Dad's jeans practically falling off him, his eyes small and tired, while he held the cards up, his thin wrist sticking out of his sleeve. One of his friends was Maksa, a boisterous man from Northern Serbia who was by far the worst player, but also the most entertaining distraction my father could wish for. He would blurt absurd things all the time, putting down his terrible hand of cards and declaring, nonsensically, "And that, my friends, is why it is important to be called Ernest."

"You talk more shit than I did when I was on morphine," Dad would say in response.

Rajko, the third player in their team, would throw his hand down, frustrated at Maksa's antics, insisting that he take the game seriously. Rajko indeed took games seriously: once he refused to talk to his wife for hours as he focused on staring at a game of chess he was playing with himself, until she finally grabbed a bishop and a pawn and threw them out a window.

And then there was my dad, who, in his healthy days had been the best player of the three, but who now increasingly lost track of which cards had passed, whether he'd declared diamonds or hearts at the start of the round. Eventually, my mother asked his friends to stop coming over because Dad was unwilling to admit he couldn't play anymore.

Dad couldn't read like he used to either, because he had trouble concentrating. He'd been the most voracious reader in our family except for maybe Grandma Xenia. When she visited us in Australia, there was a familiar pattern: when a new book came out, like John le Carré's *The Night Manager* or something by Umberto Eco, Grandma Xenia read it first, while my parents were at work. At dinner, before Dad had a chance to crack open the book himself—he always read at night in bed—Grandma Xenia would start talking about it. "These are just minor details that are unimportant to the plot," she would say, and go on to talk at length about the book, until Dad inevitably left the room, throwing his hands in the air, exasperated that she had ruined it. The biggest loser in this scenario was my mother, who would endure Grandma Xenia's recounting of the book after Dad stormed off, and then, only after Dad had read it and put his little notes in the margins, would she have the pleasure of reading the book that had already been described to her in detail.

But now Dad found it hard to concentrate on new books. Instead, he turned to Agatha Christie, rereading the mysteries he'd already consumed as a younger man, their predictable pattern all that he could endure. Eventually, he stopped with those books too, and just sat in front of the fireplace, staring at the flames.

Up until that point, I had never had much interest in religion, unless something I'd overheard or seen on television was bothering me, in which case I would pray (like when I prayed I'd never step on a syringe on the beach, or to not become morbidly obese like the mother in *What's Eating Gilbert Grape*). My parents never gave me a religious education—they themselves had been brought up without one in Yugoslavia—but they did tell me that God was an entity people prayed to; that some people believed in his existence and others didn't. I had been left to make my own choices about whether God was important to me, and generally I had decided he was not.

I'd already decided God was most likely not a bearded guy, but rather someone more gender-ambiguous. I'd known about the possibility of being both female and male ever since the first grade, when our teacher told us that a child who had a genetic difference was joining our class. When I went home and conveyed this to my mother, she proceeded to tell me all about intersex people and how this child was born with both female and male reproductive organs, and that when they got older, they'd be able to decide if they wanted to be a girl or a boy. It turned out that the child joining our class was actually a girl with Down's Syndrome. But, as usual, my mother had inadvertently managed to plant an image in my mind, and I was fascinated by gender ambiguity from that day. I loved the idea of someone not being bound by one gender; it seemed transcendent and divine.

I prayed that Dad would get better. I didn't pray to get richer, to have a smaller nose, for my parents to get along, for the family debts to disappear—all the things that had preoccupied me before. I didn't pray for our relatives, for the people dying in Yugoslavia, I didn't pray for an end to the war. Just Dad. And he got sicker and sicker.

In fact, one of the prayers I had not prayed was the one that was answered: the war in Croatia had finally come to an end.

When peace finally came, the Croatian army's last offensive, Operation Storm, had driven more than 150,000 Serbs from Croatia. Croatia was now independent. Meanwhile on the other battlefront, in Bosnia, NATO began a huge bombing campaign against the Bosnian Serbs, the international intervention hoping to finally bring that war to an end as well.

There was blood being shed, but for me, Dad trumped all those other people. It became apparent to me that there was a hierarchy to valuing life, just like my parents had turned the volume up when Yugoslavia was on the news and turned it down when Afghanistan was on. We cared about Yugoslavia more than we cared about the rest of the world, and we cared about our immediate family more than we cared about the rest of Yugoslavia. Every war in history has been driven by this hierarchy of life and death, the killing of others justified by our own unavoidable, subjective scales of human value. When Dad was lying in his bed, too feeble to speak, if someone had asked me if I would swap the lives of Bosnian villagers for Dad's, I would have immediately agreed. If I'd had the power, I would have sacrificed another kid's dad to die instead. Or any of my teachers, acquaintances, or family friends.

As my dad became sicker, I grew jealous of my friends with healthy parents and resentful of old people, who deserved their health less than my dad. If someone's grandparent died, I rolled my eyes. *So what?* I thought. *They've already lived their lives, my dad isn't even forty.* What floored me most was the moral injustice: Why did this happen to my dad, who was universally known for being a nice person? What was the point of trying to be a decent person if this was what could happen to you, to your family?

I began to weigh different types of dying against each other. The difference between dying in war versus dying from an illness; the difference between dying lucid or dying confused. Which would be worse? What would be the best way to extinguish a life? With a bullet? In a concentration camp in Croatia or Bosnia? From a long illness or a short one? How did different types of death affect the dying person, and their families? If I got distracted in class and a teacher snapped me out of it, it wasn't that I'd been daydreaming about pashing, like a normal person; more often than not, I'd been mentally rearranging my hypothetical death ranking, like a weirdo.

I felt increasingly isolated from my school friends. *The Tempest* crew had split up, all the students returning to their normal lives, and because of Dad's illness I missed a lot of the "gatherings" that were happening. There were people dating, splitting up, and partying more than ever and I was missing it all, but most of the time, I didn't feel like participating. They were experiencing something I didn't have the capacity for; I was always weighed down by my home situation, and it made my laugh shorter, my desire to join in minimal. I stayed at home, looking after Natalija or sitting in Dad's room as he lay there.

At night I still often spoke to Harry about dumb everyday school stuff. I chatted on our brand-new phone, a part of Dad's very sudden departure from his usual thrifty self. Dad had insisted on recording the answering machine message himself: "You have reached the Stefanović household, please . . . leave a message" he said stiltedly, in his shaky accented voice, sounding so sick that I was embarrassed for people to hear it. Did he not know he sounded like that? Why couldn't I do the recording, as I'd offered to do? Was this my dad's way of saying, "I'm the parent, I can still talk, I can do it myself!"? Or was it his way of leaving a mark in the world when he knew he couldn't be in it for much longer? I kept the phone by me all the time, picking up on the first ring, so people wouldn't have to hear him like that. I'd put it on the floor of the dining room, which we now called the "Nintendo room," where my sister and I spent most of our time, as Dad lay in the next room, listening to the sounds of *Donkey Kong*.

When his liver became too weak, Dad had to get a tube that

drained the bile out of his body and into a sack that hung by his hip. It was around about this time that my school friends started saying "yak bile" to each other, as a kind of joke. There was no reason for it, and no meaning behind it. It was just like when we found the word "urban" hilarious for about a month, unable to explain what was so funny, it just was. I didn't know where the term "yak bile" came from, but my friends would say it in funny voices to one another, and then crack up laughing. I knew that it wasn't related to me or my family, but it made me angry. It made me feel like my friends, healthy and stupid, were attacking my dad, who was by this point like some little, suffering animal. I was jealous that they probably didn't even know what bile was, how horrible it smelled, how it could make a person's skin and eyes yellow.

From the medications he was being fed, Dad started hallucinating again. His mother, Grandma Beba, came to Australia to look after him while our mother was at work. Meanwhile Dad, whose mind was going, would call out from his room. Once, he insisted there was a possum in there, and Grandma Beba, who didn't know what a possum was, knew that a *poskok* was a type of snake in our language. In a scene worthy of a Kusturica black comedy, she ran around with a broom, searching for a snake while Dad muttered senselessly. Grandma Beba was known not only for being easily suggestible but also for her ability for unintentional zingers. For example, she'd say things like: "When he was a child, Lola loved horses. All he talked about was horses, and he looked *so much like . . .*" (cue everyone thinking she's going to say "a horse") ". . . his father!" Now Dad came around and saw Grandma Beba searching for snakes and he said, "Oh my god, I must have been talking nonsense. Now I know what it's like to be you, Ma," to which my grandmother chuckled good-naturedly, happy to have her son back for a brief moment, even if he was being mean.

During this time, while we were embroiled in our personal drama, the Americans, under Bill Clinton, managed to engage the leadership of ex-Yugoslavia in Bosnian peace talks. Slobodan Milošević attended on behalf of the Bosnian Serb leaders, who had previously pushed him out. Now the Bosnian Serbs were exhausted, as were the other parties in this long, bloody war. Franjo Tuđman of Croatia was there, to negotiate on behalf of Croatian interests in Bosnia, as was Alija Izetbegović, the Bosnian Muslim leader.

These negotiations were filmed, and there is a scene in the BBC documentary *The Death of Yugoslavia* in which the Americans look for the first time at satellite footage of an area that Milošević and Izetbegović have been negotiating over for weeks. One of the American negotiators is confused—this area seems to be just rock: no houses, no people. The Serb and the Muslim look at the American, incredulous. "That's what most of Bosnia looks like," they say, as if he's the crazy one. The American puts his head in his hands, as if to say, "*This* is what you've been fighting over?"— and the ex-Yugoslavians continue doing what they do best, arguing.

Finally, after weeks of negotiations, the peace agreement was signed and the war in Bosnia came to an end. There were over one hundred thousand dead, and two million displaced. Cynics immediately claimed that the peace was temporary, that the war was bound to recur in about fifty years. Some said that Serbia would be at war again before we knew it, this time in Kosovo. Some used the old Yugo saying that is often applied to the Balkans: "If you build your house in the road, don't be surprised when it's knocked down." "War is over," some people rejoiced. "For now," others added.

As for us, we barely noticed.

As Dad grew sicker, our roof was invaded by rats. My parents were too preoccupied to deal with it, though, so the rats became my responsibility.

Each day, I placed a ladder beneath a hatch leading to the roof. I went up with a box of rat poison, careful not to spill it on the ground where Dante might eat it and die (being himself only slightly larger than a big rat). I'd open the hatch, and nearly fall off the ladder, ducking or weaving, because I thought dead, or half-dead, rats would come tumbling onto my head. I put my hand in the roof, feeling around where I couldn't see, until I found a little bowl, which had been emptied of poison by the rats, and I'd refill it with new poison pellets. I held my breath, my heart pounding, as if I were the one who was in lethal danger, not the rats above us or my dad in the next room. I began dreaming of rats: chasing me, climbing all over me. Rats became intertwined with illness and death in my subconscious, destined to haunt me for decades. Had my mother been concentrating on me, she would've had a psychologist's field day.

Natalija and I now avoided Dad, not just because of the smell of bile, but because he was often mean. One time when I was sitting with him, he fixed his yellow eyes on me and shouted, "Why did you dye your hair!? You look like an idiot! Who do you think you are?!" I hadn't dyed my hair, and I wasn't sure he even recognized who I was.

Later, when I was crying, my mother told me that that wasn't him talking, it was the illness, and all the medications that were poisoning his blood and mind. I tried to comfort myself: this wasn't my dad. This was the guy who hallucinated, who kicked Dante, who couldn't argue with my mother as her equal, but who yelled at her nonsensically in a hollow childish voice that inspired pity. My mother said: "Just imagine this situation we're in is a massive black cloud falling from the sky, and then be like a net. Allow it to pass through you." I pictured a net through which a black cloud is squeezed, dispersing into many pieces. I imagined holding my breath as it passed, careful not to catch the noxious substance myself.

I found myself often holding my breath, to protect myself from the things that could destroy me. I didn't want to talk about being sad, and when I saw groups of kids at school gather to comfort a girl who had been broken up with, or who'd got a bad test score, I never wished they were cooing at me. I felt beyond consolation. I had no desire to cry in front of other people, and the part of me that had dreamed about spilling forth emotionally as an actress now felt stupid. My creative energy and desire to connect with others had been silenced by sadness. I just wanted to hold my breath until everything passed.

As the weeks went on, Dad started preparing for death, in his cloudy state. He tried to put on a leather belt over his saggy pajamas, demanding, in an annoyed voice, that he had an appointment. The "appointment" that his hazy mind was reminding him of, it seems, was death.

People who weren't even close friends started calling up and insisting on speaking to Dad, telling him about dreams they'd had about him, or getting off their chests things they'd always wanted to say, even if those things had nothing to do with my dad. Some talked about their own near-death experiences, or how they needed to appreciate their families more, live life to the fullest. After a while, my mother banned these calls. She was sick of watching him lie there helpless, weak, and listening to someone unburdening themselves. When he was up to it, the two of them talked, their old arguments irrelevant now that everything was coming to an end. When she asked him if he had any wishes as far as their children were concerned, about education, or things he wanted her to impart, he said that he trusted her. He looked at her and said, "How will I get by without you?" and she didn't correct him. She didn't say that he was the one who was leaving—and that she would be left to get by.

Without telling anyone, while my dad could still get out of bed, my parents had chosen a plot at the cemetery. When they hobbled over to look at it, they found that the graveyard was divided into parts. There was an Italian Catholic part, with large, marble crypts, busts of long-dead people, and photos of nonnas and nonnos. There was a small section that was labeled Serbian Orthodox, but it was at a low-lying part of the cemetery, where it was damp and dark. My parents chose a sunny part that was nondenominational—Dad didn't want to be remembered just as a Serb; even if his ethnicity stood out here thanks to his accent and immigrant status. There were so many things he had dreamed of for himself that had nothing to do with his nationality. He had once played Romeo, he'd inhabited so many worlds of fiction, he had wanted to study literature, and he'd only just make it to forty—so many things left unexplored.

Natalija and I didn't know the death plans were under way. When our mother took us to Buci boutique, the fanciest store on our local shopping strip, and declared, "You will each buy a nice outfit," I thought she'd lost her mind. We already had a new car: a Mitsubishi Magna, burgundy-colored and sleek, only a year old when we got it. When my mother dropped me off at school in it, I wondered if kids looked over and thought we were rich. Dad had insisted on the new car, doing everything in his power to make sure we were "taken care of" when he was gone. We had driven in the new car to Centre Road, and I was trying on a pair of black-and-white herringbone pants that my mother had picked out, like we were in some film about rich American teens who go to the mall with their mother to get spoiled. The pants ballooned at the front, and I stood in front of the mirror confused.

"You've got them on back to front," the shop assistant explained, and embarrassed, I got changed again, reemerging with the pants on the right way. I had never had pants that zipped in the back, and the notion of a zip following the line of one's butt crack seemed suddenly very sophisticated. On top, I tried a shaggy black sweater with tiny threads coming off it, making me look like an elegant Muppet. Natalija got a navy-colored dress. It was only when we were in the car on the way home, our new purchases sitting in a bag by our legs, that it hit me: these were our funeral clothes.

Dad wanted to stay at home as long as possible, but when he could no longer sit up, or pee, an ambulance was called. Dante didn't even bark at the paramedics but watched with us kids, as the strangers came in with a stretcher for Dad, and he left our house for the last time, lifting his arm slightly, in a half wave.

My mother was with him at the hospital later that night, when Dad fell into a hepatic coma. He didn't feel pain, and then, he was gone. My mother sat there for a while, suddenly by herself. Then, she rang a friend who had offered to be on call in this situation to drive her home. As she was getting ready to catch her ride, she realized she'd left her house keys at home. But then she remembered: Who was the person who had never, ever left home without a key? Who had always annoyed her with his preciousness? She fished around in Dad's coat and found the key.

At dawn, our mother woke us up. Natalija and I had been sleeping on the fold-out couch in the Nintendo room, having fallen asleep mid-game. Grandma Beba was crying somewhere in the house. Our mother gave us a Valium each and told us the news. We all lay on the squeaky fold-out bed, with little Dante curled up at our feet.

A couple of days later, on the morning of the funeral, Natalija and I dressed in our new clothes. As the car inched through Melbourne's city streets during rush hour, on our way to the Serbian Orthodox church, a man thumped his fist against the roof. He was angry because we'd blocked his path, but the sound of the thump made us all gasp; imagining we'd hit a pedestrian, that there was another person dead, just like that. As we neared the church, I saw an actress from the long-running Australian TV show *Neighbours* out the window. I didn't point her out, because I didn't want our memories of Dad's funeral to feature Libby from *Neighbours*. But so many years later, she is still clear in my mind, ponytailed at the crossing.

The Serbian Orthodox church where Dad's service was held is in the inner-city suburb of Brunswick. When we arrived, all I could think about was when my mother had dragged us all to the church one Easter at the height of the war and we'd stood behind a woman in a nationalist

T-shirt that said "Greater Serbia" on the back of it, and how my dad had muttered that she should have put the stupid slogan lower, on her butt, where it belonged.

The ex-Yugoslavian diaspora turned out in droves for Dad's funeral. It was a Tuesday morning, and these people had all taken time off work to attend. Among them, I noticed Harry's dad and Alicia's dad, and I was touched that my friends had told their parents, and that they'd decided to come, even though they'd only met my dad a few times. As people filed out after the service, paying their respects, one of our family friends gripped my shoulders and shook me.

"Be strong!" he said. "You need to be strong!" like someone in a movie would say. If I hadn't been crying, I would have rolled my eyes, and if I had been braver, I would have said, "Fuck off, you don't even know me."

I couldn't stop myself from crying, wishing I wasn't surrounded by all these people. Everything happening around me seemed like a melodramatic film. I didn't want anyone to squeeze my arm, like people squeezed grieving people's arms. I didn't want people to say "it'll pass" or to start sentences with "your dad was so . . ." All of it made me sick. Everyone else's emotions seemed phony, and hypocritical, and everything they said or did was contrived and distasteful. I could think of nothing worse than being here, on what seemed like a stage, raw and helpless, with people gaping. I didn't want my mother to hug me; I didn't want my sister or grandmother to, either. All I wanted was to be away from every person I knew. I'd been yearning to be in the spotlight for so long, but now it was being delivered to me all wrong, in the form of a nightmare rather than a dream.

At the cemetery I overheard two old men we'd never met speculating about why my dad wasn't being buried in the Serbian part of the cemetery, eventually coming to the (incorrect) conclusion that he was a

Freemason. My mother turned and glared at them. My sister stood next to me in her new navy-colored dress, scuffing her shoe over and over on the concrete. "Not a single one of them brought their child," my mother whispered, looking at all her acquaintances. "They didn't want to expose their children to a funeral, but what about *my* children?" she said, looking at lonely Natalija, her voice rising. And right then, as my mother sent death glares at her friends, Davorka, the Croatian doctor my mother had made friends with when we first came to Australia, arrived with her son, Ivan. Natalija and Ivan ran around the cemetery shouting, and my mother wouldn't let anyone tell them to stop.

After the service, I noticed a cluster of Aussies in business clothes and knew they were Dad's friends from work. I realized that they probably hadn't understood a word of the funeral so far, so I walked over to them, feeling obliged to play host, for Dad's sake. *They must feel uncomfortable among all these weeping ethnic people,* I thought. Grandma Beba had even thrown herself on the coffin before Dad was lowered into the ground. Everyone had just stood there watching, as she lay on it, weeping. "Will someone help this woman, please?" my mother had said, annoyed at my grandmother's play for attention, which Dad would've found excessive and uncivilized.

"Well hello," I said, approaching my dad's work colleagues; a thirteen-year-old dressed like a grownup with pants that zipped in the back, my face puffy as Rocky Balboa's after a fight. "You must be Dad's friends from work, I've heard so much about you," I lied. They said polite things like, "we're sorry for your loss," to which I didn't know how to respond, so I kept repeating, "yes, yes," and nodding in a businesslike way.

Playing host was foreign to me, but the setting of the funeral wasn't. I remembered how in Belgrade I used to go with my grandmothers and visit the graves of family members—arrange flowers, pull up weeds, and eat ice cream. The cemeteries weren't empty, like this one, but full of old ladies and children spending their Sundays there, hearing stories of a grandpa Vladimir or a great aunt Anica. Once all these weeping people left his graveside in Melbourne, it occurred to me that my dad would now be alone. Australian cemeteries weren't busy in the way those in Belgrade were.

On the day Dad was buried, I didn't notice the lovely Italian grave opposite his, with a statue of an angel. She sits under a domed stained glass roof, where some of the panels have broken, letting the rain in, leaving stains under her eye that look like tears.

I imagine the angel watching over Dad's grave, which is made of gray marble with his name engraved on the stone, written in Cyrillic and then in the Latin alphabet below, his name appears in white marble letters, "SLOBODAN LOLA STEFANOVIČ." The stonemason got the accent wrong—so my mother used a permanent marker to make the Č into a Ć. Dad would have found it funny that they spelled his name wrong, she said—he appreciated language games and cultural mishaps and would have found this a good one: until the very last, he'd been misinterpreted by the Aussies.

Back at our place, while my mother and the funeral-goers gathered in the living room, I logged onto our family computer. It was 1996, and computers were only just starting to be used for social communication. I knew, for example, that one of our Yugo family friends had gotten divorced from his wife because he met an American woman in a romantic internet "chat room," and now, after doing some searching online, I discovered a chat room for people in mourning.

I clicked to join, and my name came up immediately as "Stefanovic."

"Hi Stef," someone typed.

"Welcome, Stef," someone else wrote.

"Hi everyone" I typed back speedily, proud of my sixty words per minute touch-typing abilities (Dad had bought us a program and I practiced to impress him).

I felt that my friends, like the people at the funeral going through the motions, couldn't understand what I was feeling. I couldn't talk to them about death, about what my family had gone through over the last year and a half. I couldn't talk to them about the guilt I felt for abandoning my dad in the end, for not wanting to talk to him anymore, for feeling alienated from him as he took on his feeble-voiced, hallucinating, weak form. I couldn't talk about the dreams I had about him all the time, where he showed up and told us that his illness had been fake, that we'd been nursing a doppelgänger, that in fact he was alive and well, that he'd been in jail for political activities instead, and now he was back. I couldn't discuss with them the feeling I had whenever I woke up and it hit me that he was dead. In the chat room, I thought that these were "my people," the ones I could actually talk to. Strangers were a good audience. I could put my thoughts and emotions out there, on the computer screen, and still be alone and protected.

In the chat room, there was a back-and-forth going on about how to handle financial considerations after the death of a loved one. I knew that Dad's company, BHP, had given us a "death benefit," a lump sum of money we used to pay off part of our mortgage, and that my sister and I were going to receive a $250 fortnightly pension for as long as we were students. *Here is my way in,* I thought, biting into some *burek* that someone had brought for the post-funeral gathering, making sure I kept it far from Dad's precious keyboard. *I'll explain our finances and join in the conversation.*

"I'm thirteen, and my dad died four days ago," I typed, and pressed Send. Boom—there it was on the screen, and already, someone was replying. I was thrilled by the novelty of this immediate conversation with real-life humans, somewhere out there.

"Sorry, Stef"

"Sorry to hear"

Having introduced myself, I hurried to add the part about our arrangement with BHP, but instead of calling it a "death benefit" as I had meant to, my brain sent the wrong message to my speedy hands and I typed "death penalty" instead, hitting Send before I realized that I was announcing to a room of internet strangers: "my dad got the death penalty."

"Oh no. I'm so sorry," someone typed.

"Stef, that's terrible," someone else added.

I stared at the stupid words I couldn't delete. Before I could witness any more reactions to my idiocy, I reached across and pressed the power button, immediately shutting the whole thing down. I hit my forehead on the desk and stayed there. I imagined people in the chat room wondering what had happened to that kid whose father was killed in the electric chair. I pictured my newly buried father turning in his grave for the slander I was spreading (and probably even more for the improper way I'd shut his computer down).

"Hope she's okay!" I imagined the people in the chat room saying.

"He must have done something pretty bad to get the death penalty."

"I hope the kid doesn't turn to a life of crime."

"These things run in families."

I got myself up from the desk and wandered into the living room, which contained what looked like the entire ex-Yugoslavian diaspora of Melbourne. And my mother, who had always complained about the diaspora, was now slumped among them as they held her. I went into my room and shut the door.

8

A Honeymoon for Mourners

T hree months after Dad's death, we booked a trip to the Indonesian island of Bali—a popular destination for Aussie tourists. We would be vacationing as a newly three-person family unit, joined by my mother's friend Davorka and her son, Ivan, who had become Natalija's closest friend. Though I knew this trip was meant to cheer us up, I couldn't help but think about the money it was costing. My mother was notoriously bad with finances (for example, she only opened mail that had "urgent" printed on it and threw everything else out), and I worried the vacation would send us into a downward spiral and I would be left to take over Dad's role as the responsible one if my mother bankrupted us.

Before we left, I listened to the Pearl Jam song "Alive" on repeat, and when Eddie Vedder sang, *"While you were sitting home alone at age thirteen, your real daddy was dying . . ."* I understood it as if he was speaking to me directly. It wasn't just Pearl Jam, though. I decided that all artistic expression about pain was specifically meant for me. I was on the same wavelength as Edgar Allan Poe when he mourned the tubercular Annabel Lee, and with Nina Simone when she sang "Why? (The King of Love is dead)" after the assassination of Martin Luther King Jr. I took Dad's old gray Levi's sweatshirt and wore it often, letting it hang baggy over my hands, as if I'd lost them in a war. I listened to his favorite Billie Holiday CD, trying to hear what Dad might have heard. I liked "Gloomy Sunday" because it suited my mood of despair: "Sunday is gloomy, with shadows I spend it all."

While I wanted to put up a wall between me and anyone who asked how I was feeling, I was happy to listen to music, watch films, read, and blubber my heart out, as long as I was alone, vulnerable to nothing but art, writing emotional, unself-aware poems inspired by Poe and Pablo Neruda. One of my poems was entitled "*Les Nuages*"—meaning "clouds" in French; another one contained the lines "I brush away all expression / The mask falls and I gasp / You look into my self and soul." The journal was secreted away to be reread by my tearful eyes only.

Natalija was eight years old, and she mourned in her own way. Mostly she watched *Jurassic Park* over and over, lost in the fantasy of dinosaurs that could crush humans to death, of kids who overcame the odds. She didn't want to talk about Dad.

As for my mother, she told me many years later that she kept a diary during this time, which she later burned because its contents were so dark. I pictured her in front of our fireplace, prodding her diary with a poker, bathed in a red glow, as her scribblings and sketches sizzled, turning into ghosts floating up the chimney to join Dad.

It was the wet season in Bali when we arrived, which meant there were fewer tourists, and vendors were especially attentive to us, running up with suitcases full of knockoff designer watches or perfumes, as I hissed to my mother, "Just don't buy anything."

On our first day, we went to an outdoor market, and Davorka, who had been to Bali before, told us we were supposed to bargain hard. She moved around eyeing objects she liked, but pretending she was underwhelmed by them. Her face—tanned, usually smiling, with an endearing gap between her teeth—now held a tight-lipped expression. Davorka would pick up a scarf, look at it halfheartedly, throw it over her ample shoulders, say "it doesn't even fit," and offer half of what the vendor asked. They would go back and forth until Davorka ended up paying about 13,000 rupiah for an item that had been marked 20,000, and we'd walk off triumphant, marveling at her mastery in saving money.

My mother would do it her own, far less effective way. First, she would elaborately fall in love with something. She'd call us all over, telling us in Serbian how much she loved it, though it was clear what she was saying whether you understood the words or not, because she would gesticulate wildly and hug the desired object to her bosom. Davorka would try and save the situation by saying, "You could get a better one in Australia." My mother, not catching on, would say, "Nonsense! In Melbourne, I would pay *ten times* what this man is asking!" My mother would turn to the vendor, throwing Davorka an "I know what I'm doing" look: "You say thirty thousand, well, I will offer you *twenty-nine* thousand!" The vendor would try for twenty-nine-and-a-half, and she would agree, delighted.

Many of the local men pointed to my oversized T-shirt with the *Pulp Fiction* film poster printed on the front: Uma Thurman lying on a bed, seductively smoking a cigarette. The men would give me a sleazy thumbs-up or wink, which made me feel dumb for wearing a shirt that seemed to advertise sex rather than announce that I was an art house connoisseur.

Every now and then, there was a huge downpour, when we would get soaked and then stay soggy, despite the heat, because of the humidity. Trying to look happy for the camera, but pale and sweaty, we posed for photos under big, beautiful flowers bowing toward us from the rain-heavy treetops.

When we got back to the hotel that first day, our mother said she wanted to go back to the market for something, and left Natalija and me in the room. After half an hour, I felt a tinge of anxiety. I remembered something she'd said recently: "You're big, I'm not worried about you. When Natalija is your age, I could die as well." I was too stunned to respond in the moment, but afterward, in the darkness of my bedroom, I pretended to answer: "What a bitch you are. I am thirteen years old, and I've just lost my father. Why would you threaten that in just five years, you'll give up and die, too?" I simultaneously hated her for saying what she'd said and felt desperately afraid, because I needed her. And what was so bad about being alive? Didn't she have Natalija and me? When someone says something hurtful, in Serbian we say, "You've bitten me on the heart," and this is what I thought as I looked out the hotel window and it started pouring.

The sunlight disappeared with the rain, and it was suddenly, aggressively, night. Across from our hotel were some stores, and their lights glowed orange through the rain. I watched a woman drape plastic over some sundresses that were hanging on a rack out in front, while her toddler watched, scratching his butt. People tried to avoid the rain by going into stores or standing under trees, and I wondered where my mother was, and if she'd taken an umbrella. Probably not, I decided. As I remembered her heart-biting comment, I didn't consider how horrible she must have felt for her to say it in the first place. She was counting down the years because she didn't want to be in the world—not even in her beloved Belgrade.

The fact that my mother hadn't taken us back there after Dad's death was a surprise to everyone. She'd decided to stay, to spare us further disruption in our lives, and she must have felt like she was sacrificing herself for our sakes.

As the rain continued, my heart sped up, and I thought, *What if she's dead too?* The sidewalk was slick. I could hear vendors yelling to each other in a language I didn't understand, and the slap of sandals on concrete, though it was properly dark now and it was hard to make out the individual people.

Natalija joined me at the window, and finally my fears of orphan-hood abated as we spotted our mother walking through the rain, short, stout, and wet. We watched her stop in front of the store across from the hotel, peer at the dresses under the plastic, and then suddenly shift her attention to a parked motorcycle, which, we only now noticed, had a small light brown monkey chained to it. My mother leaned toward the monkey, putting her hand out, and it jumped at her, bearing its teeth, straining its chain, batting at her with its claws. She jumped back, we gasped, and as our mother ran across the street toward our hotel I said to my sister, "If that thing had bitten her, she could have got ra-bies." My resentment toward my mother had returned now that I knew she was safe. I would not let her know I'd been scared.

Moments later she appeared in the room, brushing water off her-self, bringing noise into the quiet space, excited to reveal her purchase: an antique Balinese puppet, a beautiful woman with a wooden heart-shaped face and cat-eyes, her hair painted a dark brown, her mouth small and red. There were little wooden sticks attached to her hands. "I had to go back for her. Isn't she beautiful?" my mother asked, and even though I thought she was, I muttered instead: "Couldn't you have just got her tomorrow instead of running out there like a crazy person?"

Our final night in Bali was my fourteenth birthday, and my mother treated us all to dinner in our hotel. I sat quietly during the dinner, pre-tending to be bored by the adults' conversation, enjoying the delicious seafood noodles I'd ordered and glancing at myself every now and then in the large Balinese-style mirror beside me (to check my new wire-rimmed glasses and super-short nineties bangs that weren't working in the humid-ity, and to assess the shininess of my face). The waiters came out singing "Happy Birthday," and plonked a chocolate cake in front of me. Na-talija, Ivan, and I gobbled it up, and I was impressed by the check, which amounted to almost nothing, considering all the things we'd eaten.

We'd made it through international travel without Dad waiting for us at the end, holding his arms open to catch us. We were surviving. But on the inside I felt like I was missing a part. The hopeful, excited part of me, the part that could feel awed by a captured pigeon in my grandpa's hands, or the possibility of a role in a play, was gone.

When we got back to Melbourne, my mother declared that we would not be a house of mourning. We would not draw the curtains and cry, and we would not be pitied by others. This was when she burned her diary.

"The only way to fill the emptiness that your dad left in this house," our mother said, "is to invite lots of people over."

And so the parties started.

Our house soon became a hub for all of our friends and acquaintances. Stoner boys from my school who lived in the neighborhood were welcomed in for snacks. I became more popular because my mother was "super chill" about teenaged drinking and sleepovers. My sister's little school friends ran around spreading head lice and making a mess they weren't expected to clean up. And in her "coming out" of mourning, my mother dragged the ex-Yugoslavian diaspora out with her, imposing her renewed sense of adventure on our little ethnic group by staging constant get-togethers.

Her few artsy friends were happy to comply, but my mother wanted numbers, so she coerced those who were more hesitant. The ones she'd previously deemed conservative, and about whom she'd complained to my dad, were pushed out of their comfort zones and forced to join the madness, too. The door was always unlocked, and there was no Dad reading in his bedroom and complaining about mess. There were poetry recitals, game nights, and art projects, but most often, people would simply *be* there, popping in and out of our home, just to see what was going on, their continuous presence ensuring that the house was always full of voices, drowning out the haunting silence of Dad's absence.

One evening, I saw a man in drag lingering outside our place, an uncommon sight in our sleepy suburb. Eventually I recognized the tall, tanned form as Peter, the Montenegrin doctor whose office space my mother used to see clients these days. It turned out my mother was having a "Mr. Universe" party in which participants were encouraged to dress up and bring props. I entered the house via the backyard, where there was a break in the proceedings. The audience was seated on folding chairs in front of a makeshift stage, and I spotted Biljana, an old family friend who had gone to university with my dad. She looked around, half baffled, half delighted, while my sister and the other kids ran around the backyard with water pistols.

Out of nowhere, a man in a fitted police uniform appeared, and Peter, in a short skirt, followed behind him, chuckling. Peter had been waiting for this surprise guest out front. An awed hush fell over the crowd and the children stopped running to stare. The man wore snug pleather pants, and tapped his hand with a baton.

"We've had some complaints that this party is getting out of hand," he said, a hand on his hip. "I need to speak to the lady of the house."

But the lady of the house, as I could see through the window, would not be participating. She had dragged Peter into the kitchen and was berating him—she liked to be the boss at her parties, and this kind of thing, which the Mr. Universe contestants had organized without her knowledge, wasn't to her taste.

Meanwhile, the sight of a cop had taken poor Biljana back to socialist Yugoslavia, where the police were feared and respected, and she watched him anxiously.

"Well," the cop said, looking at the unfamiliar group before him: people speaking another language, some of them dressed in elaborate costumes, rowdy children peering at him, fascinated.

"If she's not here, I'm going to need another volunteer."

Biljana's hand shot up.

Heads turned.

"I volunteer, Officer," she called out in her Serbian accent, her expression solemn and resolved.

"Nice," said the cop. "Come on up!"

In her glasses and sensible clothes, Biljana walked to the cop, stone-faced, as everyone laughed and cheered.

"How dare you laugh!" she hissed in Serbian as she walked up to the front.

In her fearful state, she hadn't noticed some of the clear signifiers that this man was not the picture of law enforcement—like the tight, shiny pants and the boom box he carried. Biljana felt it was her duty, as my mother's old friend, to take responsibility for this trouble, and if she needed to go to jail, then she was willing to do so.

But as far as everyone else at the party was concerned, as she took a seat on the chair the cop provided, she was some kinky woman who, despite her mousey appearance, was big into role-playing, and this was why she sat primly, looking respectfully up at the man who now walked back and forth, slapping his baton on his hand.

To Biljana, he must have seemed like a sadist, and when one of the party guests yelled "Yeah, baby!" Biljana stared at the woman in disbelief. Who were these people who celebrated public shaming?

And then, as Biljana sat there for a few seconds longer, her face started to change ever so slightly. The cop instructed her to hold his baton between her knees, pressed Play on his boom box, and took off his massive fake policeman's hat, releasing his black shiny curls. When he whipped his head around and started dance-walking toward Biljana, it finally clicked. This man was not an upstanding member of the police force: he was a stripper, and she was about to get a lap dance.

She dropped the baton and ran into the house, leaving the policeman hanging.

But the music was pumping, and the excitement was high, so an Aussie social worker colleague of my mother's and a Serbian piano teacher jumped up and took Biljana's place, taking the policeman's pants off with their teeth, while the crowd cheered and the children watched in awe, until my mother came outside and put an end to the whole fiasco.

Six months later, when I was starting ninth grade, a man named Vanja moved into our spare room. Vanja was the son of a famous Belgrade psychology professor who had taught my mother at university. Vanja's family was Jewish, and his parents had escaped to Serbia from Hungary during the Holocaust. Though he was born in Belgrade, Vanja felt like a not-quite-legit member of the ex-Yugo diaspora since he didn't identify with any of the ethnicities that had gone to war with one another. He managed to leave Belgrade the day before his conscription papers were served, and instead of driving a tank in a war he didn't believe in, he became a taxi driver in New Zealand. Now he was in Melbourne, enjoying the freedom that taxi-driving afforded him: no boss to answer to, and plenty of waiting time in which he could read the papers and doze. Vanja had a degree in philosophy, and came from an eccentric family of his own, so he was welcomed with open arms into our household. He didn't mind the mayhem, and soon he became my mother's most devoted sidekick.

For a few sleepless weeks during semester break, Harry and his musician friends would come over to watch reruns of *Twin Peaks*, and my mother would buy us donuts and make us hot black coffee so we could pretend to be like Special Agent Dale Cooper. On the night when we watched one particularly scary episode, she made Vanja stand outside a window, and stare in at us until one of us saw him, and we all started screaming just as my mother had hoped.

On top of everything else that was going on, my mother decided to embark on a renovation of our home that would last an entire decade. The ex-Yugo community was full of laborers who now spent a lot of time at our place, smoking in the yard with my mother, striving respectfully to see her strangest ideas through.

First to go was our fireplace, which my dad had stared into during his worst days, and where my mother had burned her diary. Natalija and her delinquent prepubescent friends were allowed to graffiti the wall in our dining room before builders took it down.

One Saturday morning, when my mother was at work, I woke after an evening of drinking with my friends to find Rajko, Dad's serious card-playing friend, in my room, folding my clothes. He had let himself in through the door my mother always kept unlocked. "Your mother doesn't take care of you properly!" he said, picking up my dirty things and folding them clumsily. "Look at this mess!" He gestured at my room. My mother never came into my private space and poked around, and I was outraged to see Rajko in my unaired room, fumbling with my underthings, acting like he had any right to touch my stuff. Furious and embarrassed, I got out of bed, and pushed Rajko through our house, like a cartoon character, putting the weight of my whole body into it. I pushed him through the kitchen, past the unwashed dishes, past tiles that had been pulled up by the builders, and out the back door, which I closed and locked. "None of your business!" I yelled, adrenaline coursing through my usually lethargic body.

I knew that my mother's way of dealing-with-grief-through-chaos would have made Dad turn yet another 180 degrees in his grave—the mess, the unopened bills, the electricity that kept getting turned off because she forgot to pay. Rajko cared about us, and he was disturbed by my mother's bacchanalian approach to healing; he probably believed he owed it to my dad to make sure his children didn't grow up to be slobs. But slobs we were, and for all our infighting, the three of us stuck together whenever anyone tried to tell us what to do.

At fifteen, my friends were deep in the throes of puberty, and Alicia, and our new friend Jasmine, a super smart and cynical nerd, often came to my place where we could be together in our angst. After school, we'd climb over the gaping holes in the floor, sit in my room, and roll our eyes and talk in disaffected tones about how vacuous the sporty kids at school were. Other times, I'd hang out with Harry and his friends, and we'd drink alcohol someone's older sibling had bought, or we'd kick my little sister and her friends out of the Nintendo room and watch *A Clockwork Orange*, which I'd got from an underground bookstore in the city. Finally, I had a solid friendship group, and even though I'd never been asked to be anyone's girlfriend, I certainly wasn't unpopular. My friends and I called ourselves "alternative"—yes, I wore glasses, but I also carried vodka in a little water bottle to parties. Yes, we hung out at the library, but we also smoked bongs at the park near school. We were (to ourselves and to my little sister's group of friends at least) both complex and fascinating.

I started doing things to prove my alternative and artsy identity, such as wearing a beret. I had only once kissed a boy, at a party, but I was determined to become sexually liberated in the way an artist might be. I went to see Danish director Lars Von Trier's bizarre paranormal hospital series *The Kingdom* at an art house cinema (for the second time), where I decided to give a hand job to my date, a long-haired Aussie boy from my class, who shared my interest in avant-garde films. *Only a bohemian would be this edgy,* I thought, as we stared at the screen and I tried to get an awkward grip on my stunned companion's erection.

The next weekend, seemingly out of nowhere, Alicia started dating a nice eighteen-year-old Italian guy she'd met at the supermarket where she worked on the weekend. I was dumbfounded at her sudden graceful leap into adulthood. She informed me that boys our age were immature. I found myself torn between my bohemian, hand-job-giving self and my desire to not be left behind. So I tried to strike a balance, hanging out with my school friends half the time (going to jazz clubs where the professional musicians let Harry and some others "jam" with them, even though they were underage) and devoting the rest of my time to the new group Alicia introduced me to: second-generation immigrants— mainly Greek—from a couple of suburbs over, who smoked cigarettes and souped up their cars.

One of guys in the new group was Dan, a likeable, ponytailed nineteen-year-old virgin who called me every night. I would not be participating in a lame-ass romance with Dan, I told myself. I preferred the aloof guys, including a friend of Dan's who was a drummer in a band that tried to sound like Pearl Jam. The drummer was tall, surfy, and blond, a real Aussie, and he had a girlfriend, who was, in his own words "a psycho."

Soon after, when the drummer got drunk and declared he was "on a break" from his girlfriend, I lost my virginity to him in Alicia's parents' study. Afterward, I regretted telling him that my dad had died, and I regretted having responded when he asked when, "One year and three months ago," like a sad creep who counts months. I'd been attracted to the drummer's detachment to begin with, and I didn't want him to see that deep down, I was still the soft girl who had loved Nemanja in kindergarten, and who dreamed about justice for the hunchbacks and all those of us who were hurting but didn't know how to get help. Even though I played it cool, part of me wished he'd make me his girlfriend, tell me I was more special than a one-night stand, that I was worthwhile.

A couple of months before my sixteenth birthday, my mother, Natalija, and I went on a one-month trip overseas during the school holidays. I'd recently dyed my hair pink, trying to demonstrate that I marched to the beat of my own drum while simultaneously copying the kids I thought were cool—*I have pink hair, deal with it*, I thought whenever someone looked my way.

On the way to Europe, we had a stopover in China. My mother's best friend, Dada, now lived in Beijing with her family (most of our friends had left crumbling Belgrade to work abroad), so we were going to stay there for a few days.

After a day of sightseeing, I went out with Dada's fourteen-year-old son, Marko, whom I'd known since he was born. Our mothers had always dreamed we would grow up together, and maybe even get married one day. I was used to drinking alcohol snuck from parents' liquor cabinets at house parties, but Marko took me to a club, something I'd never experienced. It was filled with smoke and people dancing to techno, children of diplomats and entrepreneurs, a melting pot of rich kids partying and making out with each other like the end of the world was nigh. Marko walked through the crowd barely acknowledging his peers as they greeted him, his glossy black hair falling into his eyes as he parked himself at the bar. He outpaced me, four drinks to one, and I wasn't drinking slowly.

As we stood smoking outside the expat club at the end of the night, Marko told me he wanted to move back to Belgrade.

"See that smog?" he said, pointing at the sky. "Each year we live here, it takes four years off our lives." He exhaled smoke grandly, as if cigarettes, unlike smog, would bring him only health, wellness, and glamour.

As we flew toward Belgrade the next day, I thought of our hurried trips to the Great Wall and the Summer Palace, the spicy food, and the vodka I drank with Marko, which I was struggling to keep down. I thought about the diplomatic compound where his family lived, and the insane traffic. I thought about my mother and Dada, who had grown up together in Belgrade, and imagined they'd be neighbors forever, and who now found themselves living in two different enormous countries so unlike the poor, little one they'd come from, their lives having assumed entirely unpredictable trajectories. Whereas my mother's friends were a hodgepodge of ex-Yugos, Dada's crew was comprised of diplomats who she claimed were the most boring people on earth.

I listened to my Walkman, playing a mixtape Dan had made for me, recording his own introductions between songs. "This is a song that should have been titled 'Sofija,'" Dan's voice said, before "Angie" by the Rolling Stones came on. I scoffed, as I did whenever I heard him say it, but at the same time, I felt a little surge of confidence. As we started our descent into Belgrade's airport and Natalija barfed in a bag, I thought about the ways I'd changed since I was last here. I was a non-virgin, my hair was pink, men were interested in me (well, one man was, and I had the tapes to prove it), and I was fatherless. I was not the little girl I used to be.

My kindergarten friend Ana's parents had found work and moved to Damascus, Syria, but Milica (the one who had usurped my Baby-Sitters Club leadership role) and the once-unimpressive Eva were still there. Seeing teenaged Eva's flawless skin and long, silky hair and Milica's giant, glamorous sunglasses, and their simple European-chic clothes, I felt frumpy and underdressed. As we walked down the street, I couldn't help but stare at all of the women wearing skintight outfits and impossibly high heels, strutting along the streets like gravity couldn't topple them. These women had glossy hair, wore elaborate, precise makeup, and were surrounded by clouds of perfume that seemed to set them apart from mere mortals like me.

As we caught up over thick hot chocolate, my friends explained the concept of *sponzoruše* ("sponsor girls")—a derogatory term for women who dated rich men. The rise of the sponsor girls had coincided with the socioeconomic decline of Belgrade. A typical "sponsor" was a man who wore a lot of gold, who had made money from war profiteering, either on the black market or through other criminal activities. These men gave their women money to buy clothes, have their hair done, and so on. It was well known the women's style was tacky: heavy makeup, push-up bras, over-the-knee boots with pussy-length *dopičnjak* skirts. They were fashion choices that my friends frowned upon, sticking instead to more European-inspired styles, such as subtle makeup, tight jeans, and Converse sneakers—casual clothes that were neither fancy nor ill-fitting. My sloppy style of dressing, which fit into neither of these categories, did not fly in Belgrade. While my Australian friends considered it cool to shop at vintage stores and dress as if your clothes were hand-me-downs, in Belgrade it was a sign of poverty—and as the people became poorer, *looking* poor became a source of humiliation.

As I tried to fix my posture and hide my scuffed boots under the table, my friends told me about the protests they'd attended in the winter, when students and Serbian opposition parties organized a series of marches in response to electoral fraud attempted by Milošević as he ran to be reelected president. The students marched for eighty-eight days, during which they toilet-papered the Electoral Commission building and wreaked other types of havoc. I knew about the voter fraud already since my aunt had gone to the electoral office on a hunch that something fishy might be going on and found that my dead dad had mysteriously cast a vote for Milošević, the politician he spent half his life abhorring.

Listening to my friends talk about being part of a political movement stirred me, and made me remember the things I'd found exciting about politics back when I was a kid. I wanted to wake up and know more, to feel a part of something again.

Milica, Eva, and I walked over to the bookshop at the university where my mother had once taught, passing anti-Milošević graffiti and a slew of attractive students. At the bookstore, I bought a bound volume of images from the student protests my friends had talked about. It showed women trying to break the line of young policemen by kissing them, giving them roses, or trying to make them laugh; passionate young people holding ironic placards and marching through snow and rain. The protests had gone on for months, drawing crowds of two hundred thousand people. My friends told me that they'd missed months of school to attend.

"Not that our education will be recognized in the rest of the world," Milica said darkly. "We won't be able to work outside of this shitty country; Milošević has destroyed our prospects."

My Australian passport could take me anywhere in the world, while my friends' Serbian passports meant they had to jump through hoops to go anywhere. They were regularly denied visas, which had happened to Milica earlier that year when she'd wanted to visit us in Australia. I felt guilty about it, as if Australia had told my friend she wasn't good enough.

I wanted to say: "But Belgrade is great, I'd love to live here. There are so many young people, the parties are so fun, everyone is out in the city every night. In Melbourne, we have to drive from suburb to suburb, hanging out in people's backyards, while you have massive concerts, and you fight for the things you're passionate about." Instead, I just listened and said nothing because I was afraid my friends would admonish me for my privilege, that they'd ask me why I wasn't happy where I was, why I wasn't grateful to not have to worry about money or my education.

That afternoon, I picked up some pizza on the way to my grandma Xenia's apartment, and since I couldn't resist the nostalgic smell, I got a paper cone filled with whitebait as well.

My grandmother's studio apartment was 250 square feet and smelled of cigarette smoke. We sat there as Grandma Xenia piled the leftovers of the whitebait onto the slice of pizza I'd brought her, folded it over like a sandwich, and dug in.

"Why waste it?" she asked, and I questioned when she'd last eaten, as she was far more interested in smoking and weighed only seventy-two pounds. Was this her habit, not eating for days and then doing what she was doing now, eating one massive meal in huge mouthfuls at a time, like those snakes that ate sheep and then digested them for weeks? I worried she would choke when I wasn't there.

When I was a kid in Belgrade, I would often go to friends' places and there would be an old lady sitting in a nook of the apartment watching TV, or muttering to herself. Everyone would kiss the old lady as they bustled past, and she sat, swaddled in blankets, eating treats. These were grandmothers who had done their duty, looking after their grandkids while the parents worked; they'd got old, and could now kick back. This was the natural order of things: paid child care was not common, and minding and cooking for young ones was a grandparent's duty. Then when the grandparents got old, the younger family members cared for them.

When they got old, Grandma Xenia's older sisters, Olga and Mara, were looked after by my aunt Gordana. As the sisters aged well into their nineties, they would boss Gordana around, and cheerfully have baths together like when they were little, or play cards and smoke, regardless of the time of night. Willow-thin, with their matching short, loose perms, preoccupied with talking about things that had happened decades before, they chatted all day, enjoying each other's company and the comfort of living in a family home where they were loved. Now my grandma's older sisters were dead and her family was scattered across the world. She would not get to be the elder in a home full of children; she would not get to eat bacon on bread and watch game shows all day. War had upset the natural order of things.

Grandma Xenia's apartment looked the same as it had when I was a child, except now everything—Grandma included—looked like a scale model of itself. There were the Murano glass swans that had once seemed so grand, the encyclopedia of animals that had seemed so precious, the photographs of her grandchildren, who had all moved away. And my tiny grandmother sitting there like a little doll, her features smoothed by the smoke that served as a soft focus around her.

On the other side of town, I caught up on the local gossip with Dad's mother, Grandma Beba. Local gossip was my preferred topic of discussion, otherwise Grandma Beba would talk about my dad, and even though it had been awhile since he died, talking about him made me cry. Just around the corner from Grandma Beba lived Arkan the paramilitary leader and behind the massive walls of his compound, that were patrolled by armed guards, lived the tiger I'd petted as a cub. No one saw the tiger these days, though Arkan would walk his bloodthirsty dogs around; the rumor was that his idea of a joke was to let them loose on neighborhood dogs. That afternoon, I walked past there with my five-year-old cousin on the way to the bakery, and as we passed the armed guards, he jumped in a puddle, splashing them. Instead of shooting us as I'd expected, the young men with the guns said, "What a badass—he's going to be like us one day!"

Grandma Beba insisted on taking me to the town where our extended family lived, three hours southeast of Belgrade. In Serbian Orthodox culture, each family celebrates their patron saint with a feast, with each different saint being celebrated at different time of the year. This part of my family was more religious than my parents had been, and we arrived just in time for the family's Saint's Day dinner. My great-aunt Rose had spent weeks preparing the food, and, as soon as we walked in the door, Grandma Beba rushed to the kitchen to help her sister with the finishing touches. The town was small and poor, and their house was run down and musty. To avoid the older women, who kept bursting into tears and saying how much I looked like my dead father, I sat in the living room with a beautiful young woman called Anita, who had recently married my first cousin, Bojan. *Why would you stay in this shithole if you look like her?* I thought, as if beauty gave you a free pass from a life of poverty. Anita limply held a Transformer toy, while her toddler son stacked blocks. "These are all toys from when Bojan was a boy," she said.

When Bojan came back from work, he behaved just like I remembered him from the last time I'd visited as a child: he was guileless, eager to please, taking orders from his mother, Rose, never seeming to get anything right.

"You're such an idiot, Bojan, why didn't you bring the chairs from upstairs like I told you?"

Bojan jumped up, laughed as if he found the whole thing funny, and ran off.

"When I come back," he said to me, "I'll tell you about my great new job."

During dinner, Bojan explained that his boss ran a five-star recreation center, which seemed an odd fit for the town.

"Tomorrow, you'll go there with me, and we'll play tennis," he said as the phone rang and he rushed to get it.

Great-aunt Rose said, "He's at their beck and call!" and the rest of us held our tongues, as Bojan was known for being at *her* beck and call.

Bojan came in again, and sat down, then the phone rang again and he leaped out of his seat. "What can I do? They *need* me!"

My great aunt called him a moron, and we heard him talking in the other room, laughing in that apologetic, goofy way of his. The rest of the dinner was taken up by talk of whether I had a boyfriend, and news of a relative in America who had had a nose job and, in unrelated but equally exciting news, was getting divorced. We left early the next day, so I didn't get a chance to see the tennis court, or meet my first rural mafia boss, which is what some of our relatives speculated Bojan's employer might be. I was glad to leave the town, with its depressing, empty streets, its youth getting stoned amid broken-down cars.

Back in Belgrade, we had another family dinner. Some of my other relatives—cousins who had moved to Europe for business opportunities even before we left for Australia—happened to be in town at the same time as us, so it was time to visit my mother's side of the family. A cousin who was in her midtwenties and lived in Austria kept squinting at the tags on my clothes. She apparently did not find what she was looking for, since most of my things were from secondhand stores or Dangerfield—an Australian brand of edgy fashions that my friends and I adored, like the low-cut purple corduroy flares I wore most days.

"Look," my cousin said magnanimously, "all you need is to get a magazine at the start of the season."

Then, in case I didn't know what a magazine was, she said, "Like *Vogue*."

She advised me to look at the styles that were coming into fashion and then to get things that looked similar, but were cheaper. She gave me a bunch of makeup samples that she had collected, and a bottle of perfume. "It's more of a brunette scent," she said, running her fingers through her blond bob and looking at my hair, "and that pink dye seems to be growing out." My cousin was chic; her skin was smooth. And while her jeans and shirt looked simple, if you looked closely at the labels you would see that they were from Chanel or Lanvin. Her earrings were small gold hoops. "My husband got them for me when we had an argument," she said, laughing. "He knows to head to Cartier when he's done something wrong!"

Spending time with my mother's jet-setting family was very different from being with dad's family in eastern Serbia, but this dinner made me just as uncomfortable as the rural one. Natalija and I were quizzed about our knowledge of history, and if we didn't know the answers to questions like "When did the reign of the Hapsburgs end?" everyone laughed at us. If I admitted to not having read something my family considered to be an important literary work, like *The Iliad*, I'd be mocked: "And you say you're interested in literature? Ha!" Not that any of them found time to read much nowadays, but they felt that they had done the groundwork, unlike me.

A thirtysomething businessman relative who had been particularly determined to show my sister and me as ignorant, spoke to us in English "to practice," and at one point when he was recounting a conversation he'd had with a colleague, he said:

"I didn't want to be an ass-whore, but I told him what I really think. And if that makes me an ass-whore, then that's what I am."

Natalija and I tried to suppress our delight as we exchanged a look, silently agreeing we would not correct him, praying that he would refer to himself as an ass-whore in public until the end of time.

When we'd finished the meal, my gastroenterologist aunt started giving the three of us very detailed instructions for the use of her Paris home. Our plan was to tour Paris for three days en route back to Melbourne, and we were going to stay in her empty apartment.

As she was talking, she didn't seem to notice my mother start to show signs that my sister and I understood all too well—flared nostrils, her lips turning into a line. She was getting pissed off. "When you're in there, you *must* take your shoes off," my aunt said for the third time. "There is a white carpet, and you understand it is important to keep it that way." At which point, for anyone who wasn't used to the signs, it seemed as if my mother very suddenly snapped. Whether my aunt had meant to insult my mother or not, she had managed to provoke a slew of emotions that had been building, and my mother had apparently had enough of being made to feel inferior.

"How dare you tell me to take off my shoes!?" she shrieked at my aunt, standing up from the table with her large frame and gripping the sides, as if she might tip the whole thing over, dishes and all. "You think my children and I are *animals*? You don't want us to *soil* your precious apartment?"

She always hated feeling "less than" for being an immigrant in Australia, and she now felt that her own relatives were humiliating her for her apparent slovenliness. The next twenty minutes were a blur of shouting, my mother telling my aunt exactly how she felt, and my aunt biting back. Some people left the room, uncomfortable, but Natalija and I sat there, entranced, staring. As I looked at my mother, overweight, wearing her clothes that came from Target on Centre Road, I felt suddenly proud to be on her team.

I can only imagine what we must have looked like to our fancy European-transplant relatives. Crazy Koka, as my mother was known behind her back, had gone to Australia, a wilderness in which no one cared about what make of car you drove, or what designer you were wearing. I thought about the camels that roamed in the outback of Australia, how they had been brought over way back when people used to trek across the desert, before there were roads or even railways. The camels had adapted to the harsh Australian climate and eventually become feral. That's how we seemed to our relatives. Gone wild in the outback, returning with our dirty shoes, eager to trample snow-white Parisian carpet. Crazy Koka and her kids who didn't know how to dress themselves, who weren't even proficient in French. They had all laughed when I told my mother I'd been gifted a "Bvulgari" perfume, because I didn't know to pronounce it Bulgari.

"Let's go!" my mother yelled. My sister and I got up, and followed her out of the apartment, rushing to my aunt Mila's place so we could get on the phone and book a Paris hotel last-minute.

We found two rooms at the Chat Noir, in the Pigalle neighborhood of Paris. On our first evening, my mother, sister, and I sat in the café beneath the hotel, ate baguettes, and listened to a jazz band. *This is probably where Toulouse-Lautrec spent his time,* I thought, feeling like I could relax for the first time in ages. Here, unlike in Belgrade or Melbourne, I had no context, there were no stakes. I was impressed that several very old men in very old suits lived in this old hotel, and I envied them, imagining a life full of art and wine, where a maid cleaned your room every day and you were free to wander the cobbled streets eating croissants.

Harry happened to be on a high school exchange program in France, and he caught the train to Paris to see me. Leaving my family behind, we walked through Pigalle, to the Sacré-Coeur Basilica. We bought wine and walked past the Moulin Rouge to a square where we sat on a bench and drank. Suddenly, the things I had cared about—whether my relatives considered me fashionable enough, or my Belgrade friends thought I was too privileged—didn't matter. Sitting with Harry, who I was still a little in love with, talking about writing, books, and films, I reveled privately in the idea of a creative life as my salvation from all of that.

It occurred to me that my relatives who lived in Western Europe were probably trying desperately to fit in. Yugoslavians were considered Eurotrash, and my relatives wanted to distance themselves from the economic ruin and our history of fighting and war crimes that tarnished us and made us seem barbaric and uneducated. Their affected sophistication was simply a defense mechanism. There were, I realized, different ways to be an immigrant, different techniques for dealing with being out of place.

Here in Paris, on this bench, I was free. For the first time since Dad's death, I felt a tingle of excitement, the promise of stories yet to be told, the possibility that life held some excitement yet. Thanks to the beautiful environment, the company of my friend, or too much wine, an uncharacteristic earnestness took hold. *I am ready to be uniquely, unapologetically myself,* I thought. And even though I didn't really know who that was, I felt inspired to find out.

9

Sex, Bombs, and Rock and Roll

At sixteen, for the first time in my life, I started to earn my own money. After school a couple of days a week, I worked at Peter the doctor's clinic in Dandenong, an outer suburb of Melbourne. I did some admin work and awkwardly labeled little vials to be picked up by the lab, worried about getting urine or blood on my hands. With my modest wages, I bought wine, or cigarettes to share with my friends, or I saved up for items from Dangerfield. Peter didn't care if I brought my schoolbooks to work with me—it was my second-to-last year of high school and I was keen to do well so I could go on to an arts degree at university.

Peter's practice was frequented by people from all of ex-Yugoslavia, though most of the patients were Bosnian Serbs. Considering that some of the people who crossed paths at Peter's had been enemies during the war, I often wondered which of them were nationalists, and how they all felt about the other people in the waiting room. It was hard to tell. There was a rumor that someone had their eye taken out at a local bar thanks to a nationalistic dispute, but mostly I saw people being friendly, sometimes even hugging and kissing.

Peter was one of those gregarious doctors who was beloved by his patients (and also the kind who smoked, partied, and dressed in drag for select parties). He served as a conduit between his patients and the unfamiliar Australian medical system. Part of my job was to placate people in the waiting room as he ran late, while laughter emanated from his examination room. He'd come out slapping his patients on the back, a look of relief on their faces, like they'd finally been understood in a country where everything was foreign.

The clinic operated like an ex-Yugo outpost, and even though I'd gone out of my way to avoid the community in the past, I now enjoyed my role as an authority behind the reception desk, and I particularly liked the disposable income I was receiving, for doing not much. People told jokes from back home, swapped opinions on whose home-preserved sausages were best, and slipped in "Havaya" or other Aussie-Yugo slang into their speech. Every now and then a non-Yugo would appear in the clinic, and there would be a sudden hush, as if we'd been busted doing something illicit. The staff and patients would switch to speaking English, with varying degrees of success. One patient, by the name of Jagoda—a Yugoslavian botanical name as common as Rose or Heather in English—introduced herself to an English-speaking physiotherapist (who had come to see a couple of Peter's patients) by translating her name literally: "Hello, I am Strawberry!" she declared.

From where I was sitting, the atmosphere seemed lighthearted. But I soon realized that perception wasn't always accurate. Many of Peter's patients who had taken factory jobs in Australia were suffering from injuries—ranging from the consequences of repetitive strain to serious injuries sustained from accidents involving heavy machinery. People were often seeking compensation from their employers, and in such cases Peter dictated as I typed and refined his reports, bringing to his clinic my excellent control of English and speedy touch typing skills.

Most ex-Yugos, and even the average Australian, could not afford to see a psychologist. However, when they were injured at work, counseling sessions were covered by their employers. More often than not, Peter referred his injured patients to my mother, who rented a room at his clinic twice a week. Even though their technical reason for seeing her was because of their work-related pain or depression, my mother's clients inevitably ended up talking about the war. It was only because they'd lifted something heavy and slipped a disk, or their hands got crushed in a machine, that my mother's clients were able to share their old traumas.

Through her clients, my mother was drawn into the heart of the war. While in the past she had been at a distance—first as a Belgrade intellectual protesting in the streets, and then as an immigrant watching the Western news and trying to interpret what was actually happening in her homeland—now she was getting first-person accounts that painted a new picture. Her focus was zoomed right in on the suffering of individuals, case by case.

My mother hadn't worked with refugees before. In Belgrade, she tutored psychology students, her research was mostly focused on children, and in her private practice in Melbourne, she counseled couples and individuals dealing with common issues such as anxiety, relationship problems, and depression.

While their individual experiences were foreign to her, my mother shared with her new clients a language and a collective memory of a faraway place called Yugoslavia, which had existed before the wars. For her clients, having someone say, in a familiar language, "I understand what you're talking about," turned out to be extremely important, and her practice quickly grew. After all, my mother and her clients had all been born under Tito, they'd all been taught the same songs in primary school, they knew the taste of creamy *kajmak* spread and what "Brotherhood and Unity" had once meant.

When I typed up her reports as part of my admin duties at the clinic, I pointed out to her how many people suffered from insomnia, and she said that not a single one of them could sleep. "They relive the war in their dreams," she said. The dead of night was when my mother's clients were visited by their terrors: not having enough food for their babies, being in a concentration camp, watching a cell mate die from a beating. "Once you get down to talking about it, it's not about Serbs, Croats, and Bosnians," my mother said one day, after a client of hers had left with red-rimmed eyes. "War is the same all over the world. It's about the extremes of human experience, people being pushed to their limits."

Even though the Bosnian war had officially ended three years earlier, for these people it was still going, and it would continue for the decades to come. To outsiders they may have seemed like any other forgettable foreigners living in their Housing Commission apartments, with their strange language, their accents, their dark clothes, smiling automatically in the way browbeaten people do to avoid being told off, leaning forward, straining their ears to understand what Aussies were saying to them. But these were individuals with their own specific nightmares. Even under warm blankets, in a snowless climate, they felt the cold from a faraway winter, and each night they woke, their hearts racing.

As Peter and my mother worked, I poked around in files, or listened closely in the waiting room. And in this way, I got a glimpse beyond the sometimes slapstick veneer of our diaspora's roasted piglets and bawdy jokes. I found out the backstory of a woman with a perm whose brother had died by losing his head and an arm (he was sliced from his neck, through his torso, until his arm and head were removed). I heard about the Bosnian Serb who was a prisoner of war in a Bosnian Muslim camp. His job was to "swap" corpses, dragging dead Serbs for burial on the Serbian side, and taking dead Muslims and dragging them back for burial on the Muslim side. The dead on both sides were people he knew personally, who had lived in his town. He was like Sisyphus, rolling a boulder up a hill each day only to have it roll back down, but instead of a boulder it was heavy corpses, and his brutal penance for dragging his dead neighbors through the mud was that he still heaved them now, every night, in his sleep. Did he wake up questioning why he'd survived and they'd died, or did he wonder whether he was alive at all?

I started to absorb images far more specific than my imagination had previously conjured. Like the couple whose daughter committed suicide with a hand grenade on their balcony in Sarajevo. The family was unable to move because of the war, and for several years they had to sit with a hole in the wall as a reminder. There was the woman who blamed herself for her son's poor performance at school because when he was a baby and they were on the run, her milk dried up and he almost died. The couple who couldn't decide whether to sell the home in Bosnia in which a relative's throat had been slit, or keep it—what was the more respectful thing to do? The teens who now suffered from low self-esteem because they'd grown up in European refugee camps in their old clothes and their too-small shoes, the butt of jokes from local kids who lived near the camps. The man who served in a battalion that was later accused of war crimes. (When asked if he had participated in the atrocities, he said: "I didn't have to participate. Each time we arrived at a place, the commander asked for volunteers. The same men always volunteered to rape or kill.")

"I don't even know if it's psychology, what I do," my mother said one day, after a particularly grueling batch of sessions. "I just listen. When I listen to them, I validate: that they survived, that they are alive," and after the listening, she said, "I try to help them find something in the world that interests them still, a reason to keep on living."

Up until my time at Peter's, I had simplified the act of war in my mind: people shot at one another, many died, many were made refugees. On immigration forms, people could tick a box that said "refugee," which whittled their stories down to that: they were humans seeking refuge. But now I realized war could not be explained easily. It was full of individual stories, and the people at Peter's were just a tiny portion of the refugees all over the world, who had fled their homes in Afghanistan, Rwanda, Vietnam. War doesn't actually end when a date is stamped on it for the textbooks, when the headlines are printed, when the newscasters announce it. After the tanks roll out and the bodies are buried, those left alive are left with nightmares, anxiety, twitches, and a fear that is passed on to their children. War isn't just about men with guns; it's about old people and mothers and children, and those not yet born.

Through my report-writing for the clinic, I became a tiny mouthpiece: "Ms. X has suffered from anxiety ever since shrapnel lodged in her stomach." I stated facts, helping Peter and my mother send information into the world in order for their patients to receive benefits they deserved. I was in the unique position of being an English-speaking fly on the wall, and beneath my Serbian-receptionist-schoolgirl costume, I dreamed of being a serious writer. English was the language of my favorite books, and I wished I could command it like Angela Carter or John Steinbeck did. I loved reading fiction, but more and more, nonfiction spoke to me: I knew that telling stories like my grandma Xenia had told me was a powerful way of showing the world to people.

As I observed the scenes at Peter's clinic, I wanted to be the person who put the patients' stories into the world, into English. I wanted to explore the mix of dark humor and tragedy that was always present in the waiting room, the sense that everything here was somehow tainted by the history and geography of a place very far away. But these were stories that had a beginning, and a middle, but no real end, with the last line reading, "And then they lived with PTSD ever after." Would anyone want to hear them? Secretly, I hoped Westerners' eyes would be opened by what they learned from my writings; I could do something that might even be useful. At the same time, I was insecure enough to discourage myself before I even started. What could I say that would make any difference to anyone?

So I held back, and became a sort of reception-dwelling spy, someone who listened but didn't comment, someone who observed but never felt qualified to outwardly sympathize like my mother. Hearing the details of war made me remember who I was and where I came from. And it reinforced that my Australian friends and I were different, and we always would be. If, at the start of my high school life, I'd been trying to fit in, to shut the door to my past, it would never work now. The door was ajar, and all sorts of voices were wafting through— some of them spoke of homemade brandy, some hummed folk songs, and others spoke of centuries of turmoil, the words "cock" and "your mother" thrown in every few sentences for good measure. This was my language. Yugoslavia had gripped me again.

Just as my interest in Yugoslavia was being rekindled, things took a new turn back home, the violence moving to the region of Kosovo, placing our troubled region on the world stage once again.

Since his rise to power, Milošević had reduced the autonomy of Kosovo, giving more power to Serbs. Kosovo Albanians had been subject to the shutdown of their Albanian-language media outlets, and were increasingly losing their jobs. A separatist Albanian movement was created with the aim of gaining independence from Serbia, and a paramilitary group calling itself the Kosovo Liberation Army (KLA) launched attacks against the Yugoslav army and police in Kosovo. The Serbian paramilitary was sent in, and people were being killed.

"We Serbs are a minority over there!" a Bosnian Serb who had been driven out of Bosnia said to no one in particular in Peter's waiting room, "They want to drive us out of Kosovo, too!?" The Serbs dubbed the KLA terrorists, while Albanians saw them as freedom fighters. As for me, now that I was trying to form my own opinions separate from what I was told by my elders, I was torn. I was watching the Albanian deaths, watching the Serbs being painted as villains, and hearing the Serbs in Peter's clinic citing our holy places in Kosovo, the monasteries that people held dear, saying that this was our mecca, our Jerusalem, a place that could not be taken.

Via executive order, U.S. President Bill Clinton declared a national emergency, stating that the actions of Serbia in "promoting ethnic conflict and human suffering, threaten to destabilize countries of the region . . . and therefore constitute an unusual and extraordinary threat to the national security and foreign policy of the United States." When Serbian forces refused to withdraw from Kosovo, a U.S.-led NATO intervention was planned. "The Americans want to bomb us," was how the Serbs in Peter's clinic put it, another Yugo adding, "Clinton wants to take attention away from his blow job." I couldn't help but wonder if this was all paranoia, or if Western politicians were in fact just as self-serving as those back in Yugoslavia.

Even though the NATO intervention had not gained approval from the UN Security Council, and was considered legally dubious by some, Australia was one of the many nations that supported military action, and Prime Minister John Howard announced to the press that: "History has told us if you sit by and do nothing, you pay a much greater price later on." The Serbian patients in Peter's waiting room pretended to spit at the TV—listing in true Yugo spirit all the places they'd like to fuck Howard's mother. But Howard's statement didn't make me angry, it gave me a chill. The people in Peter's waiting room didn't spend all day with Aussies like I did. This was the same unpleasant feeling I got when friends' parents expressed their opinions on the Yugoslavian wars, when I was in a taxi speaking Serbian with a friend and the taxi driver threatened to kick us out if we didn't speak English. I was now living in a country that directly supported the bombing of Yugoslavia, and it made me feel personally attacked. I felt for the Albanian population of Kosovo, as we watched news reports of aggression against them, but mostly I felt for my friends and family, who were living in a place that would be bombed because of a leader they did not elect.

In March 1999, the NATO bombing campaign began. While NATO had hoped it would be quick, and that Milošević would capitulate and withdraw his troops, it would end up being nearly three months before the bombing was over. The bombs were aimed at military targets and mostly focused on the Kosovo region and other areas in rural Serbia, but there were also targets within Belgrade.

Watching the news, my mother, her friends, and I deliberated among ourselves why the U.S. couldn't have sent someone to assassinate Milošević ten years earlier.

"He was the West's 'man,' and now they feel like they've lost control, so they're punishing the population who opposed him all along!" my mother's friends said.

I wondered what my dad would think of all of it, remembering the protests he took me to—protests whose principal aim was preventing a war—all those years ago. He'd always been pro-West, teasing my mother for what he called her nationalism. What would be his take on this new situation, where the West was responsible for bombing Serbia?

As bombs fell, our family and friends had to take shelter in the basements of their apartment buildings. Most of the bombs were dropped directly on Kosovo, and NATO referred to the resulting deaths of civilians with the disturbing military term "collateral damage."

The weekend after the bombing began, I went with my mother and sister to a protest in front of the U.S. consulate. The crowd of several hundred people comprised family friends, patients from Peter's clinic, and others I didn't know. One old man holding a sign that said "Stop NATO" kept repeating in a heavy accent, "Vorning vorning, bombs are folling!" and "Clinton killa!" through a megaphone. There were also thuggish-looking guys with nationalist tattoos, and when several news crews arrived, they were quick to point their cameras at these Serbian nationalists who were chanting and throwing rocks at the consulate, and an old lady with no teeth holding up a sign saying "Clinton is devil."

"Of course they want to make us look like assholes," my mother said, as a camera operator got right up in the face of some guy yelling "FUCK AMERICA AND FUCK AUSTRALIA!" One of my family friends who was peacefully protesting piped up, "Hey, why don't you film us instead?" A motherly looking woman went up to the young thugs who were jumping up on one another's back and shouting "SER-BIA! SERBIA!"—purposely jostling the people around them. The woman tried to scold the young men, and one of them told her to fuck off, in English, in an Aussie-Serb accent, making me think he was one of those Serbian nationalists who had been born in Australia and had quite a lot to say about a place he'd never been to.

I silently judged these guys, who had likely grown up writing "wogs rule, skips pull" on the trains and who saw this as their chance to take a stab at the West, throwing stones in order to feel some power, when they were usually marginalized. I pictured them actually visiting the Serbia they'd romanticized, or heard about from their parents. When would they realize that they were deluded? That they didn't even speak the language? When the local Serbian people laughed at them, and their ideas of what the country was like? I wished they would go to Serbia, and put their money where their mouths were—"You'd change your story soon enough," I wanted to say, remembering my mother's clients.

Even though we were all technically there to oppose the bombing of our country, the people gathered at the protests couldn't quite get through the protest without snapping at one another. There's a

saying in our language "Two Serbs, three opinions," meaning that we can never agree on anything. Our national slogan, "*Samo Sloga Srbina Spašava*," means "Only Unity Can Save the Serbs," as if our forefathers who coined the term knew that our Achilles' heel would always be our self-destructive tendencies.

Alicia and I went to her boyfriend's place that night, and we sat around smoking in his parents' shed. A second-generation Turkish guy named Hass was there. When I first met him a few months earlier, Hass had said, "So, you're Serbian. Have you got a bit of Turk in ya?"—and plenty of my people did, thanks to the five-hundred-year Ottoman occupation. (I once heard our neighbor in Belgrade say, "All of us would be blond and blue-eyed, if it wasn't for the Turks," and only as a teenager did I come to realize what he'd meant.)

"I don't think so," I'd said to Hass.

"Do you *want* a little bit of Turk in ya?" he'd asked, winking, and everyone had laughed, including me.

Now I mentioned to my friends that I'd been at the anti-NATO protests. Though I'd never heard him say anything political before, suddenly Hass said, "Your people are getting what they deserve. They're fucked up, they don't know how to rule themselves. They were better off when they were under us."

By "us" he meant the Ottoman Empire. It occurred to me that just like when I'd learned from Ms. Danica about the Serbs being the "moral winners" against the oppressive Ottomans in Kosovo, I was pretty sure Hass was repeating a patriotic myth that had been passed to him by his elders. Hass was second generation and I was first, but both of us were swaddled in an ethnic identity we couldn't shake: our last names and the way we spoke and looked set us apart and reminded us always of where we had come from.

I know now that we all drag around the prejudices and unfulfilled

dreams of our elders, suffering the lot of migrants with tenuous links to home, wishing we were other than insignificant minorities getting lost in the vast world of the West. But when Hass said that my people were getting what they deserved, instead of laughing politely, or pretending not to be offended, I said "fuck you" and went home.

I was elated that I'd actually told someone to fuck off, but at the same time, I also felt shame, that old feeling of wanting to be liked, of wanting to toe the line. I thought about the Australians who publicly declared that immigrants should "go home." Yet here I was, instead of just trying to "pass," to not make noise, telling someone to fuck off. My confidence level had reached a new milestone and, for the first time, I thought: *I don't need to apologize for myself.*

Every day after school, I boarded a train and traveled forty minutes to the city, then caught the tram to the U.S. consulate. I thought of the students in that book I'd bought about the anti-Milošević protests. So many times, I'd looked at their faces and imagined being among them: young, cool, passionate. I remembered going with my dad to nightly demonstrations as a kid, and as I stood in front of the U.S. consulate, I thought: *This is in my blood. This is what Dad taught me to do.*

The protests were smaller on weekdays as compared to the weekend, but I made sure I went to them all. I started hanging around with a group of young people who were a few years older than me, some of them students who had come to Australia only in the last few years. Until now, my Yugo interactions had been restricted to family friends and their kids, but these young people were different. I'd met them not through my family, but on my own—at a protest just like the ones my friends went to in Belgrade.

There was a couple in their midtwenties who hosted a Yugo night at a club in the center of Melbourne, which I managed to get into, even though I was underage. The club attracted various young people from

our community, from rockers, to guys with unbuttoned shirts in leather jackets, to women in tiny golden miniskirts.

Many of the conversations I had with my new friends were about how we wished we were back in Belgrade. We would talk about what a drag it was being in Australia. With my new friends, I was happy to renounce Australia and my love for its language, and to dream of the Belgrade that they described, which was somehow more sophisticated than the one I knew, full of fascinating people, while, the way we painted it, the Australia that we lived in was inhabited by barbarians and oppressors.

After the club that first time, at three in the morning, we went to Melbourne's Little Italy, and sat in a restaurant open twenty-four-seven. It was a big group of us, all speaking in our language. Some in the group were recent refugees who barely spoke English. One classic example was when a Bosnian guy wanted ice in his drink and asked for "vater, brrrr" as he pretended to shiver. We only spoke in English when it was time to order, and suddenly my friends were rendered foreign, stilted, some of them mispronouncing certain words. Meanwhile I was accent-less, and when it was my turn, I ordered as quickly as possible. I felt like my English made me sound like "one of them," meaning the oppressors.

I had never felt more Serbian. My new friends and I shared stories we'd heard, some of them true, some rumors, about farmers who had taken down bombers by shooting at them; about young people who ignored the sirens that told them to go to their basements and instead sat on rooftops, drinking and watching the bombing like it was fireworks; about the animals in Belgrade Zoo who were traumatized by the bombs, including the lion that had taken to eating its own paws in distress. We found confidence by sticking together, by glorifying the place we'd come from. As we drank, we spoke loudly, daring passers-by to say something, so we could snap at them; roar like lions in a cage. But everyone left us alone, and to the other people on Lygon Street in the middle of the night, we might have seemed like any other group of drunk foreigners.

People continued to gather at our house to watch the news and discuss politics. As if they could hear us through the TV, we'd call the NATO pilots idiots when they used an old map and accidentally bombed the Chinese embassy thinking it was a military target. We worried for Aunt Mila, as it was rumored that Radio TV Serbia would be bombed. And one day, it was. The station had been deemed a legitimate military target, as it was spreading Milošević propaganda. Sixteen people died. My aunt hadn't been on shift that night, but some people she'd worked with had died. "And they hadn't been Milošević's people," Aunt Mila said.

The NATO campaign was the first in which the brand-new stealth bombers were used, and when one of them was taken down by Serbian missiles, we celebrated, on our feet clapping and jeering at the TV, "How does *that* feel!?"

I put on music that my new Yugo friends and I listened to, and my mother's friends joined in singing—these Yugo rock songs had come out when they were young themselves, before Yugoslavia dissolved. A particular favorite was "Look Homeward, Angel" by the beloved Serbian singer Bora Čorba. The song's title came from the Thomas Wolfe novel and was meant to highlight the poverty and political instability of Yugoslavia. As we all sang, I thought about all the damage the war had wrought over the last decade.

And now, in the wake of the NATO bombs falling, we sang the end of the song with the West in mind: "*May they feel poverty, fear, and pain on their own skins.*" The last bit really stuck with me. I looked at the bald, privileged Australian prime minister, John Howard, and I looked at sleazy, privileged Bill Clinton, at Milošević with his underground bunker, and I hated them. I thought: *the people who suffer will always be those who happen to be poor and weak, and the greedy, fortunate bullies will prosper.* I thought about my mother's clients, many of them apolitical, who were the victims of power-hungry leaders. I remembered the taxi driver who threatened to kick my friend and me out of the car for not speaking English even though we were teenagers and in the middle of nowhere, and I lumped him in with the rest of them: Clinton, Howard, Milošević, Australian taxi driver—I wanted them all to drop dead. *May they feel it on their own skins,* I thought.

Back in Serbia, anti-Western sentiment grew to an all-time high. The opposition movement, which had looked to the West for help in the past, now had trouble dealing with the fact that it was American-led NATO forces bombing them. It was hard to promote a Western-style democracy when you were being bombed by the West. Infighting among opposition groups did nothing to curb the popularity of Milošević, and just like we were annoyed at the Western news, we became annoyed at the opposition parties, who were bickering among themselves instead of uniting against Milošević. Milošević's popularity blossomed again, as he commiserated with the people, appearing on television to renounce the Western attacks, and to use them as proof that he was right and his opponents were wrong: We *were* being threatened by foreign powers. We *were* the victims and the martyrs, as our national myths told us.

That weekend, Harry had been hanging around my place, where we were meant to be studying for an English exam. Actually, we were eating nachos and watching a Coen brothers film, as I put the finishing touches on a handmade sign. It said "WHERE IS YOUR STEALTH?"—referring to the bomber that had recently been taken down by Serbian forces. "I understand that you don't want your country to be bombed, but celebrating the death of a pilot isn't nice," he said.

Harry's point touched a nerve—the sign *did* go against my assertion that I was a pacifist. But instead of thinking about it some more, and working through my reaction, I pretended that Harry hadn't said anything. Instead of engaging with his comment, I thought about my little cousin in Belgrade who hid behind the couch when he heard a truck or a helicopter, thinking it was a bomber flying overhead. I thought about my friends from kindergarten who had been denied visas to leave the country and who would be going to university soon just like me, except their degrees would be worth nothing because Yugoslavia was a shithole. That could have been me.

And even though Harry knew me well, I decided that he didn't understand me the way my Yugo friends understood me. Of course I would still hang out with him at school, and goof around like we always had, but I would not forget that he was an Aussie. If I'd looked more closely, I might have seen that Harry and I had many more things in common than I had with my Yugo friends, with whom I had just one thing in common: ex-Yugoslavia. Still, even though it was only a nonexistent land that bound me to the Yugos, that community was what I currently needed. So I ignored Harry, listened to Yugo rock on my headphones on the Melbourne tram to the consulate, and glared at anyone who looked over at me and my sign.

A few weeks into the bombing, I was dancing in the club with my friends, nodding my head and mouthing the words to the angsty Yugo rock song "What Am I Supposed to Do?" I lip-synced in the direction of my friend Jovana, who sang back. The song was from the Croatian new wave band Azra and had come out in 1979, but we listened to it as if it was still on the charts. When Yugoslavia started to crumble, Yugo rock crumbled with it, but we still held on, singing at the top of our voices in a Melbourne club, pretending like the culture and art in our country hadn't come to a standstill twenty years earlier.

Jovana drew my attention to a guy who was looking over at us, also singing along to Azra. He was tall and tanned and even though he was clearly "one of ours," with his big nose and olive skin, for a second something about him reminded me of how I pictured Native American hero Winnetou from my favorite childhood book. He was handsome, and his look told me he was kind, confident, and wise. He and I locked eyes and sang the chorus.

"*He* seems all right," Jovana said, appraising the guy glancing at me. Her approval was based on his music taste, and the absence of thick gold chains and hair gel. He gave me a wide, sincere smile. "You dropped this," he said, bringing over a bobby pin that may or may not have fallen out of my hair, which I'd pinned up in little twists. In my attempt to look casual, I forgot to take the bobby pin from him, and he held it between us like a strange little microphone. He was nineteen and his family was from Sarajevo, although they'd lived in Serbia for a few years before coming to Australia. That meant he was a refugee. His name was Blaža (the *ž* pronounced like the *j* in *je m'appelle*). He talked to me, relaxed, like he didn't even notice my protective older friends looking over from the DJ booth. He also didn't seem to care that his friends were looking over at us and nudging each other, as he stooped (he really was very tall) to hear me better, like he was hanging on my every word. Whereas I liked to roll my eyes, smirk, and make ironic comments, he seemed like a genuinely happy person. My heart leapt at being singled out like this, as Blaža ignored every other girl walking by and seemed delighted by everything I said. "What a weird guy," I said to my friends afterward, playing it cool, as he kept looking over at us from where his friends stood.

After a seventy-eight-day campaign, NATO stopped bombing Serbia, when Milošević agreed to withdraw Yugoslavian forces from Kosovo, provided that Kosovo would be politically supervised by the United Nations and that there would be no independence referendum for three years. Our daily protests against the bombing finally came to an end. The casualties of the yearlong war stood at over thirteen thousand people, most of them Kosovo Albanian civilians. Milošević declared victory, and in a way he had won; Kosovo was still Serbian, and he'd managed to gain back popular support during the bombing. Reports of civilian deaths from the bombing campaign varied widely, and have been estimated at between five hundred and twenty-five hundred. Yugoslavia reported that the damage sustained to the country amounted to $26 billion.

The following week, I rushed home after school on a Friday to put on a lot of makeup and a floral maxi dress that I'd borrowed from Alicia, which I paired with a choker. Blaža picked me up for a date wearing a carefully ironed light blue shirt and black jeans. We drove to the city in his shiny new Subaru RX, which he'd just bought that day and was extremely proud of, but I didn't notice, and he never mentioned it because he didn't want to show off.

We went to a tiny Italian restaurant that had been recommended to him by friends. There were little candles on the tables, and the whole thing resembled the kind of adult date scene I'd only seen in films. My family didn't go to restaurants, and my friends and I stuck to cheap casual places. The lighting gave off a flattering orange glow, and I didn't feel like saying something smart-ass about how clichéd it was. I didn't feel like this was stupid; I felt like Blaža actually cared about me, and wanted to treat me to something lovely. And I found myself wanting to know all about him. We did not split some fries like I would have with my friends, but instead each of us ordered from the menu. And as we talked, a classic, old school romance seemed like just the thing I wanted, just like when I was a little girl watching romantic films, before I became my wizened seventeen-year-old self.

I don't remember what we talked about, except that I found out that Blaža worked with his dad as a builder and carpenter, but his dream was to be a photographer. When we finished eating, he insisted on getting the check, and the little bobby pin that had fallen out of my hair the night I met him fell out of his wallet. I went to pick it up, but he got it instead, tucking it back in his pocket, as if it was precious.

On the way home, he made a showy U-turn without noticing a

Melbourne tram, the same tram that had taken me to the consulate each day after school. The tram hit the back right corner of his brand-new car, and Blaža hid his distress well, pulling over and calmly talking to the tram driver, but privately wondering what his parents would say, as he'd been saving up for the car all year. We drove home happy, despite the damage, Blaža pointing out a huge spiral structure he and his dad had built in the Toyota showroom on the highway near my place. I made a note of it, so I could point it out to people in the future. Perhaps I'd say, "My boyfriend made that."

10

Welcome Not-Home

Blaža and I started dating as my last year of high school began. He came over when I wasn't studying and took large black-and-white photos of me, lovingly approving of the dramatic dark lipstick and beret I wore for the occasion. The childhood Disney princess side of me stirred, and in our private time together I felt confident enough to coo at him, to be soppy and loving in a way my cynical, withdrawn self would not normally have allowed.

I was excited about the next stage of my life, which meant focusing less on my new Yugo friends and nights out, and more on what was coming up. At school, I had my old gang: Harry, Jasmine, and Alicia. After school, I had a real boyfriend. And if I got a high enough score on my end-of-year exams, I'd be accepted into the prestigious University of Melbourne, my top college choice.

Jasmine and I had become supernerds and were applying to take on a university subject to accelerate our studies. When we were ac-

cepted, we took the tram to the university once a week, quizzing ourselves for various upcoming exams as we went deeper into the city
center and farther from the suburban life we would soon be able to
transcend.

Our tram stop was right near where my ex-Yugo friends and I
had sat around late at night eating pizza after the club. But now I was
not Yugo-me, who wore makeup and spoke another language with
her friends, but a studious almost-adult, in my ugly McKinnon High
School uniform and with my heavy backpack. Jasmine and I entered
the University of Melbourne's beautiful old campus, with its sandstone
buildings, courtyards where students would sit reading or smoking,
lawns where barefoot hippies played hacky sack. We sat proudly in the
lecture hall with legitimate university students and listened to our professor talk about Caravaggio's use of shadow and how it reflected his
personal turmoil, or Jacques-Louis David's painting *The Death of Marat*
and how it revealed the artist's Jacobin politics.

Our lecturer used words like "pastiche" and "avant-garde" and Jasmine and I pretended like this language was completely normal, like
this was exactly where we belonged—rather than in our actual high
school, where people expressed themselves in other ways, such as when
a kid called Boris stole a car from his dad's used car lot and drove it onto
the back of the school football field.

Jasmine and I breathed in the possibilities of this new world,
dreaming about college-student life. Sitting there in the lectures, I often
thought about the university in Belgrade where my parents had once
studied, where fascinating young people chatted about politics and
music, and I felt myself rising to their level.

To complement the identity we were trying to assume, Jasmine and
I started smoking thin, menthol cigarettes that I'd procured using a fake
ID. The cigarettes were colorful, which I hoped would work to spark
conversations with fellow students, rather than making us seem more
childlike with our pink and turquoise cigarettes, in our school frocks,
as we stood outside the campus after class, waiting for Blaža to pull up

in his Subaru and take us home, all the way through the city and back to the burbs.

While we waited, Jasmine and I buoyed each other's feelings of self-importance. Many of our classmates intended to keep living in the suburbs after they grew up, but we felt sophisticated, bound for interesting lives in the city. Not only were we in an accelerated program at a university, but our ethnicity took on a new meaning here. I came from Europe, not far from where Caravaggio and David had painted their masterpieces, and Jasmine's family had come from China—a place that our lecturer recognized for its rich cultural history. As we learned about art and revolution, we felt more significant than we normally did in our day-to-day immigrant lives.

In Blaža's car, Jasmine and I talked with the authority of experts about the concepts that had been introduced to us only hours before in class. Sometimes, he asked basic questions, and I became exasperated, lecturing him like I was suddenly an art history scholar, and he was a mere amateur photographer whom I had once been charmed by. And then I felt guilty afterward, and then I did it again, and the cycle would continue in an endless loop.

As I was becoming an "adult" over in Melbourne, Serbia was going through its own rite of passage. Though Milošević had enjoyed a surge in support after the NATO bombings, it was now waning, and a student group called Otpor, meaning "resistance," was enjoying a popularity that previous opposition groups hadn't managed to muster.

The Otpor members were inspired by the writings of American political scientist Gene Sharp, who advocated for nonviolent resistance. Otpor's activities were often aimed at degrading the government, and making Milošević seem small, powerless in the face of their youthful exuberance. Blaža and I delighted at news of their antics, at hearing how Otpor members from the town of Kragujevac broke into a poultry farm and attached white flowers to the heads of turkeys, in imitation of Mira Marković, Milošević's wife and political collaborator, who wore a flower in her hair. They released the turkeys on the streets and the police ran around trying to catch them, to the joy of townspeople and journalists, who had been tipped off and were snapping photos of the absurd scene, which were then widely distributed. Resistance suddenly seemed attractive.

Otpor seemed fresh, strong, and united. Their cheerful resistance was welcomed by the people of a depressed Serbia, where unemployment, poverty, and dissatisfaction were at an all-time high.

The Serbian people had been humiliated and felt left behind by the world. Those who had previously been pro-Western were still smarting from being bombed by NATO. And now these energetic students decided they were going to fix it, from the inside, by themselves. The youth of Serbia felt capable of bringing about the changes that their parents had failed to enact, and their parents felt a surge of hope with the younger generation.

The young people were empowered not just by their energy and their growing numbers, but also by their technological knowledge, which superseded that of Milošević's aging government. It was 1999, and young people had the advantage of being savvy users of new technology. The students had built a bilingual website, they had a dedicated marketing team, they used cell phones and the internet to communicate with one another, and managed to avoid being shut down by the regime, which had a history of suppressing opposition. Suddenly, Milošević seemed like a parent trying to work the internet, while his kids laughed at his incompetence.

As revolution stirred, Blaža and I were excited to learn that the tiger-owning paramilitary leader Arkan had been assassinated, by a cop with ties to the underworld. Politics back home were interesting again, and we couldn't help but be drawn into the excitement. With Blaža, whose cheerfulness made him a favorite of my mother and sister, we sat at our place, chatting in our language, excitedly discussing rumors that Arkan had been killed by Milošević because he knew "too much," as Milošević suspected that his reign was coming to an end. Some speculated that Arkan was working for the West, though I wasn't sold on this theory, which had been applied to everyone over the years—Tito was said to be working for the West, as were Milošević's opponents and Milošević himself.

On New Year's Eve 1999, Otpor staged a huge outdoor concert in Belgrade. They spread rumors that the Red Hot Chili Peppers would be headlining, and tens of thousands of revelers showed up in their Chili Pepper T-shirts under heavy winter coats. As the clock counted down to the New Year, however, the crowd was presented with images on a massive projector: names and photographs of people who had been killed during Milošević's wars. They were told that there would be no band. They had nothing to celebrate, as this had been another year of war and oppression. The people of Belgrade were told to go home. They'd been given something to think about, and like chided children, they left. The message was: "We must bring him down."

In the spring of 2000, as I was preparing for my final exams, posing for my photographer boyfriend, and attending my weekly art history class at the university, Milošević called for an early election in the hopes that he still had enough support to secure power for another four years. Otpor, which now had seventy thousand members, took to the streets. They distributed nearly two million stickers, which simply said, "*Gotov je*" ("He's finished"), and were plastered on cars, bathrooms, and walls across Yugoslavia.

As the election neared, the numerous political parties opposing Milošević were still split. Otpor exerted pressure on these groups, and eventually managed to achieve something unheard of: eighteen different political parties came together under one banner to form the Democratic Opposition of Serbia (DOS), united in one mission—to topple Milošević.

The poor and exhausted people of Yugoslavia came out to vote in droves, most of them (according to polls) wearing shoes that were over ten years old. They shuffled to the polling booths, which were wallpapered with "He's finished" stickers.

Back in Melbourne, we heard the news—DOS had won. The community gathered at our place, and I joined twelve-year-old Natalija in a crazy dance. It was the end of the bad news reports that had been with us our whole lives! We jumped around hugging and screaming, singing along to the song "All of Yugoslavia Is Dancing to Rock and Roll."

Unwilling to accept defeat, Milošević asked for a second round of voting, and in response, DOS called for a general strike. And for the first time in ten years, the protestors in Belgrade gained a powerful ally—the workers. Forty thousand miners joined the strike, meaning the country's thermoelectric power would come to a standstill. We cried and laughed at the thought of our country rumbling, finally rising up in a revolution. Milošević went on TV, trying a tactic that had worked for him in the past. He announced that his opponents were funded by the West, and that Otpor and the DOS would bring foreign troops into Serbia, insinuating that they were puppets of the NATO forces. But the miners didn't budge. The people took to the streets of Belgrade. The police, who had been in secret talks with Otpor, took their posts, but agreed to not attack the protestors.

And then, the best part: from five directions, makeshift convoys converged on the capital. The fed-up people from the small towns, some of them riding actual tractors and bulldozers, made their way to Belgrade. Photos of farmers waving the Otpor flag and their fists in the air reached us and we shouted to no one in particular: *"GOTOV JE!"* (*"HE'S FINISHED!"*) This was "the Bulldozer Revolution."

The people of Serbia broke into parliament. Falsified votes for Milošević were found inside and tossed from the windows onto the streets. The DOS coalition took control of parliament, and Milošević was forced to concede defeat. After all the violence and unnecessary deaths that had plagued Yugoslavia over the last ten years, Milošević had been brought down through peaceful means. This was what my dad had dreamed of. I remembered when we used to light candles in the Belgrade park, calling for peace when the wars were just starting, and I pretended he was alive now, picturing him healthy and happy in Melbourne, celebrating the long-awaited peace with us.

My family and our ex-Yugo friends were delirious. Blaža brought over a bottle of champagne and my mother, twelve-year-old Natalija, and I drank it. Three months after the revolution, my mother's college friend and doctor of philosophy Zoran Đinđić became the prime minister of Serbia. He was pro-Western and his idea was to make Serbia modern—to join the European Union and fix the damage that had been done over the decades. Slobodan Milošević—the reason we left Yugoslavia, the reason Blaža's family had to flee Sarajevo—would soon be sent to the Hague. I only realized that a weight had come off my shoulders when it was no longer there. Milošević had been in our lives since I could remember, and now, he was gone.

In the last few weeks of 2000, I turned eighteen, finished high school, and had my wisdom teeth extracted. I felt tenderness around the removal sites in my mouth, which I constantly poked with my tongue.

Instead of waiting for December, when my exam scores would arrive, I used the small savings I'd gathered from working at Peter's (and a substantial donation from my mother) to travel with Blaža to Europe. Thrilled by our upcoming adult adventure, we bought thermal underwear to keep us warm, and gifts for our friends and relatives in the form of little stuffed koalas.

A week before we left Melbourne, we received news that Marko, Dada's son, the one I went out with in Beijing, had died from an overdose. I sat in the living room with my sobbing mother, stupidly thinking about how I'd made plans to see Marko in Belgrade the next week (his family had moved back there a few years earlier) and wondering if he'd thought about that the night he died. I'd last seen Marko when we had visited them in Beijing, and he was fourteen, drinking at the expat club. As he got older, Marko had developed a drug problem and had recently had an implant inserted under his skin, which was meant to stop him from consuming drugs and alcohol. But Marko had cut out the implant with a knife, gone out on a bender, and died the same night, after visiting all his favorite nightspots, dragging himself from one to another.

As I thought of Marko, the image of him in Beijing, wise beyond his years, cynical, eager to tell me how the world really worked, soon faded and was replaced by another memory, which was contained in an old videotape. I didn't need to watch the video to remember what was on it—seeing "1986" in my dad's handwriting on the video's spine was enough to remind me of its contents, which I'd watched over and over as a kid. The video was shot when I was three and Marko was two, in his family's courtyard on a sunny summer day in Belgrade, when Yugoslavia was still intact. Our mothers are wearing flowing dresses and smoking cigarettes, their voices so similar: they'd talked to each other every day since they were five, their mannerisms fusing. I'm wearing blue overalls, probably handed down from one of my boy cousins, and a red plastic headband with a plastic bow. Marko's grandmother had taken him to a hairdresser that morning, and his long, shiny black hair was gone, replaced with a boyish haircut his mother hated. Marko puts my hair band on his freshly shorn head, and starts walking slowly up and down the courtyard, pausing every now and then to look at us like a catwalk model, our mothers making loud exclamations of admiration—"Look at you, Marko!" "You're so beautiful!"—and he smiles winningly, batting his giant eyes.

He'd looked much the same when I'd seen him in Beijing; he was one of those people you could recognize from a baby picture, except when I saw him, his hair was long again, bangs flopped carelessly into his face. Last time I was in Belgrade, a friend had pointed out that in Serbia, if you take drugs you don't have a drug of choice, like ecstasy or cocaine, you just *take drugs*, whatever you can get your hands on. That's the difference, my friend said, between privileged people in the West taking drugs recreationally, and people taking drugs in a ruined, hopeless country.

I was still reeling from the news of Marko when Blaža and I arrived at our first stop, London, where everything was double the price we'd expected, and December was colder and wetter than we'd dreaded. On our first day, I bought two pairs of Doc Martens, a classic pair for me, and knowing that she still thought everything I wore was cool, I also got a garishly green limited-edition pair for my sister, weighing down my suitcase. We lived off fries and premade sandwiches at Boots pharmacy, and by the time we left for Belgrade a few days later, I felt soggy and tired.

On the flight to my hometown, my jaw started ticking, like a watch, where my wisdom teeth used to be. Blaža noted that my face had swelled a little, and as we landed, the plane full of Yugos clapped and shouted "*Bravo, majstore!*" ("Bravo, maestro!") to the pilot as they always did, but I felt like opening my mouth would be a mistake, so I sat there tight-lipped, like some Western traveler who didn't know how to show appreciation for a smooth landing. We rode a taxi from Belgrade Airport to my aunt Mila's house, my face ticking faster and more forcefully. I watched dirty, small Belgrade unfold, as I pressed my face to the cold window. I saw the remnants of the NATO bombings, buildings with holes in them, but Blaža saw other things. He squeezed my hand, excited about the young people gathering around kiosks and clubs, but all I could do was keep thinking I saw Marko among them, and then wonder if he'd been to these places the night he died.

We stayed with Aunt Mila, whose idiosyncratic habits I usually found charming (she drank tea at 10 a.m. every morning, from a pot, like an English person; she had a hot bath every night around midnight; she still used a typewriter for her work). She had separated from my uncle Tim, their sons were still abroad, and now that the apartment was just hers, she lived exactly as she liked. I had, however, forgotten about her insistence on keeping all the windows open, no matter the time of year. When we arrived and I told her the place was freezing, she said, "Oh, please," and rolled her eyes. The only source of heat was the big radiator in the living room, and I leaned directly on it, letting my hands thaw on the ceramic tiles.

I decided to have a bath and ran the hot water, which produced an incredible cloud of steam, making the icicles around the open window start to melt and drip into the bath. I got in and let my body go red from the heat. When I came out, Aunt Mila looked at my face and said we needed to go see the dentist who lived down the street. Which was pretty convenient, as that was approximately as far as I could walk in my feverish state.

The dentist's mother opened the door. "Is your son home?" my aunt asked.

"My god, what is wrong with the boy?" the old lady asked, looking at my disfigured visage, wrapped in a scarf.

I tried to say that I was a woman, but it came out as a whistling sound. The old lady led us to a basement-slash-homemade-dental-clinic, where her middle-aged son, slightly annoyed that we had interrupted his dinner, told me my wisdom teeth scars had become infected. He lanced something in my mouth, drained a lot of pus, gave me antibiotics, pocketed the cash we offered, and went back to his cabbage rolls, the smell of which pervaded the place. I went home with antibiotics and instructions on how to press my jaw in a way that would squeeze out the gathering infection.

On our second night there, Blaža and I wandered the streets past crowded bars, steam coming out of our mouths from the cold, surrounded once again by the sounds of our language. Blaža put his arm around me, and I imagined the sentiment was "Isn't it great to be home?" but I didn't feel at home. Was the reason I couldn't enjoy myself because my mouth was so sore, or something else? Because the city had never been real to me as an adult, I was unaware of the good places to drink, unfamiliar with the city's rhythms.

The vendors were selling *ćevapčići,* but I could only tolerate liquids, sipping juice from a straw, popping painkillers every few hours. In my exhausted, medicated state, Belgrade seemed strange and ugly in a new way, the horror of Marko's death quashing any charm it once held. And the more cheerful Blaža was, the more annoyed I got at him, and the more frustrated with myself for being this way.

As we walked, it occurred to me that when I said I "missed" Belgrade, to Blaža or my friends, I wasn't actually thinking of this place. I barely knew it. Instead, I missed a small cluster of memories from my early childhood. My Belgrade was a place from another time, where I lived with my young parents. The Belgrade I stood in now seemed like a lie. I'd expected it to welcome me, and hold me the way my parents had done when I was a child, and now I was disappointed. As we trudged along the streets, it became apparent that the place I missed was my life before anything bad ever happened.

Because I couldn't eat solid foods for a week, I rapidly lost weight, and I soon found myself a less-glamorous pus-spitting version of the waifish girls of Belgrade's streets, who still glided effortlessly about as I'd remembered them. I refused to go out at night, preferring to meet friends and family for coffees during the day, and only if I had to. I had never been angry at a place before, but I found myself hating Belgrade, transferring the blind hatred I'd once held for Milošević to the city itself.

I saw my kindergarten friend Milica briefly, and she watched as I dribbled coffee into my mouth, tilting my head from side to side, trying to avoid the sites of my infection. I imagined she was resentful of me when I talked about my exams and university plans, even though I hadn't been accepted yet. The education system had been slowly eroded by Milošević's regime and I knew I was an outsider. I hadn't been present for the protests, I wasn't a cool Otpor kid, I hadn't fought for the right to be a student the way my friends had.

I would blame my infected mouth for the fact that I had no interest in going anywhere, the idea of Belgrade itself filling me with an unreasonable dread. Blaža and I didn't talk much, and if he tried to, I pointed to my mouth and made an excuse, and felt myself withdrawing into myself, shrinking away from his touch, and becoming deaf to his chirpy take on life.

As my mouth recovered, my attention was taken by a pimple-like lump on my vagina. I found myself spending all my waking hours thinking about my genitals. Did I have a serious disease? After serving me relatively well for eighteen years, my body was apparently falling apart, in solidarity with Yugoslavia. Rather than wait a few weeks and see a doctor in Australia, I decided I needed this new problem seen to, pronto. However, I was convinced that if I went to a local doctor, it would somehow get back to my relatives, specifically my gastroenterologist aunt, whom we hadn't spoken to since her fight with my mother, and who would now be able to accuse our family of not only being slobby, but also possessing diseased genitals. Instead of venturing into a hospital where my aunt might have colleagues with loose lips, I found an ad for a clinic on the outskirts of town, and took Blaža with me. The clinic was called Lady Medica, and there was a neon love-heart above the door. A casual woman about my mother's age examined both me and Blaža and concluded that I had genital warts, while he was perfectly healthy. Before we could have an awkward conversation about how I alone could have contracted an STD, the doctor said that I'd probably got it from a hotel towel, and that it happens all the time. I scheduled an appointment for the following week to have the warts removed.

To my relief, Blaža went to visit friends in Bosnia while I stayed in Belgrade, free to watch films in Aunt Mila's apartment, recover from my dental problems, and wait for my vaginal warts removal appointment without any pressure to have fun. I met up with Marko's younger brother Alex, and we just stood around for a while.

"I don't really know why we've met up, there's nothing to talk about," he muttered, looking at the ground. And really, there was nothing to talk about, so we said goodbye. He left me at the bookstore in the university's faculty of philosophy. I had once loved this bookstore. Now I walked through it, running my hand over books, repeating to myself, "I don't care."

Without the pressure of Blaža, who wanted to go out and see the city and have a nice time, I was free to be a recluse. Our Australian cell phones didn't work over here, and if he tried to call my aunt's landline from Bosnia, I kept the conversations short; I was afraid if I stayed on the phone longer, I would start crying for no reason, or that I would snap at him.

Every few days, I walked around the Red Star soccer stadium to get to my grandma Beba's place. I'd been told to be careful, as a friend had been bitten on the butt by a stray dog near the stadium. The number of strays had increased in the last couple of years, and the rumor was that a lot of people had abandoned their pets because they couldn't afford to keep them, including big purebreds like German shepherds and Dobermans, who had mated with the previously scrappy stray-dog gene pool, making strays bigger and more fierce than they'd been in the past. The bombing, other people said, had made the dogs crazy. But much as I imagined them in their mighty packs as I walked alone, I didn't see any strays; there was just the wind whipping around the stadium and the sound of faraway voices.

Like a huge chunk of the population, Grandma Beba had become obsessed with *Kassandra*, a Venezuelan telenovela that had made its way onto the airwaves. Even though I was her beloved grandchild, when it came to *Kassandra*, I played second fiddle, though I was invited to sit with her on the couch to watch. "She is an orphan in a banana plantation," Beba explained breathlessly, bringing me up to speed before the show started. Kassandra herself was beautiful and honest; two men wanted her—one the audience was rooting for, the other a scoundrel—but Kassandra didn't know that. *Kassandra* had taken Serbia by storm, and my grandmothers weren't the only ones who were addicted to it. It was the most popular show on television, and the obvious reason seemed to be that it provided people with an escape from their dreary lives in a country that was still, despite the new leadership, economically ruined. Those who had expected everything to be fixed by the fall of Milošević were disappointed, and the brightly colored world of *Kassandra* took them to a place far from gray Serbia.

One afternoon, we were supposed to watch with my great-uncle Alek, who was visiting from eastern Serbia, and as we waited for him to arrive I thought about the tragedy that had befallen their family. His son, my first cousin Bojan, had killed himself the previous year. It turned out that Bojan's boss—the one who owned the recreation center—was part of the mafia, as we had suspected. Bojan had been tasked with driving a van full of alcohol from Romania into Serbia. He was caught at the border and the smuggled liquor was confiscated. Bojan was held responsible by his boss, whose cronies had been forcing him to personally pay back the money for the lost alcohol. Bojan's family knew he was in trouble, but he never told them the full story, or how desperate he was becoming. He'd sold everything he owned, and when he ran out of options and the pressure and threats didn't stop, he hanged himself. On the day of his funeral, his parents got a call from the mafia, saying the family had inherited Bojan's debt. Now Bojan's elderly father was in Belgrade to sell his coin collection.

The doorbell rang just as the show was about to begin, and my grandmother ushered my great-uncle in. I hardly had time to offer my condolences before the credits started rolling and my two elderly relatives became entranced. I remembered Bojan's beautiful wife Anita and their young son playing on the linoleum floor of their old house and wondered what they would do now.

When the commercials came on, we had a chance to catch up a little, and I asked how my great-uncle and my great-aunt Rose were doing. "We're the saddest family in this country," he told me, as my grandmother opened a tin of *vanilice*, a shortbread-jam cookie she had made. I started thinking about that phrasing, "the saddest family in this country," as if it was something measurable, like it was possible to measure my relatives' sadness compared to that of Marko's parents, or all the people who were still miserable, whose situation had barely changed since the fall of Milošević. Why had I thought a revolution was like a magic wand? As if a democratic government could wipe out the mafia just like that. As if it could erase the lingering problems of the depressed people.

The show came back on. As Kassandra argued with the evil man who was trying to seduce her, and my elderly relatives watched rapt, my mind drifted from the banana plantation to the genital wart operation I was going to have that night, which I hadn't mentioned to my family.

In the taxi to the clinic, I started looking for my seat belt, then stopped, remembering that no one wore seat belts here. In the scathing tone my ex-Yugo friends and I used to complain about Australians, I said: "I live in Australia, where we pay *ridiculous* fines for not wearing seat belts."

"Well, here in Serbia, we pay with our lives," the driver responded.

I thought about how people who live in poor countries have shorter life expectancies, and my eyes started filling with tears again, thinking about all the years Marko and Bojan had taken off theirs.

When I arrived at the clinic, the neon love-heart above the entrance flickered and then went out, like in a horror film. I walked in to find the doctor and her young assistant illuminated by flashlights they held under their faces like members of the Baby-Sitters Club preparing to tell spooky stories around a campfire.

The doctor assured me there was no need to call a taxi, and that she could operate just fine despite the electricity having been cut, and she took all the cash I had left for this vacation and led me by the hand into the pitch-black operating room. I had a brief flashback to Madame Marie's story of the Hunchback of Notre Dame.

In the freezing cold, I was instructed to strip and lie on a table with my legs spread, as the assistant spotlighted my vagina with her flashlight. She made me feel simultaneously uncomfortable and at home: she eyeballed my vagina impassively, and even rested her cheek on my thigh at one point sleepily. The doctor explained that she wasn't able to use her "usual" instruments because of the power outage, but her confident tone made me think this wasn't the first time she was required to use tools from preelectrical times.

I lay there limp as the doctor injected me with a couple of local anesthetics and then got to work with tools that made scraping and cutting sounds. But instead of thinking about the medieval circumstances, I cried, as I had done every day in Belgrade, not from the pain, but because lying in that cold dark place, everything felt hopeless. The doctor, assuming I was crying because of my wart removal, tried to cheer me up.

"Sister, this is nothing," she said. "These warts are tiny. You should see when we get women from the country coming here to give birth. They've never even been to a gynecologist. I find warts the size of grapes and have to remove them during labor, 'cause they can't even give birth!" She laughed heartily, and her assistant joined in.

I was sent home with some vaginal suppositories, and another round of antibiotics. A few weeks later, when I saw my gynecologist back in Melbourne, I was told that I hadn't had warts, and that the lumps that had been removed by torchlight were probably just cosmetic blemishes, the equivalent of pimples. I was told that I was duped by the doctor, who was trying to make a buck. But in the moment, ignorant to all of this, I hobbled to a taxi believing myself to be STD-free and went back to my aunt's apartment so I could go to bed at 8 p.m., and the next morning cross off another day on the calendar, counting down the time I had left in Belgrade.

"Did you have a nice time with your friends?" Aunt Mila asked.

"Oh yes," I said, imitating the gusto of a person who had been guzzling cocktails, rather than someone with an antibacterial tablet fizzing inside her.

While I was gone, my mother had called to let us know the letter had arrived. I'd aced my exams, and in a few months, I'd be going to my first-choice college.

A few days later, healing from two infections, I left my diseased homeland and got on a plane, eager for once to fly far away, back to Melbourne, which seemed full of hope. And as we flew toward Australia and away from my birthplace, I felt like I was coming home.

11

The School of Life

I was about to start university, and after a year of dating, the comfortable relationship I had with Blaža felt increasingly stifling. I didn't want to speculate about how many kids we might have, and whenever Blaža dreamed aloud about our future, I was silent. I wanted to immerse myself in college, to live the idealized life I'd dreamed about with Jasmine. I wanted to be someone new, who was not tied to a Yugo boyfriend, or confined to the Yugo diaspora. The weight of his arm around me felt suddenly heavy, and his text messages became annoying. On my sister's birthday, Blaža gave her a beautiful spiral bookcase he'd made based on a design we'd seen in London. The night after, I finally ended it. Once he left, I cried, running my hand over the carefully crafted, meticulously painted bookshelf, and I wondered if I would ever find someone as kind again.

In March, I started university. I still lived at my mother's place, and each morning I got in my new-to-me Toyota and drove an hour into the city, blasting music. As a first-year arts student at the University of Melbourne, I had the freedom to take courses in subjects as varied and impractical as I wanted. I took a course entirely dedicated to Hong Kong cinema prereunification with China and one called "The European Spectacle" in which we learned about the abject theater of the absurd. I took "Art, Pornography, Blasphemy, Propaganda," which explored how those categories blurred into one another in literature and in the sordid lives of authors. I continued to study French, which I'd kept up through high school, and in class I sat next to a blond Aussie named Laurence who loved riding bicycles, smoking weed, and had excellent conversational French.

My favorite was a linguistics class in which we learned about Anna Wierzbicka, a linguist who writes about how translation can cause cultural clashes. She believes it is difficult to translate certain emotions from one culture to another, when words don't have an exact equivalent, and we try to squash them into a definition that doesn't fit. This can lead to cultural misunderstandings, and to people feeling like they haven't been heard.

How often had I misunderstood people, or been misunderstood thanks to the clumsiness of language, and the dominance that one language, like English, exercised over others? What about kids whose immigrant parents failed to communicate with them because they had been raised on different languages that could never quite meet? I jotted down Serbian phrases I had always regretted not being able to translate properly. There were songs, of course, so poetic in the original, that always sounded not quite right in English. It was also hard to translate terms of endearment. In English, people used terms like "honey" and "dear," but we called our loved ones "my sun" or "my soul," neither of which translated well, especially as calling a lover "my sun" sounds creepy when you say it out loud. There were also diminutives and augmentatives, which made expressions so much more colorful. In English, if we are talking about a child's hand we might call it a "little hand," while in my language we just add a suffix to hand, making it something like a handlet, or handsie, handkin. There are diminutive dogs, diminutive bridges, diminutive books. Blaža had used diminutive pet names when talking to me; instead of having a button on my coat, I had a little button—in English what would you call that? A buttonette?

I had massive folders full of materials I was supposed to read for my courses, and I discovered it took me a long time to grasp certain academic language, or intentionally complicated literature, to get to the point. In high school, I had never had problems with reading assignments, though I would often read a sentence over several times to make sure I got the gist. Now I was reading sentences three times over, blaming myself for being an ethnic and struggling with English somehow, still. Everything would take me three times as long as it took everyone else, I insisted to myself, calculating the disadvantage I had.

But then, I knew that if these readings were in Serbian, they would take me even longer. So which was it? Was I a jack-of-all-trades, or a master of none, unable to wrap my head completely around my second language because my first one stubbornly forbade it? Why couldn't people write in a way that was easy to understand? Surely, it's less taxing to write a simple sentence than a complex one. It was deliberate, I told myself, a way of pushing out a certain part of the population from the world of intellectual pursuits.

The first few months of university were sunny and exciting—Jasmine and I sat with our new friends in a courtyard under a gigantic oak tree rolling cigarettes. Or we hung out at another place on campus that served sushi and good, strong coffee. Sushi was only just becoming popular then, and I will never forget the exotic smell of the café—pickled ginger mixed with freshly roasted coffee beans. We sat on the grungy couches, ate our salmon rolls, and talked about our new lives, brimming with new people and stimulating ideas. Jasmine took a performance art class with a guy who, in the name of art, put ice blocks into his butt while lying on a sheet of ice. The point of the piece was unclear to us, but we respected his dedication. Some of my classmates had parents who were lawyers, or composers, or poets, or who owned apartments in London. There were international students from Singapore in my journalism classes, and we rolled our eyes at one another because our professors were too old-fashioned to teach us about online journalism.

One bright day when the air smelled like leaves and coffee, my new friend Laurence and I walked toward our French class, as our professor came down the hall from the other direction. Out the window, we saw students sprawled on the lawn, and in a late-teenaged silly rebel kind of way, Laurence and I decided to ditch class and enjoy the freedom outside.

In our excitement, we ran all the way out the building and onto Lygon Street with its Italian restaurants, and as we ran, I thought about all the things we could suddenly do now that the world was open to us: we could have a beer at one of the pubs, grab a hazelnut ice cream from New Zealand Natural, a cannoli from Brunetti's Italian patisserie, or eat takeout Indian sitting on the grass under the tree. And at that moment, not paying attention to where we were going, we crashed directly into Blaža, who immediately dropped the hand of the young woman he was walking with.

Confused, I said hello in our language, then switched to English, introducing Laurence, who wiped sweat from his brow, not realizing this was an important moment. I looked at Blaža and his new girlfriend, who looked exactly like a Yugo Cameron Diaz. Had I made the wrong decision in breaking up with him? As Cameron Diaz tried to absorb how she'd found herself with her hand suddenly unheld, I wondered if by ending my relationship and taking a step back from my ex-Yugo friends I'd shut the door to my culture, leaving myself lonely.

Later, as Laurence perused the books on the bargain table in Readings bookstore, I pretended to do the same, but instead I thought about Blaža and his new girlfriend, and also about our last trip to ex-Yugoslavia. The Yugos aren't my people, I told myself, at the same time remembering that I never felt like an Aussie either. I considered whether I could get away with calling myself "a citizen of the world" should anyone ask.

The following two years of undergraduate study passed in a blur of learning, parties, and short romances. Student life was luxurious. We were expected to sit for hours reading and pontificating, and I cherished the fact that I only worked at Peter's a couple of shifts a week, not having to worry about rent. In my life as a student, I was able to reinvent myself, or to exist just like everyone else did, and the campus was an eclectic mix of kids from all over the place. My creative writing and journalism classes became my favorites, and in August I got tickets to the Melbourne International Film Festival, where I was entranced by the documentaries from all over the world and reminded of how much I loved film.

When I finished my undergraduate degree, I was accepted to the Victorian College of the Arts (VCA), where I was one of nine students chosen to study documentary film on a graduate level.

Nearing the end of my first semester at VCA, we were supposed to be working on a short film project leading up to our end-of-year assessment. My classmates had pursued their specific interests: a former social worker was filming someone struggling with depression, another student who loved walking was filming a spiritual trek.

I still didn't have a topic, and I drove to the airport a couple of times a week, trying to find inspiration for my film. I loved driving, and I had time on my hands, as well as a semilegitimate excuse to observe strangers, so I would go there to watch people reuniting, their emotions raw in that white-tiled space, and I'd hold back tears as I spied, pretending to be waiting for someone, too. Once, lurking at arrivals near midnight, I spotted a friend from high school waiting for someone. Her Israeli boyfriend appeared and they fell into each other's arms, kissing passionately, as I withdrew behind a large post, embarrassed by the fact that I had no good reason for being there. If they saw me, what would I say? "No, I'm not waiting for anyone, I am actually a big baby who likes observing strangers' bodies smooshing together at an international terminal." Or would I admit to them and myself that being there reminded me of the happiest times in my life, hugging loved ones tightly in the fluorescent light, breathing in the stale scent of airplane and unbrushed teeth? Would I explain that, for me, this chaotic, badly lit terminal represented a Disney-grade happy ending?

Often, I stood in the arrivals hall, thinking: *Why can't I be little again?*—remembering each of my parents holding my hand and saying "fly, fly, fly" as I swung in between them—down Knez Mihailova Street, where we could smell the chestnuts roasting. I wanted to live in places that no longer existed, with people who were gone. My grandma Xenia, who had died at ninety-one, was vivid in my mind whenever I got a face-full of cigarette smoke, and my dad was a little voice in my head that said: *Try to remember everything we ever did, or those moments will be lost.* I imagined him watching me from some other-world, or perhaps he was a star in the sky, or dust particles the air that surrounded me. Or—for all I knew about the afterlife—he was reincarnated as some mysterious, glowing deep-sea creature, who had no idea what Yugoslavia was, what a daughter was, how to code on a computer. I let my imagination run, picturing this bizarre version of my father obsessed only with plankton, gathering it by using a light at the end of his unusual head, chomping on it with some spiky teeth so unlike my dad's.

"You know the famous line from *Casablanca*?" my dad said once when I was nine and we were coming back from lighting candles in the park. *Casablanca* was his favorite film. "There's a line: 'He's looking at you, kid.' When Humphrey Bogart says that to Ingrid Bergman, he means: 'God is looking over you, kid.'" It was the only time I remembered my dad talking about God; it was out of character for him, and out of character for Humphrey Bogart's fast-talking, worldly Rick.

Later, after it was too late to tell my dad, I found out the line is actually: "*Here's* looking at you, kid," a grammatically incorrect shortening by Bogart, who should have said: "Here's to looking at you." In the world of *Casablanca*, when everyone was about to flee Paris and become displaced thanks to Nazi occupation, Rick didn't tell Ilsa that God was looking at her. Rather, he wanted to toast the idea of them staying alive and together as the world fell apart. "I hope I get to continue looking at you," is what he meant. Bogart's line was grammatically incorrect, and so my dad had misunderstood it. This was exactly the sort of thing that irked him, people bending the rules of language like it was nothing.

But, as I found out in my linguistics class, language is ever-changing, and like people, it shifts over the years, incorporating new words and grammatical structures. It is actually less rigid and scary than it seems at first. It is even possible that one day "havaya" will become a legitimate greeting in the West, incorporated into the lexicon thanks to ethnics like us misunderstanding "how are you" and creating a whole new greeting of our own.

One of those days at the airport, thinking about the things that mattered to me, I decided I might as well make a film about people traveling away from and toward each other again. That weekend, during my shift at the clinic, Peter pinned up a new flyer on the noticeboard, and there it was: the perfect setting in which to examine immigration, war, diaspora, and, it turned out, boobs.

In my language, beside a photo of a woman wearing not much, the flyer advertised the Miss Ex-Yugoslavia competition. "Young women, sign up!" it encouraged members of our community. I knew that young women from the Yugo club would be looking at this with interest, and maybe some of Peter's clients would attend. The flyer promised that "The winner gets a return ticket to ex-Yu!"—to whichever part of that former country she wanted to visit. And rather than picturing my terrible recent trip to Belgrade, I saw myself once again as a five-year-old splashing naked in the Croatian shallows where we used to go on holidays before the wars. Before I could think too much about it, I sent in two photos of myself, filled out the admission form, and added a request to record the event for my film school project.

Epilogue: Miss Ex-Yugoslavia

Dressed in a pink bikini and high heels, Nina from Sarajevo opens the door of the dressing room a crack and we contestants stick our heads out. Through the cloud of cigarette smoke, we see people in the audience holding hands, dancing in a circle called the *kolo* while folk music blares. Groups of men, their arms around each other's shoulders, sway from side to side, singing along to the music at the top of their lungs. A belly dancer makes her way around the room, gathering tips in her belt and bra. It's the last part of the competition, the swimsuit portion, and for the first time, Nina seems nervous. "I don't wanna do this. I do *not* want to do this."

"Stick together! Stick together!" Tina, the blond Slovenian, says like we're a group of schoolchildren, and we all grab one another's hands and file out to the side of the stage. Wearing a bikini with high heels is a very unnatural combination, especially at night, in a club, where everyone else is fully dressed. Before each of us goes onstage, we look back at the rest of the girls desperately, like a lamb going to the slaughter. "You can do it," we whisper to one another, then cheer each girl as she takes the stage.

Nina, regaining her calm, stands in front of the judges in her fragile glory: her thin limbs, her visible ribs. Her foot that was injured by a bomb shows no signs of trauma, her confident gait gives no indication that anything was ever wrong. She comes off the stage elated.

Next up is Zora, from Montenegro, her dark hair cascading. With her youthful glow, she walks to the end of the runway and stops. Zora is wearing a wrap-skirt around her waist, and with one movement, she rips it off, revealing a small bikini bottom underneath. This surprise reveal of flesh sends the crowd into even wilder applause than when Nina made her touching comment about Yugoslavian unity earlier in the night. The judges nod approvingly as Zora tosses her hair over her shoulder and stalks back down the runway.

When it's my turn, in my clumsy heels and not much else, I am lifted by the roar of the audience onto the stage. I am buoyed by the cheers. I pause in this surreal nearly-naked-as-the-day-I-was-born moment and muster a sassy shoulder-shrug and a smile for the ex-Yugo diaspora. And the next thing I know, I've done it, and I am climbing back down the stairs, feeling euphoric.

We run backstage to put on cocktail dresses as the judges make their final decision, and once we are called back to the stage, we go on together, sharing the spotlight for the first time. We've been given a sugary cocktail each, and we stand sipping, as the hosts, Bane and Monica, lead the audience in a round of applause for all of us.

Bane addresses us, sincerely. "Dear girls. You are all equally nice! And not only outside, inside as well." There are nods of agreement from the audience.

"And now we're ready to announce the runner-up," Monica says, pulling out a small, plastic crown.

"It's Nina!" Barely hiding her disappointment at not winning, Nina puts her drink down on the ground, and lets Monica place the crown on her head. Slowly, she walks to the end of the runway and pauses before the crowd. Though most people are cheering, there are some shouts from those who believe Nina deserved to win the whole competition. Later, there will be speculation about the judging panel, which contained no Bosnians. People will assert that the so-called "unified" ex-Yugoslavian event was biased, tilted to favor certain nationalities over others—the same complaints we have always had about one another. There are people yelling "Shut up!" to each other in the various dialects of ex-Yugoslavia, as the crowd settles once more for the big announcement.

"And now, for the winner of the Miss Ex-Yugoslavia competition . . . Zora!" Upon hearing her name announced, Zora hands her drink to Tina and then puts her hands over her mouth, in a delayed shock reaction. Just as she's finished parading her sash and crown, we are about to file offstage, when Monica stops us.

"But wait, there's more!"

"We have here a prize for Miss Personality!" Bane says, chuckling.

"The prize for Miss Personality goes to So-oooo-fija from Serbia!"

I choke on my cocktail as the crowd roars. I have just won a personality prize at a beauty competition, and it's not even a joke. I look over to the judges, to see if they're genuinely smiling or taking the piss. I suspect they decided to give me a prize because I know them personally, because I've clearly tried so hard with my hair, and possibly because my mother is their counselor. But I don't care. I've won something.

Monica gestures to the runway and I walk down it one last time, as Bane announces grandly, "Sofija's prize is a *hun*dred-dollar voucher to Just Jeans! Sofija, you're gonna have some niiiiiiice jeans."

The final scene of my student film shows me, aged twenty-two, accepting my award, and looking out at my community. In the audience my sister is cheering for me, as is my mother and her clients, the builder who renovated our bathroom, and the man with the groin cyst. Maybe my dad's ghost is there too, laughing at the absurdity of his daughter onstage wearing a plastic crown, in front of a crowd of ex-Yugoslavians.

Crowned Miss Personality of a country that doesn't exist, I shrug and turn away.

Acknowledgments

Thank you to my mother and my sister for generously allowing me to put our lives on paper. Thank you for reliving and sharing; for reminding, correcting, and supporting me.

Thank you to the experts who worked on this memoir, who were patient, wise, and encouraging through this strange process. You made this book so much better: my agent, Marya Spence; my editor, Daniella Wexler; and my publisher, Judith Curr, and her team at Atria Books. Thank you also to Stephanie Mendoza, Jackie Jou, Suzanne Donahue, Isolde Sauer, and Albert Tang. Thank you, Clare Mao.

Thank you, Kimberly Burns, for your PR expertise.

Thank you to Cate Blake and the Penguin Random House team in Australia.

Thank you to the ex-Yugoslavian community (those who feature in this book, and those who do not). To the people in the diaspora, as well as those who stayed. My friends and family, whose stories inspire me.

I want to acknowledge the people who died or suffered in the wars, and those who still suffer.

And the people who have died whose names I know: Lola, Ksenija, Milan, Tim, Misko, Dada, and Marko.

Thank you to my other families:

The Moth—the wonderful people who encouraged me to tell stories onstage when I first moved to New York. Thank you for sending me to new places and showing me that people want to hear what I have to say. It gave me the confidence to write this. Thanks to story whizzes for working on stories with me (Jenifer Hixson, Kate Tellers, Meg Bowles, and Catherine Burns—I'm so lucky!).

Women of Letters—Michaela McGuire, Marieke Hardy, and Trish Nelson, who gave me the opportunity to host an extraordinary literary salon, where I'm inspired each month by incredible women.

The Wing—speaking of women, thank you to The Wing for providing me with a space to work and socialize, surrounded by New York's most talented.

Thank you to the team at Joe's Pub, for the support over the last three years, as well as taking a chance on our latest immigration venture, *This Alien Nation*.

Those who read this book in detail: Lorelei Vashti, whose support buoys me and whose opinion I value so much. To Harry Angus and Luke Walker for their trusted opinions. To Ivan Berger and Josh Strong for their expertise.

To friends, family, and colleagues who have read things, or given advice, included me in their projects, chatted about immigration, and inspired me: Lauren Cerand, Mona Chalabi, Sophie Cunningham, Maša Dakić, Sarah Darmody, Imogen Dewey, Noah Erlich, Xochitl Gonzales, Maeve Higgins, Abeer Hoque, Matt Huynh, Benedikt Josef, Elmo Keep, Susan Kent, Daniel Kitson, Hanna Kopel, Benjamin Law, Angela Ledgerwood, Sandi Marx, Michaela McGuire, Alicia Mitic, Abbas Mousa, Trish Nelson, Biljana Novaković, Bojana Novaković, Sam Pang, Liam Pieper, Milica Popović, Jon Ronson, John Safran,

Matthew Sandager, Ronnie Scott, Neboysha Simic, Mila Stanojević, Estelle Tang, and Danusia Trevino.

Thank you to the Millay Colony for letting me stay and dream there for a while.

Thank you, Payton Turner, for the cover and the little illustrations that I love so much!

Thank you to Michael, whose love and encouragement have always been unwavering, and much needed. Thank you for being an excellent reader and thinker, as well as all the other things you do that make me so fortunate.